Something to Celebrate
365 Days a Year!

From time-honored traditions to spur-of-the-moment fun, *Taste of Home Holiday & Celebrations Cookbook* makes home entertaining as stress-free as it is heartwarming, delightful and delicious. Simply turn to any of the 267 never-before-published recipes found here for a get-together that's sure to impress.

'TIS THE SEASON. The most wonderful time of the year is quite easily the most memorable, too, especially with this chapter's merry mix of menu and entertaining ideas. Dazzle Christmas guests with 112 recipes for tempting starters, elegant entrees, seasonal sides and irresistible desserts.

Choose from a variety of yuletide main dishes, including Apple-Glazed Holiday Ham, Portobello-Stuffed Pork Roast, Halibut with Citrus-Olive Sauce and Cranberry-Stuffed Beef Tenderloin.

Put a creative spin on holiday entertaining with complete menus for a festive Wine Tasting Buffet, Not So Silent Night Karaoke Party, Feast of the Three Kings and Sparkling Midnight Supper. When you're feeling crunched for time, rest easy knowing you can still throw a fabulous party thanks to the Last Minute Christmas Party and Make Ahead Yuletide Brunch offerings.

And because the season isn't complete without a few sweets, you'll find dozens of goodies, including 12 Days of Cookies and Candies and Dazzling Mint Desserts.

GIVING THANKS. Show your appreciation for family and friends with a from-the-heart Thanksgiving meal, featuring Roasted Sweet Potato Soup, Rosemary Roasted Turkey, Pecan Sausage Stuffing, and Brown Sugar & Almond Pumpkin Custard Pie. If your sweet tooth craves even more desserts, you're sure to enjoy pleasing pies, cheesecakes and other confections in the Awesome Autumn Desserts section.

EASTER GATHERINGS. Greet the season of all things new with fresh spring party themes. Charm guests with an Elegant Easter Garden Party that spotlights Rosemary Roasted Lamb, Carrot Soup with Orange & Tarragon, and Spinach and Artichoke Bread Pudding, plus, for dessert, Coconut Chiffon Cake.

You'll find tasty recipes showcasing spring's finest produce in the Spectacular Spring Sides section and dozens of baked specialties with Easter Bread Basket.

SPECIAL CELEBRATIONS. Let the celebration continue all year long with 88 crowd-pleasing recipes for a Game Day Gathering, St. Patrick's Day Party, Japanese-inspired Cherry Blossom Celebration, Summer Harvest Get Together, Vampire Themed Halloween and more! You're sure to find some colorful new favorites in this popular section of the book.

SIMPLY STUNNING DECORATING IDEAS. You'll also get inspired by dozens of eye-fetching centerpieces (just turn to page 197 for Bells of Ireland Beauty), clever decorations (don't miss the shabby-chic Glass Jar Chandelier on page 147) and fun party favors (see the Cheering Station Setup on page 179).

With flavorful foods, engaging party plans and no-fuss decorating tips, *Holiday & Celebrations Cookbook* makes sharing your table and your home effortless and enjoyable throughout the year!

Would you like to see one of your family-favorite recipes featured in a future edition of this timeless treasury? See page 256 for details!

taste of home

HOLIDAY & Celebrations

VICE PRESIDENT, EDITOR-IN-CHIEF: Catherine Cassidy

VICE PRESIDENT, EXECUTIVE EDITOR/BOOKS: Heidi Reuter Lloyd

CREATIVE DIRECTOR: Howard Greenberg

FOOD DIRECTOR: Diane Werner, RD

SENIOR EDITOR/BOOKS: Mark Hagen

PROJECT EDITOR: Julie Schnittka

EDITOR: Sara Lancaster

CRAFT EDITOR: Shalana Frisby

ASSOCIATE FOOD EDITOR: Annie Rundle

ASSOCIATE CREATIVE DIRECTOR: Edwin Robles Jr.

ART DIRECTOR: Gretchen Trautman

PROJECT GRAPHIC DESIGN ASSOCIATE: Juli Schnuck

CONTENT PRODUCTION MANAGER: Julie Wagner

COPY CHIEF: Deb Warlaumont Mulvey

COPY EDITOR: Alysse Gear

RECIPE ASSET MANAGEMENT SYSTEM: Coleen Martin

RECIPE TESTING AND EDITING: Taste of Home Test Kitchen

ADMINISTRATIVE ASSISTANT: Barb Czysz

FOOD PHOTOGRAPHY: Taste of Home Photo Studio

NORTH AMERICAN CHIEF MARKETING OFFICER: Lisa Karpinski

VICE PRESIDENT/BOOK MARKETING: Dan Fink

CREATIVE DIRECTOR/CREATIVE MARKETING: Jim Palmen

The Reader's Digest Association, Inc.

PRESIDENT AND CHIEF EXECUTIVE OFFICER:
Tom Williams

EXECUTIVE VICE PRESIDENT, RDA, AND PRESIDENT, NORTH AMERICA:
Dan Lagani

Taste of Home Books
© 2011 Reiman Media Group, LLC
5400 S. 60th St., Greendale WI 53129

International Standard Book Number (10): 0-89821-953-1
International Standard Book Number (13): 978-0-89821-953-1

Cover photo of Rosemary Roasted Turkey (p.115) by Jim Wieland. Food styled by Diane Armstrong. Set styled by Stephanie Marchese.

Back cover photos: Portobello-Stuffed Pork Roast (p. 48), Caprese Scallop Stacks (p. 37), Stunning Squash Vase (p. 117), Bourbon Chocolate Pecan Pie (p. 135).

For other Taste of Home books and products, visit
ShopTasteofHome.com

table of CONTENTS

'TIS THE *season*

Ham for the Holidays 6
Last Minute Christmas Party 16
Make Ahead Yuletide Brunch 24
Wine Tasting Appetizer Affair 34
Classic Christmas Entrees 46
Dazzling Mint Desserts 58
12 Days of Cookies & Candy 66
Sparkling Midnight Supper 76
Not So Silent Night Karaoke Party 86
Feast of the Three Kings 96

GIVING *thanks*

Traditional Thanksgiving Dinner 108
Turkey Day Leftovers 118
Awesome Autumn Desserts 126

EASTER *gatherings*

Elegant Easter Garden Party 138
Easter Bread Basket 148
Spectacular Spring Sides 158

SPECIAL *celebrations*

Game Day Gathering 170
Crazy for Cupcakes 180
St. Patrick's Day Party 188
Cherry Blossoms Celebration 198
Romantic Picnic for Two 208
Congrats to the Grad 214
Summer Harvest Get Together 224
Vampire Themed Halloween 236

Index 246

'TIS THE
season

Whether you're welcoming Father Christmas with a traditional holiday dinner or simply spreading good cheer at an open house, this colorful section is sure to make your yuletide merry and bright. Turn the page for hints on planning a dinner honoring the three kings, baking up a platter of buttery cookies, hosting a delightful cocktail party and creating a Christmas sing-along friends won't soon forget!

The incredible aroma of a sweet and salty ham baking in the oven is a wonderful way to welcome family and friends in the door during the Christmas season.

Apple-Glazed Holiday Ham is certain to impress guests. But best of all, the recipe is easy on the cook, because the ham bakes unattended for hours before being brushed with the fast-to-fix glaze.

For more tried-and-true recipes that never seem to go out of style, you can depend on delightful White Wine Sangria and Cheese-Stuffed Twice-Baked Potatoes.

Round out your classic, comforting meal with a yuletide trimming such as Lemon-Scented Broccolini.

DOWN-HOME DINNER
(PICTURED AT RIGHT)

Apple-Glazed Holiday Ham (p. 10)
Cheese-Stuffed Twice-Baked Potatoes (p. 10)
Lemon-Scented Broccolini (p. 14)
White Wine Sangria (p. 9)

ham for
THE HOLIDAYS

Countdown to
Christmas Dinner

A Few Weeks Before:

- Prepare two grocery lists: one for nonperishable items to purchase now and one for perishable items to purchase a few days before Christmas Day.

- Order a bone-in spiral-sliced ham (7 to 9 pounds).

- Bake Greek Olive Bread. Let cool, place in a heavy-duty resealable plastic bag and freeze.

Two Days Before:

- Buy remaining grocery items.

- For Flourless Chocolate Cake with Peanut Butter Ice Cream, make the ice cream and sauce.

Christmas Eve:

- Set the table.

- Prepare the glaze for the ham; cover and chill.

- Make the onion-date mixture for Onion-Date Baked Brie; process 3/4 cup with dates and vinegar. Refrigerate the blended and unblended onion-date mixtures in two different covered containers.

- Bake and assemble the Cheese-Stuffed Twice-Baked Potatoes; cover and store in the refrigerator.

- For the Mixed Greens with Lemon Champagne Vinaigrette, prepare the dressing, wash and dry the greens, and seed the pomegranate. Store in separate containers in the refrigerator. Toast the walnuts; let cool and keep in a covered dish at room temperature.

- Remove cauliflowerets from the head for Roasted Cauliflower; wash and dry. Place in a resealable plastic bag; chill.

Christmas Day:

- In the morning, bake the Flourless Chocolate Cake. Cool completely, loosely cover and store at room temperature.

- Thaw Greek Olive Bread at room temperature.

- Roast Apple-Glazed Holiday Ham. Reheat glaze; baste and continue baking as directed.

- An hour before guests arrive, prepare White Wine Sangria; chill.

- Just before guests arrive, make Onion-Date Baked Brie.

- Bake Squash au Gratin alongside ham.

- Remove the ham and squash from the oven. Increase the temperature to 425°. Bake Roasted Cauliflower and Cheese-Stuffed Twice-Baked Potatoes.

- Prepare Lemon-Scented Broccolini.

- Assemble and toss Mixed Greens with Lemon Champagne Vinaigrette.

- For dessert, serve Flourless Chocolate Cake with Peanut Butter Ice Cream.

squash au gratin

(PICTURED AT RIGHT)

This is a fabulous-tasting dish that has an awesome aroma while baking. Tart apples add a fruity flavor.

Deb Williams | PEORIA, AZ

5-1/2 cups thinly sliced peeled butternut squash

1/2 teaspoon salt

1/4 teaspoon pepper

1/8 teaspoon ground nutmeg

2 tablespoons olive oil, divided

1 cup heavy whipping cream

2 medium tart apples, peeled and thinly sliced

1 cup (4 ounces) crumbled Gorgonzola cheese

In a large bowl, combine the squash, salt, pepper, nutmeg and 1 tablespoon oil; toss to coat. Transfer to a greased 11-in. x 7-in. baking dish; pour cream over top.

Cover and bake at 325° for 30 minutes. In a small bowl, toss apples in remaining oil. Spoon over squash. Bake, uncovered, for 25-30 minutes or until squash is tender. Sprinkle with cheese; bake 3-5 minutes longer or until the cheese is melted. **YIELD:** 9 servings.

white wine sangria

(PICTURED ON PAGE 7)

Lime, kumquats and two types of oranges infuse this quick and easy cocktail with an unforgettable citrus taste.

Joyce Moynihan | LAKEVILLE, MN

3 bottles (750 milliliters each) white wine

1-1/2 cups brandy

3/4 cup orange liqueur

1/2 cup sugar

1 large navel orange, sliced

1 medium blood orange, sliced

3 kumquats, sliced

1 medium lime, sliced

In a large pitcher, combine the wine, brandy and orange liqueur. Stir in the sugar until dissolved. Add the remaining ingredients. Refrigerate for 1 hour before serving. Serve over ice. **YIELD:** 18 servings (3-1/2 quarts).

apple-glazed holiday ham

(PICTURED ON PAGE 7)

Each Christmas, I'm asked to prepare this entree. I'm happy to oblige because it's easy to assemble, bakes for a few hours unattended and is delicious!

Doty Emory | JASPER, GA

1 bone-in fully cooked spiral-sliced ham (7 to 9 pounds)

1/2 cup packed brown sugar

1/2 cup unsweetened applesauce

1/2 cup unsweetened apple juice

1/4 cup maple syrup

1/4 cup molasses

1 tablespoon Dijon mustard

Dash ground ginger

Dash ground cinnamon

Place ham on a rack in a shallow roasting pan. Bake, uncovered, at 325° for 2 hours.

In a small saucepan, combine the remaining ingredients. Cook and stir over medium heat until heated through. Brush ham with some of the glaze; bake 30-60 minutes longer or until a meat thermometer reads 140°, brushing occasionally with remaining glaze. **YIELD:** 15 servings.

cheese-stuffed twice-baked potatoes

(PICTURED ON PAGE 6)

This is the first recipe I made when I initially became interested in cooking. No one can resist the creamy filling inside the crispy potato skins.

Cyndy Gerken | NAPLES, FL

8 large baking potatoes

1/4 cup olive oil

1/2 teaspoon salt

1/2 teaspoon pepper

FILLING:

3/4 cup butter, cubed

2-1/2 cups (10 ounces) shredded cheddar cheese

1 cup heavy whipping cream

1/2 cup sour cream

1/4 cup shredded Parmesan cheese

1/2 teaspoon salt

1/2 teaspoon pepper

3 tablespoons minced chives, divided

Scrub and pierce potatoes; rub with oil. Sprinkle with salt and pepper. Bake at 375° for 1 hour or until tender. When cool enough to handle, cut each potato in half lengthwise. Scoop out the pulp, leaving thin shells.

In a large saucepan, melt butter. Add the cheddar cheese, whipping cream, sour cream, Parmesan cheese, salt and pepper.

In a large bowl, mash the pulp with cheese mixture. Stir in 2 tablespoons chives. Spoon into the potato shells. Place on baking sheets. Bake, uncovered, at 375° for 25-30 minutes or until golden brown. Sprinkle with remaining chives. **YIELD:** 16 servings.

mixed greens with lemon champagne vinaigrette

(PICTURED AT RIGHT)

Every forkful of this spectacular salad has a crunch from walnuts, a burst of flavor from pomegranate seeds and a smooth finish from its easy vinaigrette.

Ray Uyeda | MOUNTAIN VIEW, CA

4 cups torn leaf lettuce

4 cups fresh spinach

2 cups fresh arugula

3/4 cup chopped walnuts, toasted

1/2 cup pomegranate seeds

1/2 cup olive oil

2 tablespoons Champagne vinegar

2 teaspoons lemon juice

1 teaspoon Dijon mustard

1 shallot, finely chopped

In a salad bowl, combine the leaf lettuce, spinach and arugula. Sprinkle with walnuts and pomegranate seeds.

In a small food processor, combine the remaining ingredients. Cover and process until blended. Transfer to a small pitcher or bowl; serve with salad. YIELD: 10 servings.

greek olive bread

The dough for this delicious bread is great to work with, making it easy
to knead in the olives and feta cheese. The subtle taste would complement any entree.

Tiffany Hartpence | LANDER, WY

1 package (1/4 ounce) active dry yeast

1/4 cup warm water (110° to 115°)

1 cup warm 2% milk (110° to 115°)

6 tablespoons olive oil, divided

1 tablespoon sugar

1 teaspoon salt

3-1/2 cups all-purpose flour

1/2 cup crumbled feta cheese

1/3 cup Greek olives

In a large bowl, dissolve yeast in warm water. Add the milk, 4 tablespoons oil, sugar, salt and 1-1/2 cups flour. Beat on medium speed for 3 minutes. Stir in enough of the remaining flour to form a soft dough.

Turn onto a floured surface; knead until smooth and elastic, about 6-8 minutes. Place in a greased bowl, turning once to grease the top. Cover and let rise in a warm place until doubled, about 1 hour.

Punch down dough. Sprinkle with cheese and olives; fold and knead lightly until combined. Shape into an 8-in. round loaf. Place on a greased baking sheet. Brush with remaining oil. Cover and let rise in warm place until doubled, about 40 minutes.

With a sharp knife, make four shallow slashes across top of loaf. Bake at 375° for 25-30 minutes or until golden brown. Remove from pan to wire rack to cool. **YIELD:** 1 loaf (16 slices).

roasted cauliflower

Roasting is a unique way to prepare cauliflower. Seasoned with
a wonderful blend of herbs, this side is simple enough for weeknight dinners.

Leslie Palmer | SWAMPSCOTT, MA

3 cups fresh cauliflowerets

2 tablespoons lemon juice

4-1/2 teaspoons olive oil

1 garlic clove, minced

1 teaspoon dried parsley flakes

1/2 teaspoon dried thyme

1/2 teaspoon dried tarragon

1/4 teaspoon pepper

1/4 cup grated Parmesan cheese

In a large bowl, combine the first eight ingredients; toss to coat. Transfer to an ungreased 15-in. x 10-in. x 1-in. baking pan. Bake at 425° for 15-20 minutes or until tender, stirring occasionally. Sprinkle with cheese. **YIELD:** 4 servings.

CHOOSING THE BEST

When purchasing fresh cauliflower, look for a head with compact florets that are free from yellow or brown spots. The leaves should be crisp and green, not withered or discolored. Tightly wrap an unwashed head of cauliflower and refrigerate for up to 5 days. Before using, wash and remove the leaves at the base and trim the stem.

flourless chocolate cake with peanut butter ice cream

(PICTURED AT RIGHT)

This luscious dessert features a chocolaty cake, peanut butter ice cream and a smooth coffee-flavored sauce. Every element can conveniently be made in advance.

Rebekah Beyer | SABETHA, KS

ICE CREAM:

1/2 cup 2% milk

1/4 cup sugar

2 egg yolks, beaten

1/4 cup creamy peanut butter

3/4 cup half-and-half cream

1 teaspoon vanilla extract

CAKE:

5 eggs, separated

1 pound semisweet chocolate, chopped

1/2 cup plus 2 tablespoons butter, cubed

1/4 teaspoon cream of tartar

1 tablespoon sugar

SAUCE:

2 egg yolks

2 tablespoons sugar

1 cup heavy whipping cream

2 teaspoons instant espresso powder

1-1/2 teaspoons coffee liqueur

Chopped chocolate

In a large heavy saucepan, heat milk and sugar until bubbles form around sides of pan. Whisk a small amount of hot mixture into egg yolks. Return all to the pan, whisking constantly.

Cook and stir over low heat until mixture is thickened and coats the back of a spoon. Quickly transfer to a bowl; stir in peanut butter until blended. Place in ice water and stir for 2 minutes. Stir in cream and vanilla. Refrigerate for several hours or overnight.

Fill cylinder of ice cream freezer two-thirds full; freeze according to the manufacturer's directions.

For cake, let eggs stand at room temperature for 30 minutes. In a small heavy saucepan, melt chocolate and butter over medium-low heat. Remove from the heat; whisk in egg yolks.

In a large bowl, beat egg whites and cream of tartar on medium speed until soft peaks form. Gradually beat in sugar on high until stiff glossy peaks form and the sugar is dissolved. Fold into the chocolate mixture.

Transfer to a greased and floured 13-in. x 9-in. baking pan. Bake at 325° for 20-25 minutes or until set. Cool completely. Cut into 12 pieces.

For sauce, in a small bowl, whisk egg yolks and sugar. In a small saucepan, heat heavy cream and espresso powder until bubbles form around the sides of pan. Whisk a small amount into yolk mixture. Return all to pan, whisking constantly. Cook until thickened. Remove from the heat; stir in liqueur. Refrigerate until serving.

Serve cake with ice cream and sauce. Garnish servings with chopped chocolate. **YIELD:** 12 servings.

lemon-scented broccolini

(PICTURED ON PAGE 7)

Even the most finicky eaters will eagerly enjoy this vegetable seasoned with lemon pepper, lemon peel and lemon juice. If you prefer, use broccoli instead.

Kim Champion | PHOENIX, AZ

2-1/2 pounds broccolini or broccoli spears

6 tablespoons butter

1 tablespoon plus 1-1/2 teaspoons lemon juice

1 tablespoon lemon-pepper seasoning

1 teaspoon grated lemon peel

1/4 teaspoon salt

In a large saucepan, bring 4 cups water to a boil. Add broccolini; cover and cook for 5 minutes. Drain and immediately place broccolini in ice water. Drain and pat dry.

In a large skillet, melt butter. Stir in the lemon juice, lemon pepper, lemon peel and salt. Add broccolini; cook over medium heat for 5-7 minutes or until tender. **YIELD:** 12 servings.

onion-date baked brie

Many baked Brie recipes call for a fruity topping, but my family favors this savory version. I even use the onion-date mixture at the table as a relish.

Allene Bary-Cooper | WICHITA FALLS, TX

2 large onions, sliced

2 tablespoons olive oil

2 garlic cloves, minced

1/4 teaspoon ground ginger

1/8 teaspoon salt

1/8 teaspoon cayenne pepper

1/2 cup dry red wine or beef broth

1/4 cup red wine vinegar, divided

6 ounces pitted dates, coarsely chopped

1 round (8 ounces) Brie cheese

Assorted crackers or French bread baguette slices

In a large skillet, saute onions in oil until tender. Add the garlic, ginger, salt and cayenne; cook 1 minute longer. Stir in wine and 2 tablespoons vinegar. Bring to a boil; cook until liquid is almost evaporated. Cool slightly.

Place the dates, 3/4 cup onion mixture and remaining vinegar in a food processor; cover and process until finely chopped.

Place Brie on a baking sheet. Spoon date mixture over Brie; top with remaining onion mixture.

Bake at 350° for 10-15 minutes or until heated through. Serve with crackers or baguette slices. **YIELD:** 8 servings.

under-glass place card

(PICTURED AT RIGHT)

Add an element of surprise to your traditional table setting by presenting your guests' place cards in a new way.

First place a pretty pinecone on the plate at each setting, then tuck in a computer-printed or hand-written place card.

You can also employ other holiday trinkets, such as mini ornaments, small bells or even tiny wrapped packages. For an eclectic, contemporary look, consider using a variety of items.

Place the wine glasses you'll be using at dinner upside-down over each of the place cards. If desired, tie a ribbon to the stem of each glass.

A Christmas Cracker Napkin Fold (see the instructions below) provides a festive finishing touch.

CHRISTMAS CRACKER NAPKIN FOLD

Christmas crackers are a common sight during the holiday season. There's no need to buy any when you can make them out of dinner napkins. Simply fold a square napkin in half, then roll up. (If you like, tuck a few pieces of candy inside.) Tie each end of the roll with ribbon.

Maybe your plans for Christmas dinner have changed at the last minute. Perhaps the holiday season is so hectic that you simply didn't have time to plan a merry menu until the day before. Or possibly you just need formal, no-fuss recipe ideas in your back pocket for spur-of-the-moment entertaining.

No matter the circumstances, you can present festive fare that looks elegant but comes together easily.

Make a quick stop at the grocery to pick up readily available tenderloin steaks. Once home, simply season the beef and then pop it in a skillet for an elegant entree of Steak au Poivre.

Mashed potatoes are wonderful but time-consuming. This year, prepare easy Spectacular Fingerling Potatoes instead! And while an assortment of sides is nice, it's unnecessary. Opt for Lemon-Butter Brussels Sprouts, which have awesome appeal for all.

FESTIVE FAST FOOD
(PICTURED AT RIGHT)

Steak au Poivre (p. 20)
Lemon-Butter Brussels Sprouts (p. 20)
Spectacular Fingerling Potatoes (p. 22)

last minute
CHRISTMAS PARTY

Easy Outline for a No-Fuss
Christmas Meal

The Day Before Before:

- For Grapefruit in Honey-Thyme Sauce, peel and cut the grapefruit into slices; cover and chill. Make the sauce; cover and store in the refrigerator.

- If using frozen brussels sprouts for Lemon-Butter Brussels Sprouts, thaw in the refrigerator. Halve fresh or frozen sprouts and chill.

Early in the Day:

- Combine the dressing ingredients for BLT Wedge Salad; cover and chill.

- Make the topping for Spicy Apple Dip. Refrigerate in a covered container.

Just Before the Party:

- For Spicy Apple Dip, place the cream cheese on a serving plate. Top with sauce; set out with crackers or cookies.

- Make the Oil & Vinegar Dipping Sauce; let stand 10-15 minutes. Slice the bread. Set out.

30 Minutes Before Dinner:

- Make Spectacular Fingerling Potatoes and Lemon-Butter Brussels Sprouts. Cover dishes until ready to serve.

- Prepare Steak au Poivre.

Just Before Dinner:

- Assemble the BLT Wedge Salad.

- For Grapefruit in Honey-Thyme Sauce, reheat the sauce over low heat, then drizzle over grapefruit and garnish with thyme.

spicy apple dip

(PICTURED AT RIGHT)

Here's a fun way to use up apple preserves. Or be creative and change up the jelly and preserves to develop a variety of flavor combos. My favorite is apple jelly with orange marmalade.

Crystal Bruns | ILIFF, CO

1 package (8 ounces) cream cheese, softened

1/2 cup apple jelly

1/2 cup apricot preserves

1-1/2 teaspoons prepared horseradish

1-1/4 teaspoons ground mustard

1 teaspoon pepper

Assorted crackers or gingersnap cookies

Place cream cheese on a serving plate. In a small bowl, combine apple jelly, preserves, horseradish, mustard and pepper until blended. Pour over cream cheese. Serve with crackers or cookies. **YIELD:** 4 servings.

oil & vinegar dipping sauce

I came up with this homemade dipping sauce after eating something similar at my favorite Greek restaurant. It goes wonderfully with fresh-baked bread and a glass of white wine.

Tracy Field | BREMERTON, WA

4 garlic cloves, minced

1/2 cup olive oil

1/3 cup balsamic vinegar

Sliced French bread baguette

Place garlic in a small bowl; pour oil and vinegar over top. Let stand for 10-15 minutes. Serve with baguette slices. **YIELD:** 1 cup.

steak au poivre

(PICTURED ON PAGE 17)

*This elegant entree can be prepared in under 30 minutes! Tender meat and
a great peppery flavor are accompanied by a rich cream sauce and fresh shiitake mushrooms.*

Barbara Pletzke | HERNDON, VA

4 beef tenderloin steaks (6 ounces each)

1 tablespoon coarsely ground pepper

1/2 teaspoon salt

1 tablespoon plus 2 teaspoons olive oil,
divided

2 cups sliced fresh shiitake mushrooms

1 tablespoon minced fresh thyme

2 tablespoons brandy

2 tablespoons heavy whipping cream

Sprinkle steaks with pepper and salt. In a large skillet over medium heat, cook steaks in 1 tablespoon oil for 4-5 minutes on each side or until meat reaches desired doneness (for medium-rare, a meat thermometer should read 145°; medium, 160°; well-done, 170°). Remove and keep warm.

In the same skillet, saute mushrooms in remaining oil. Add thyme; cook 1 minute longer. Remove from the heat. Add brandy; cook over medium heat until liquid is evaporated. Stir in cream. Serve with steaks. **YIELD:** 4 servings.

lemon-butter brussels sprouts

(PICTURED ON PAGE 17)

*Kick up ordinary brussels sprouts with olive oil, garlic, lemon juice and wine.
Even those who say they don't care for sprouts will ask for seconds.*

Jenn Tidwell | FAIR OAKS, CA

2 garlic cloves, minced

3 tablespoons olive oil

1 pound fresh or frozen brussels sprouts,
thawed and halved

1/4 cup white wine

1/2 cup chicken broth

4 teaspoons lemon juice

1/2 teaspoon dried thyme

1/4 teaspoon salt

1/4 teaspoon pepper

2 tablespoons butter

1 teaspoon grated lemon peel

Minced fresh parsley

In a large skillet over medium heat, cook garlic in oil for 1 minute. Add brussels sprouts; cook for 5 minutes. Add the wine, stirring to loosen browned bits from pan. Stir in the broth, lemon juice, thyme, salt and pepper.

Bring to a boil. Reduce heat; cover and simmer for 8-10 minutes or until sprouts are tender. Stir in butter and lemon peel until butter is melted. Garnish with parsley. **YIELD:** 4 servings.

grapefruit in honey-thyme sauce

(PICTURED AT RIGHT)

It takes just four ingredients to create this beautiful—and tasty—dish. Serve it as a first course or a side. Honey and white wine really allow the natural flavor of grapefruit to shine through.

Deirdre Dee Cox | MILWAUKEE, WI

3 large grapefruit

1/2 cup white wine or white grape juice

1/4 cup honey

2 tablespoons minced fresh thyme

Peel grapefruit. Cut into slices on a cutting board; reserve the juices and set the grapefruit aside.

In a small saucepan, combine the wine, honey, thyme and reserved juice. Bring to a boil. Reduce heat; simmer, uncovered, for 13-15 minutes or until liquid is reduced to 1/2 cup.

Arrange grapefruit slices on four plates; drizzle with sauce. YIELD: 4 servings.

SECTIONING A CITRUS FRUIT

Cut a thin slice off the bottom and top of the fruit. Rest the fruit, cut sides down, on a cutting board. With a sharp paring knife, remove peel and white pith from fruit.

Hold fruit over a bowl and slice between the membrane of a section and the fruit until the knife reaches the center. Turn the knife and follow the membrane so the fruit is released. Repeat until all sections are removed.

spectacular fingerling potatoes

(PICTURED ON PAGE 17)

My children absolutely love these tender "mini" potatoes. Fingerling potatoes can be found at the farmers market and specialty grocery stores, though Yukon Gold would work, too.

Michelle Herren | LAS VEGAS, NV

1 pound fingerling potatoes

3 tablespoons grated Parmesan cheese

3 tablespoons minced fresh parsley

2 tablespoons olive oil

1 tablespoon minced fresh rosemary
or 1 teaspoon dried rosemary, crushed

1 tablespoon butter, melted

1/4 teaspoon salt

1/4 teaspoon pepper

Place potatoes in a large saucepan and cover with water. Bring to a boil. Reduce heat; cover and cook for 10 minutes. Drain. Transfer to a greased 15-in. x 10-in. x 1-in. baking pan. Combine the remaining ingredients; drizzle over potatoes and toss to coat.

Bake, uncovered, at 425° for 8-10 minutes or until tender, stirring once. YIELD: 5 servings.

blt wedge salad

The homemade dressing really makes this simple, quick-to-fix salad shine. You get so much flavor without a whole lot of work. Making the dressing in advance and refrigerating will intensify the flavor. Adding blue cheese crumbles is a great option as well.

Crystal Holsinger | SURPRISE, AZ

1/2 cup 2% milk

3 tablespoons lime juice

1 cup mayonnaise

1 shallot, finely chopped

1 tablespoon ranch salad dressing mix

1 teaspoon pepper

1 garlic clove, minced

1 medium head iceberg lettuce

1-1/2 cups grape tomatoes, halved lengthwise

2/3 cup crumbled cooked bacon

Crumbled blue cheese, optional

In a small bowl, whisk milk and lime juice; let stand for 5 minutes. Whisk in the mayonnaise, shallot, ranch dressing mix, pepper and garlic until blended.

Cut lettuce into four wedges. Drizzle with dressing; top with the tomatoes and bacon. Sprinkle with the blue cheese if desired. YIELD: 4 servings.

fast & festive decor

(PICTURED AT RIGHT)

Easy-to-prepare menu items make it a breeze to entertain on a moment's notice during the Christmas season.

But what to do about decorating? Here are three ways to present everyday holiday items in simply stunning ways.

EASY ORNAMENT CENTERPIECE. Pluck a few ornaments from your evergreen and set them on a long, rectangular serving tray. (Or make a quick stop at a discount store to buy an inexpensive pack.) Adorn the display with fresh pine cones and pine boughs, artificial leaves and berries, or any of your favorite yuletide trinkets.

PRETTY POINSETTIA DISPLAY. Get more bang for your buck from the poinsettia plants you likely have scattered throughout your home. Snip off several stems from the plants and place inside some water-filled vases or bottles. You can help stabilize the stems by adding floral stones to the vases.

FIRE-AND-ICE ARRANGEMENT. Even if you don't live in a cold climate, you can create a snowy scene at your table. Just pour coarse sugar or sea salt into a shallow serving bowl. Place pillar candles of varying heights on top, making sure they sit securely in the sugar or salt. Then tuck in a few small pinecones taken from an evergreen in your own yard.

lanning time to get together with a few friends, relatives or neighbors during the Christmas season can be a scheduling challenge.

Between office parties, school plays, open houses and sit-down dinners, your evenings are likely full. So think about hosting a late-morning brunch!

You don't need to get up at the crack of dawn to start cooking. The recipes in this chapter all have make-ahead elements to them.

The batter for Overnight Yeast Pancakes with Blueberry Syrup is made the night before. Just pour onto the griddle in the morning.

Both the Strawberry Citrus Slushies and Berries in Yogurt Cream can be prepared a day in advance and assembled before serving.

Last-minute fuss stays to a minimum with these do-ahead dishes!

OVER-EASY BREAKFAST
(PICTURED AT RIGHT)

Overnight Yeast Pancakes
with Blueberry Syrup (p. 26)
Berries in Yogurt Cream (p. 26)
Strawberry Citrus Slushies (p. 28)

make ahead
YULETIDE BRUNCH

overnight yeast pancakes with blueberry syrup

(PICTURED ON PAGE 25)

Nothing says "good morning" like these fluffy pancakes topped with a fruity homemade syrup. When I don't have the time to make the syrup, I'll sprinkle a few blueberries over the batter when I spoon it onto the griddle.

Katie Wollgast | FLORISSANT, MO

1 package (1/4 ounce) active dry yeast

1-1/2 cups warm buttermilk (110° to 115°)

1 cup all-purpose flour

1 cup whole wheat flour

1/4 cup sugar

3 teaspoons baking powder

1 teaspoon baking soda

1/2 teaspoon salt

2 eggs

2 tablespoons canola oil

1 teaspoon vanilla extract

SYRUP:

1 cup fresh or frozen unsweetened blueberries

1/2 cup water

1/4 cup maple syrup

2 tablespoons sugar

2 teaspoons cornstarch

1/8 teaspoon salt

In a small bowl, dissolve the yeast in buttermilk; let stand for 5 minutes.

Meanwhile, in a large bowl, combine the flours, sugar, baking powder, baking soda and salt. Whisk the eggs, oil and vanilla; stir into dry ingredients just until moistened. Stir in yeast mixture. Cover and refrigerate for 8 hours or overnight.

To make pancakes, pour batter by 1/4 cupfuls onto a hot griddle coated with cooking spray; turn when bubbles form on top of pancakes. Cook until second side is golden brown.

Meanwhile, in a small saucepan, combine the blueberries, water, syrup, sugar, cornstarch and salt. Bring to a boil. Reduce heat; simmer, uncovered, for 5-7 minutes or until blueberries pop. **YIELD:** 18 pancakes (1 cup syrup).

berries in yogurt cream

(PICTURED ON PAGE 24)

Yogurt, cream, brown sugar and fresh fruit are all you need to wake up your taste buds on mornings you'd rather sleep in. Save time by having guests assemble their own parfaits.

Michelle Stillman | LANCASTER, PA

1-1/2 cups (12 ounces) plain yogurt

1-1/4 cups heavy whipping cream

1/2 cup packed brown sugar

5 cups assorted fresh fruit

Place yogurt in a large bowl; whisk in cream. Sprinkle with brown sugar but do not stir. Cover and refrigerate for at least 3 hours.

Just before serving, stir cream mixture. Divide among 10 dessert dishes. Top with berries. **YIELD:** 10 servings.

butterscotch maple scones

(PICTURED AT RIGHT)

Loaded with rich butterscotch flavor, these tempting scones could also be dessert. Wedges look so pretty drizzled with the maple glaze.

Lisa Varner | CHARLESTON, SC

1-1/2 cups quick-cooking oats

1 cup chopped walnuts

2 cups all-purpose flour

1/4 cup sugar

2 teaspoons baking powder

1/2 teaspoon salt

2/3 cup cold butter

1/2 cup maple syrup

1/4 cup 2% milk

1/4 cup heavy whipping cream

1 egg

1 teaspoon vanilla extract

1 cup butterscotch chips

GLAZE:

1/2 cup confectioners' sugar

2 tablespoons maple syrup

1 teaspoon vanilla extract

Spread oats and walnuts on a baking sheet. Bake at 375° for 8 minutes or until lightly browned, stirring occasionally. Remove to wire racks to cool.

In a large bowl, combine the flour, sugar, baking powder, salt and oat mixture. Cut in the butter until the mixture resembles coarse crumbs.

In a small bowl, whisk the maple syrup, milk, cream, egg and vanilla; stir into crumb mixture just until moistened. (Dough will be soft.) Stir in chips.

Transfer dough to a greased baking sheet. Pat into a 7-in. circle. Cut into eight wedges, but do not separate. Cover and refrigerate overnight. Bake at 400° for 25-30 minutes or until golden brown.

Meanwhile, combine glaze ingredients; drizzle over scones. Serve warm. **YIELD:** 8 scones.

coconut waffles

So tender they almost melt in your mouth, these waffles have a hint of coconut flavor in every bite.
We like to top the golden stack with whipped cream and a drizzle of chocolate sauce for an indulgent morning treat!

Kathy Angeley | TUCSON, AZ

1-3/4 cups all-purpose flour

2 tablespoons sugar

1 tablespoon baking powder

Dash salt

3 eggs

1 can (13.66 ounces) coconut milk

6 tablespoons butter, melted

1/8 teaspoon coconut extract

3/4 cup flaked coconut

Chocolate ice cream topping
and whipped cream

In a large bowl, combine the flour, sugar, baking powder and salt. In another bowl, whisk the eggs, coconut milk, butter and extract. Stir into dry ingredients just until moistened. Fold in coconut.

Bake in a preheated waffle iron according to manufacturer's directions until golden brown. Serve desired amount of waffles with whipped cream and chocolate topping.

To freeze waffles, arrange in a single layer on baking sheets. Freeze overnight or until firm. Transfer to a resealable plastic freezer bag. Waffles may be frozen for up to 2 months. **YIELD:** 8 waffles.

TO USE FROZEN WAFFLES: Reheat waffles in a toaster. Serve with chocolate topping and whipped cream.

strawberry citrus slushies

(PICTURED ON PAGE 24)

Ordinary juice is just fine for everyday breakfasts. But when hosting a holiday brunch, our Test Kitchen staff members suggest you serve something a little more special, such as this pretty and refreshing beverage.

STRAWBERRY PUREE:

1/2 cup frozen unsweetened sliced strawberries, thawed

2 tablespoons confectioners' sugar

2 tablespoons water

CITRUS SLUSH:

3/4 cup sugar

3/4 cup water

3/4 cup lemon juice

2/3 cup orange juice

4-1/2 cups ice cubes

Place the strawberries, confectioners' sugar and water in a blender. Cover and process until blended; transfer to a small bowl. Cover and chill until serving.

In a small saucepan, bring the sugar and water to a boil. Cook and stir until sugar is dissolved. Remove from the heat; cool to room temperature.

Just before serving, place the lemon juice, orange juice, ice cubes and sugar syrup in a blender. Cover and process until it reaches a slushy consistency. Divide strawberry puree among four chilled glasses. Top with citrus slush. Serve immediately. **YIELD:** 5 servings.

bananas foster baked french toast

(PICTURED AT RIGHT)

Mmm...bananas foster for breakfast! This yummy baked French toast serves up all the taste of the spectacular dessert in fine fashion.

L. G. Nasson | QUINCY, MA

3 large bananas, sliced

2/3 cup packed brown sugar

1/2 cup butter, melted

1/2 cup heavy whipping cream

1/2 teaspoon ground cinnamon

1/2 teaspoon ground allspice

1/4 cup chopped pecans, optional

12 slices egg bread

1-1/2 cups 2% milk

3 eggs

1 tablespoon sugar

1 teaspoon vanilla extract

In a large bowl, combine the bananas, brown sugar, butter, cream, cinnamon, allspice and pecans if desired. Transfer to an ungreased 13-in. x 9-in. baking dish. Arrange bread over banana mixture. Place the milk, eggs, sugar and vanilla in a blender; cover and process until smooth. Pour over the bread. Cover and refrigerate for 8 hours or overnight.

Remove from the refrigerator 30 minutes before baking. Bake, uncovered, at 375° for 35-40 minutes or until a knife inserted near the center comes out clean. Let stand for 10 minutes before serving. **YIELD:** 6 servings.

corned beef & cranberry hash

The make-ahead convenience of this deliciously different hash makes it a standby during the busy holiday season. Fresh cranberries bring sweet-tart flavor to a traditional breakfast dish.

Carolyn Cope | ALLSTON, MD

2 cups cubed red potatoes

2 cups cubed cooked corned beef

1/2 cup fresh or frozen cranberries, thawed and chopped

1/3 cup chopped onion

1/4 cup chicken broth

1 tablespoon minced fresh parsley

1 tablespoon stone-ground mustard

1 small garlic clove, minced

1/4 teaspoon dried thyme

1/4 teaspoon pepper

1/8 teaspoon ground nutmeg

5 tablespoons butter, cubed

Place the potatoes in a small saucepan and cover with water. Bring to a boil. Reduce the heat; cover and cook for 10-15 minutes or until tender. Drain.

In a large bowl, mash 1 cup of potatoes. Stir in the corned beef, cranberries, onion, broth, parsley, mustard, garlic, thyme, pepper, nutmeg and remaining potatoes. Cover and refrigerate for 3 hours or overnight to allow flavors to blend.

In a large skillet, melt butter. Stir in meat mixture. Cook and stir over medium-high heat for 15-20 minutes or until lightly browned and heated through. YIELD: 4 servings.

overnight baked oatmeal

My husband and I spent a long weekend at a bed-and-breakfast not far from our home. The owners shared this delicious recipe with me, which I've made my own after a couple of simple changes.

Jennifer Cramer | LEBANON, PA

2 eggs, lightly beaten

3 cups 2% milk

2 cups old-fashioned oats

3/4 cup packed brown sugar

1/4 cup canola oil

1-1/2 teaspoons ground cinnamon

1 teaspoon salt

1/4 cup dried blueberries

1/4 cup dried cherries

1/4 cup sliced almonds

In a large bowl, whisk the eggs, milk, oats, brown sugar, oil, cinnamon and salt. Stir in blueberries and cherries. Pour into a greased 8-in. square baking dish. Cover and refrigerate for 8 hours or overnight.

Remove from the refrigerator 30 minutes before baking. Uncover and stir; sprinkle with the almonds. Bake, uncovered, at 350° for 45-50 minutes or until a thermometer reaches 160°. Serve warm. YIELD: 9 servings.

ham & cheese strata with sun-dried tomatoes

(PICTURED AT RIGHT)

Brimming with ham, cheese and sun-dried tomatoes, this pretty breakfast casserole feeds a crowd while adding visual appeal to your brunch's spread. It's elegant comfort food at its best.

Kim Deane | FENTON, MO

1 cup cubed fully cooked ham

1 cup sun-dried tomatoes (not packed in oil), chopped

1 tablespoon minced fresh parsley

1-1/2 teaspoons minced chives

1 loaf sourdough bread (1 pound), crust removed and cut into 1-inch cubes

2 cups (8 ounces) shredded cheddar cheese

12 eggs

1-1/2 cups 2% milk

1/2 cup heavy whipping cream

1 teaspoon salt

1/4 teaspoon coarsely ground pepper

1/8 teaspoon ground nutmeg

1/8 teaspoon cayenne pepper

1 tablespoon butter, melted

In a small bowl, combine the ham, tomatoes, parsley and chives. Place half of the bread in a greased 13-in. x 9-in. baking dish. Layer with half of the ham mixture and half of the cheese. Repeat layers.

In a large bowl, combine the eggs, milk, cream, salt, pepper, nutmeg and cayenne. Pour over top; drizzle with butter. Cover and refrigerate overnight.

Remove from the refrigerator 30 minutes before baking. Bake, uncovered, at 350° for 45-50 minutes or until a knife inserted near the center comes out clean (cover loosely with foil if the top browns too quickly). Let stand for 10 minutes before cutting. **YIELD:** 12 servings.

make-ahead monkey bread

Frozen bread dough makes this ooey-gooey breakfast treat a snap to make. I have used it for Christmas because I can prepare it the night before, which allows me to join the family in seeing what Santa left under the tree.

Judith Gordon | TEXARKANA, AR

3/4 cup packed brown sugar

1 package (3-1/2 ounces) cook-and-serve butterscotch pudding mix

1 teaspoon ground cinnamon

1 cup chopped pecans

1/2 cup butter

20 frozen bread dough dinner rolls, quartered

1 teaspoon lemon juice

In a small bowl, combine the brown sugar, pudding mix and cinnamon. In a greased 10-in. fluted tube pan, layer a third of the pecans, 1/3 cup brown sugar mixture, 2 tablespoons butter and half the rolls. Repeat layers. Top with lemon juice, remaining pecans, brown sugar mixture and butter; cover and refrigerate overnight.

Remove from the refrigerator 30 minutes before baking. Bake, uncovered, at 350° for 30-35 minutes or until golden brown. Immediately invert the bread onto a serving platter. Serve warm. YIELD: 1 loaf (12 servings).

south of the border citrus salad

Orange, grapefruit and jicama add color and texture to this out-of-the-ordinary fruit salad. Sometimes I'll toss in slices of mango and cucumber for additional pizzazz.

Mary Fuller | SEATAC, WA

3 medium oranges, peeled and sliced

3 medium pink grapefruit, peeled and sliced

1-1/2 cups cubed peeled jicama

2 tablespoons minced fresh cilantro

2 tablespoons lime juice

1/4 teaspoon ground cinnamon

In a large bowl, combine all ingredients. Arrange on a serving platter; refrigerate until chilled. YIELD: 7 servings.

MAKE TIME FOR JICAMA

A jicama (HEE-kah-mah), also known as a Mexican potato, is a root vegetable resembling a turnip. It has thin brown skin, white flesh, a crunchy texture and a sweet, nutty flavor similar to a water chestnut.

Look for small jicamas (large ones tend to be woody and fibrous) that are firm and unblemished. Store whole in the refrigerator for up to 2 weeks. Once cut, wrap in plastic wrap and use within a week.

Before using, wash jicama in cold water. Peel the skin and then cut or slice as desired. It will not discolor after cutting.

Jicamas: Louise Lister/StockFood.

overnight baked eggs bruschetta

(PICTURED AT RIGHT)

I like to take advantage of time with family and guests when I'm preparing a meal. Because most overnight brunch recipes are so similar, I came up with a breakfast bruschetta.

Judi Berman-Yamada | PORTLAND, OR

1 tablespoon cornmeal

1 tube (13.8 ounces) refrigerated pizza crust

3 tablespoons olive oil, divided

1-1/2 cups (6 ounces) shredded part-skim mozzarella cheese, divided

3/4 pound sliced fresh mushrooms

3/4 teaspoon garlic powder

3/4 teaspoon dried rosemary, crushed

1/2 teaspoon pepper

1/4 teaspoon salt

2 cups pizza sauce

1/8 teaspoon paprika

1 tablespoon white vinegar

9 eggs

2 ounces fresh goat cheese

1/2 cup French-fried onions

Fresh basil leaves

Sprinkle cornmeal into a greased 15-in. x 10-in. x 1-in. baking pan. Unroll pizza dough; press to cover bottom of pan. Brush with 1 tablespoon oil; sprinkle with 3/4 cup of mozzarella cheese. Bake at 400° for 8 minutes.

In a large skillet, saute mushrooms in remaining oil until tender. Stir in the garlic powder, rosemary, pepper and salt. Remove 1 cup of mushrooms; sprinkle over the crust. Combine the pizza sauce and paprika; add to the skillet.

Place 2-3 in. of water in a large skillet with high sides; add vinegar. Bring to a boil; reduce heat and simmer gently. Break cold eggs, one at a time, into a custard cup or saucer; holding the cup close to the surface of the water, slip each egg into water.

Cook, uncovered, until whites are completely set and yolks are still soft, about 4 minutes. With a slotted spoon, lift eggs out of water. Arrange eggs over mushrooms.

Spoon pizza sauce mixture around eggs; sprinkle with remaining mozzarella cheese. Crumble goat cheese; sprinkle over eggs. Cover and refrigerate overnight.

Remove from the refrigerator 30 minutes before baking. Sprinkle with onions. Bake, uncovered, at 400° for 10-15 minutes or until golden brown. Garnish with basil. **YIELD:** 9 servings.

osting a special hors d'oeuvre-inspired cocktail party during the Christmas season doesn't mean you have to spend a fortune on fully stocking your bar.

You can create an affair to remember by serving a selection of both red and white wines that pair perfectly with your assorted homemade appetizers. (Look for the wine suggestions after each recipe in this chapter.)

Feed the spirit of your yuletide guests with such offerings as Brie and Wild Mushroom Soup, Caprese Scallop Stacks, Cheese Crisps with Ricotta Dip and Baked Figs.

WINING AND DINING
(PICTURED AT RIGHT)

Brie and Wild Mushroom Soup (p. 36)
Caprese Scallop Stacks (p. 37)
Cheese Crisps with Ricotta Dip (p. 36)
Baked Figs (p. 40)

wine tasting
APPETIZER AFFAIR

brie and wild mushroom soup

(PICTURED ON PAGE 35)

I obtained this recipe at a local home and garden show a few years ago.
The rich, comforting soup is sure to please on chilly winter days.

Patrice Bruwer-Miller | WYOMING, MI

2 cups cream sherry

1/4 cup butter, cubed

1 pound assorted fresh mushrooms
(such as shiitake, cremini and oyster)

8 shallots, finely chopped

1/3 cup minced fresh parsley

1 tablespoon lemon juice

1/3 cup all-purpose flour

4 cups beef broth

1 round (8 ounces) Brie cheese, rind
removed, cubed

1 cup heavy whipping cream

1 teaspoon salt

1/2 teaspoon white pepper

Place sherry in a small saucepan. Bring to a boil; cook until reduced by half. Set aside.

In a Dutch oven, melt butter. Add mushrooms and shallots; saute until tender. Add the parsley and lemon juice. Stir in flour until blended; gradually add broth and reduced sherry.

Bring to a boil. Reduce the heat; simmer, uncovered, for 8-10 minutes or until thickened. Stir in the cheese until melted. Add the whipping cream, salt and pepper; heat through (do not boil). **YIELD:** 16 servings (1/2 cup each).

SUGGESTED WINES: Chardonnay, Pinot Noir

cheese crisps with ricotta dip

(PICTURED ON PAGE 34)

This Italian-style appetizer is the perfect combination of salty and sweet.
My kids gobble up the crisps even without the fruity dipping sauce!

Naylet LaRochelle | MIAMI, FL

3 slices pancetta or bacon, finely chopped

1 tablespoon olive oil

1-1/2 cups grated Parmesan cheese

1 cup ricotta cheese

1/2 cup apricot preserves

2 tablespoons minced fresh basil

In a small skillet, cook pancetta in oil over medium heat until crisp. Drain on paper towels. Drop Parmesan cheese by tablespoonfuls onto parchment paper-lined baking sheets about 1 in. apart. Sprinkle with pancetta. Bake at 400° for 5-6 minutes or until crispy and golden brown. Remove from pans.

Combine ricotta cheese and preserves; sprinkle with basil. Serve with crisps. **YIELD:** 2 dozen (1-1/2 cups dip).

SUGGESTED WINES: Chardonnay, Sauvignon Blanc, Chenin Blanc

caprese scallop stacks

(PICTURED AT RIGHT AND ON PAGE 35)

Scallops and zucchini put a creative and tasty twist on the traditional caprese recipe. The red and green colors make it perfect for the Christmas season.

Roxanne Chan | ALBANY, CA

1 medium zucchini

12 sea scallops (about 1-1/2 pounds)

4 tablespoons olive oil, divided

1/4 cup chopped roasted sweet red peppers

1 tablespoon pine nuts, toasted

1 tablespoon lemon juice

1 garlic clove, minced

1 teaspoon dried currants

1 teaspoon capers, drained

1/2 teaspoon Dijon mustard

1/4 teaspoon grated lemon peel

Watercress, optional

Cut zucchini into 1/3-in.-thick slices; place in a steamer basket over 1 in. of water. Bring to a boil; cover and steam for 1-2 minutes or until crisp-tender.

Meanwhile, cut the scallops in half horizontally. In a large skillet, saute scallops in 1 tablespoon oil until firm and opaque. Remove and keep warm.

To serve, place zucchini slices on a serving plate. Layer each with a scallop half, some chopped roasted pepper and a scallop half. In a small bowl, combine the pine nuts, lemon juice, garlic, currants, capers, mustard, lemon peel and remaining oil; spoon over stacks. Garnish with watercress if desired. **YIELD:** 1 dozen.

SUGGESTED WINES: Chenin Blanc, Sauvignon Blanc, Pinot Grigio

roasted garlic & sun-dried tomato toast

*During the busy holiday season, I really love special appetizers
that are actually easy to prepare. This recipe fits the bill.*

Krist Wilcox-Borsher | PAWCATUCK, CT

4 whole garlic bulbs

1 can (14-1/2 ounces) beef broth

1 cup olive oil

1 package (3-1/2 ounces) sun-dried tomatoes
(not packed in oil), chopped

1 French bread baguette (10-1/2 ounces),
cut into 1/2-inch slices

Remove papery outer skin from garlic (do not peel or separate cloves). Cut top off of each garlic bulb. Place garlic in a 9-in. deep-dish pie plate. Add the broth, oil and tomatoes.

Bake, uncovered, at 425° for 30-35 minutes or until garlic is softened. Cool for 10-15 minutes. Place baguette slices on ungreased baking sheets. Bake at 425° for 4-6 minutes or until toasted.

Squeeze softened garlic into a small bowl; spread over baguette slices. With a slotted spoon, top each slice with the tomatoes. **YIELD:** 3 dozen.

SUGGESTED WINES: Beaujolais, Chianti, Sauvignon Blanc

warm olive bruschetta

*Cream cheese and ripe olives add heartiness to the
usual bruschetta with tomatoes. The flavors blend beautifully.*

Lori Harmon | BILLINGS, MT

24 slices French bread baguette
(1/4 inch thick)

3 tablespoons olive oil

1 celery rib, chopped

1/2 cup chopped pimiento-stuffed olives

1 can (2-1/4 ounces) sliced ripe olives,
drained and chopped

1 tablespoon prepared Italian salad dressing

2 garlic cloves, minced

3/4 cup spreadable chive and onion
cream cheese

3/4 cup chopped cherry tomatoes

Place bread on ungreased baking sheets; brush lightly with oil. Bake at 400° for 3-4 minutes or until lightly browned.

Meanwhile, in a small bowl, combine the celery, olives, salad dressing and garlic. Spread cream cheese over toast; top each slice with 2 teaspoons olive mixture. Bake for 6-8 minutes or until heated through. Top with tomatoes. **YIELD:** 2 dozen.

SUGGESTED WINES: Cabernet Sauvignon, Sauvignon Blanc

beef tenderloin lollipops

(PICTURED AT RIGHT)

Bite-sized beef cubes are easy to pop in your mouth as you mingle at parties. Sweet caramelized onion and salty blue cheese add unforgettable taste.

Bonnie Hawkins | ELKHORN, WI

3 large onions, halved and thinly sliced

2 tablespoons olive oil

3 tablespoons butter, divided

1 beef tenderloin roast (2 pounds)

1/4 teaspoon salt

1/4 teaspoon pepper

2 cups (8 ounces) crumbled blue cheese

In a large skillet, saute onions in oil and 1 tablespoon butter until softened. Reduce the heat to medium-low; cook, stirring occasionally, for 30 minutes or until deep golden brown.

Meanwhile, cut roast into 1-1/2-in. cubes; sprinkle with salt and pepper. In a large skillet over medium heat, brown beef in batches in remaining butter.

Transfer beef to an ungreased 15-in. x 10-in. x 1-in. baking pan; top with onions and blue cheese. Bake at 350° for 8-10 minutes or until the beef reaches desired doneness (for medium-rare, a meat thermometer should read 145°; medium, 160°; well-done, 170°). Insert skewers into appetizers. **YIELD:** 2-1/2 dozen.

SUGGESTED WINES: Cabernet Sauvignon, Merlot

HOW MUCH WINE TO BUY?

Typically, cocktail parties last around 3 hours, with the average person having 1 glass of wine per hour. A standard-size bottle of wine (750 ml.) yields about 5 servings, so buy accordingly. Because you don't know who prefers red or white wine, you may want an equal number of both. And don't forget to offer water and soda as well.

baked figs

(PICTURED ON PAGE 34)

Here's a nice change from traditional savory offerings. To keep these
flavorful figs warm during your party, serve them in a chafing dish.

Deirdre Dee Cox | MILWAUKEE, WI

3/4 pound dried figs

3/4 cup orange juice

1/4 cup orange liqueur

1/8 teaspoon ground cloves

1/4 cup sugar

Whipped cream

Prick holes in figs with a fork; place in a greased 8-in. square baking dish. In a small bowl, combine the orange juice, liqueur and cloves. Sprinkle sugar over figs; pour juice mixture over the top.

Bake, uncovered, at 325° for 45-55 minutes or until tender, basting occasionally with juice mixture. Serve warm with whipped cream. **YIELD:** about 1-1/2 dozen.

SUGGESTED WINES: White Zinfandel, White Merlot, Riesling

salmon & cream cheese potatoes

Everyone enjoys these elegant-looking appetizers. You can assemble
them several hours ahead of time and refrigerate until guests arrive.

Marie Rizzio | INTERLOCHEN, MI

12 small red potatoes

2 packages (3 ounces each) cream cheese, softened

2 tablespoons sour cream

2 tablespoons snipped fresh dill

2 tablespoons grated lemon peel

1 tablespoon capers, drained

1/4 teaspoon salt

1/8 teaspoon coarsely ground pepper

3 ounces smoked salmon fillet, flaked

Fresh dill sprigs, optional

Place potatoes in a large saucepan and cover with water. Bring to a boil. Reduce heat; cover and simmer for 15-20 minutes or until tender. Meanwhile, in a small bowl, combine the cream cheese, sour cream, dill, lemon peel, capers, salt and pepper.

Drain potatoes; cut in half. Cut a thin slice from the bottom of each potato half to level if necessary.

Dollop cheese mixture onto potatoes, 2 teaspoons on each. Top with salmon. Garnish with dill sprigs if desired. Chill until serving. **YIELD:** 2 dozen.

SUGGESTED WINES: Chardonnay, Pinot Grigio, Sauvignon Blanc

onion tarts with balsamic onion jam

(PICTURED AT RIGHT)

I came up with this recipe when I needed to use up some puff pastry. Now this spur-of-the-moment snack makes a regular appearance on my entertaining menus.

Teddy Devico | WARREN, NJ

3 large sweet onions, chopped

1/2 cup butter, divided

5 bay leaves, divided

2 small fresh sage sprigs, divided

2 fresh thyme sprigs, divided

4 garlic cloves, minced

1/4 cup balsamic vinegar

3 tablespoons brown sugar

2 tablespoons molasses

1 package (17.3 ounces) frozen puff pastry, thawed

3/4 cup grated Parmesan cheese

In a large skillet, saute onions in 1/4 cup butter until softened. Add 3 bay leaves, 1 sage sprig and 1 thyme sprig. Reduce heat to medium-low; cook, stirring occasionally, for 30-40 minutes or until onions are deep golden brown. Add garlic; cook 2 minutes longer. Discard bay leaves, thyme and sage. Cool slightly.

Place onion mixture in a food processor; cover and process until blended. Transfer to a small saucepan. Add the vinegar, brown sugar, molasses and remaining bay leaves, sage, thyme and butter. Bring to a boil; cook and stir until thickened, about 10 minutes. Discard bay leaves, sage and thyme.

Unfold puff pastry; cut into 1-1/2-in. squares. Transfer squares to greased baking sheets. Dollop a scant teaspoonful of onion jam in the middle of each square; sprinkle with 1/2 teaspoon cheese.

Bake at 400° for 10-15 minutes or until golden brown. Serve warm or at room temperature. **YIELD:** 6 dozen.

SUGGESTED WINES: Chenin Blanc, Chardonnay, Pinot Noir

parmesan truffles

(PICTURED AT FAR RIGHT)

*These individual Parmesan cheese balls begin with a base of
whipping cream and garlic. Rolling them in minced parsley lends a festive holiday color.*

Melissa Zawaduk | ST. ALBERT, AB

3/4 cup heavy whipping cream

2 garlic cloves, minced

2 cups grated Parmesan cheese

Additional grated Parmesan cheese and/or minced fresh parsley

Assorted crackers

In a large saucepan, bring cream and garlic just to a boil, stirring occasionally. Reduce heat to low; stir in cheese, 1/2 cup at a time, until smooth.

Transfer to a bowl; cool to room temperature, stirring occasionally. Refrigerate for at least 2 hours or until firm. Shape into 3/4-in. balls; roll in additional cheese and/or parsley. Serve with crackers. **YIELD:** 3 dozen.

SUGGESTED WINES: Chardonnay, Chenin Blanc, Sauvignon Blanc

tomato rosemary hummus

*Crispy pita chips are the perfect accompaniment to a creamy hummus
infused with the appealing flavors of tomato and rosemary.*

Crystal Heaton | ALTON, UT

1 medium onion, chopped

3 tablespoons olive oil

4 garlic cloves, minced

2 cans (15 ounces each) garbanzo beans or chickpeas, rinsed and drained

1 can (6 ounces) tomato paste

1 tablespoon minced fresh rosemary
or 1 teaspoon dried rosemary, crushed

1/2 teaspoon salt

1/4 teaspoon pepper

Baked pita chips

In a large skillet, saute onion in oil until softened. Reduce heat to medium-low; cook, stirring occasionally, for 20-30 minutes or until light golden brown. Add garlic; cook 2 minutes longer.

Cool slightly. Transfer onion mixture to a food processor. Add the beans, tomato paste, rosemary, salt and pepper; cover and process until smooth. Serve with chips. **YIELD:** 3 cups.

SUGGESTED WINES: Barbera d'Asti, Chianti, Pinot Grigio

FREEZING FRESH ROSEMARY

Rosemary is a hearty herb that freezes well for future use. Simply wrap sprigs in foil. Place in a freezer bag and freeze for up to 3 months. When using, remember that frozen rosemary has a stronger flavor than fresh.

garlic-herb mini flatbreads

(PICTURED AT RIGHT)

The dough for our Test Kitchen's homemade crackers is easy to work with. And with such wonderful flavor, these are worth the time it takes to prepare them.

2 cups all-purpose flour

1/3 cup shredded Asiago cheese

5 tablespoons sesame seeds

1 tablespoon dried minced garlic

1 teaspoon baking powder

1/2 teaspoon salt

1/2 teaspoon dried rosemary, crushed

2/3 cup plus 2 tablespoons water, divided

1/3 cup olive oil

1 egg white

TOPPING:

2 tablespoons shredded Asiago cheese

1 tablespoon dried minced garlic

1 tablespoon sesame seeds

1 teaspoon dried rosemary, crushed

In a small bowl, combine the first seven ingredients. Gradually add 2/3 cup water and oil, tossing with a fork until dough forms a ball. Divide dough in half; roll each portion into a 12-in. x 8-in. rectangle directly onto a greased baking sheet. Pierce dough with a fork.

Whisk egg white and remaining water; brush over dough. Combine topping ingredients; sprinkle over the top.

Score dough into 2-in. squares. Bake at 400° for 15-20 minutes or until golden brown. Immediately cut along the score lines; cool on pans on wire racks. Store the crackers in an airtight container. YIELD: 4 dozen.

SUGGESTED WINES: Blanc de Blancs, Cava, Pinot Noir

polenta mushroom appetizers

Mushroom lovers will fall for this appetizer that has the flavor of Stroganoff. When I can't find tubes of prepared polenta, I make instant polenta according to package directions and cut out pieces with cookie cutters.

Patricia Nieh | PORTOLA VALLEY, CA

2 tubes (1 pound each) polenta, cut into 1/2-inch slices

3 tablespoons olive oil

1/2 pound sliced baby portobello mushrooms

1/2 pound sliced fresh shiitake mushrooms

1 tablespoon chopped shallot

1 tablespoon butter

1 garlic clove, minced

1/4 cup white wine

1 tablespoon minced fresh parsley

1/2 teaspoon minced fresh thyme

1/2 cup heavy whipping cream

1/4 cup grated Parmesan cheese

Place polenta on greased baking sheets; brush with oil. Bake at 425° for 15-20 minutes or until edges are golden brown.

Meanwhile, in a large skillet, saute mushrooms and shallot in butter until tender. Add garlic; cook 1 minute longer. Add the wine, parsley and thyme; cook and stir until liquid is evaporated. Add cream; cook and stir until thickened. Stir in cheese.

Top each slice of polenta with a rounded tablespoon of mushroom mixture. **YIELD:** 2 dozen.

SUGGESTED WINES: Cava, Chardonnay, Fino Sherry

roasted curry chickpeas

Our Test Kitchen staff members coat chickpeas with simple seasonings to make a low-fat snacking sensation. It rivals calorie-laden varieties sold in stores.

1 can (15 ounces) chickpeas or garbanzo beans

2 tablespoons olive oil

1 teaspoon salt

1/4 teaspoon pepper

2 teaspoons curry powder

1/2 teaspoon crushed red pepper flakes

Rinse and drain chickpeas; place on paper towels and pat dry. Place in a greased 15-in. x 10-in. x 1-in. baking pan; drizzle with oil and sprinkle with seasonings. Toss to coat. Bake at 450° for 25-30 minutes or until crispy and golden brown. **YIELD:** 1 cup.

SUGGESTED WINES: Gewurztraminer, White Merlot, White Zinfandel

wine pairing cards

(PICTURED AT RIGHT)

Your guests can certainly sip on whichever type of wine they prefer while nibbling on the appetizers at your Christmas party.

But it can be fun to encourage them to pair specific wines with certain dishes in order to enhance the already wonderful flavors of the foods.

Take the guesswork out of what spirits complement which appetizers. Assemble several wine pairing place cards listing each dish and its corresponding wine suggestions. Then set them out on the appetizer table and near your bar area.

Don't feel like you need to offer every type of wine suggested in this chapter. Consider planning the menu so you can offer two red wine choices and two white wine options.

If you're preparing a dish of your own, ask the wine expert at your local liquor or specialty grocery store for advice.

Unless you're a sommelier, don't worry about having all the perfect pairings. Entertaining should be fun!

HOW TO MAKE WINE PAIRING PLACE CARDS

A few everyday items are all you need to make attractive Wine Pairing Place Cards for your appetizer party. For each base, use a hot glue gun to hold six wine bottle corks together; let dry. Tie a ribbon around the base if desired.

Hand-write or use a computer to list the appetizers you're serving and the suggested wines to pair with each dish. Print on card stock or glue paper to card stock so it is rigid and stands upright. Slip the paper between the two columns of corks. Set on the appetizer table and beverage station.

Unlike any of the other holidays, the busy Christmas season spans several weeks. During that time, there are countless opportunities to entertain friends and relatives.

Take the worry out of what to make for every merry occasion by turning to this recipe-packed chapter.

Are you hosting a formal sit-down dinner with the family? Portobello-Stuffed Pork Roast, Halibut with Citrus-Olive Sauce and Pistachio-Crusted Chicken Breasts are impressive entrees.

For more casual gatherings, you can't go wrong with mouthwatering ideas such as Pasta and White Bean Soup with Sun-Dried Tomatoes and Mozzarella-Stuffed Meatballs.

MAJESTIC MAIN COURSE
(PICTURED AT RIGHT)

Portobello-Stuffed Pork Roast (p. 48)

classic
CHRISTMAS ENTREES

portobello-stuffed pork roast

(PICTURED ON PAGE 47)

Tart cherries and earthy mushrooms come together in a savory stuffing for pork tenderloin.
The sauce, prepared with port wine and balsamic vinegar, makes every bite even better.

Linda Monach | CHESTNUT HILL, MA

1 package (6 ounces) dried cherries

3/4 cup ruby port wine or grape juice, warmed, divided

3 large portobello mushrooms, divided

1 medium onion, finely chopped

3 tablespoons olive oil

6 garlic cloves, minced

1-1/2 cups soft bread crumbs

1/3 cup chopped pecans

1/2 teaspoon salt

1/4 teaspoon pepper

3 tablespoons plus 1/4 cup balsamic vinegar, divided

1 boneless pork loin roast (3 to 4 pounds)

CHERRY PORT WINE SAUCE:

1/2 cup ruby port wine or grape juice

1/2 cup balsamic vinegar

1/4 cup chicken broth

3 garlic cloves, minced

1/2 cup heavy whipping cream

In a small bowl, combine cherries and 1/2 cup wine. Let stand for 5 minutes. Drain cherries, reserving wine; set aside.

Chop one mushroom. In a large skillet, saute onion in oil until tender. Add garlic; cook 1 minute longer. Remove from the heat. Add the bread crumbs, pecans, salt, pepper, 3 tablespoons balsamic vinegar, 1/2 cup cherries and chopped mushroom.

Starting about a third in from one side, make a lengthwise slit in the roast to within 1/2 in. of bottom. Turn roast over and make another lengthwise slit, starting from about a third in from the opposite side. Open roast so it lies flat; cover with plastic wrap. Flatten to 3/4-in. thickness; remove plastic. Spread stuffing mixture over the meat.

Roll up jelly-roll style, starting with a long side. Tie pork at 2-in. intervals with kitchen string. Place on a rack in a shallow roasting pan. Slice remaining mushrooms; brush with 1 tablespoon vinegar. Arrange around pork.

Bake at 350° for 1 hour. In a small bowl, combine remaining vinegar and reserved wine; brush over the pork. Bake 1 to 1-1/2 hours longer or until a meat thermometer reads 160°. Let stand for 10 minutes before slicing.

For sauce, in a small saucepan, combine the wine, vinegar, broth, garlic and remaining cherries. Bring to a boil; cook until liquid is reduced by half. Stir in cream; simmer for 5 minutes. Serve with pork and mushrooms. **YIELD:** 8 servings (1 cup sauce).

halibut with citrus-olive sauce

(PICTURED AT RIGHT)

This poached halibut is one of my favorite fish entrees. The lovely sweet and salty sauce has incredible flavor, texture and color.

Gloria Bradley | NAPERVILLE, IL

2-1/2 cups orange juice, divided

1/3 cup white wine

2 tablespoons lime juice

2 tablespoons chopped shallot

1/4 cup butter, cut into four pieces

2 tablespoons chopped sweet red pepper

1 tablespoon chopped pitted green olives

1 tablespoon chopped Greek olives

3 garlic cloves, minced

1 teaspoon dried oregano

4 halibut fillets (6 ounces each)

In a small saucepan, bring 1-1/2 cups orange juice, wine, lime juice and shallot to a boil; cook until liquid is reduced to 1/2 cup, about 15 minutes. Reduce heat to low; gradually whisk in butter until butter is melted. Remove from heat; stir in red pepper and olives. Keep warm.

In a large skillet, bring the garlic, oregano and the remaining orange juice to a boil. Reduce the heat; add fillets and steam, uncovered, for 8-10 minutes or until fish flakes easily with a fork. Serve with sauce. **YIELD:** 4 servings.

SLICING SHALLOTS

Shallots are part of the onion family and can be cut in the same way.

First, remove the papery outer skin. Place the shallot on a cutting board and slice off the root end. Cut vertically through the shallot.

Then cut across the shallot in the opposite direction. The closer the cuts, the finer the shallot will be chopped.

cranberry-stuffed beef tenderloin

Fresh cranberries and cranberry juice lend a satisfying sweet-tart taste to beef tenderloin. Serving plated dishes to guests makes for a pretty presentation.

Carolyn Cope | ALLSTON, MD

1 cup fresh or frozen cranberries, thawed

1/4 cup dry red wine or beef broth

2 shallots, chopped

1 tablespoon butter

1 beef tenderloin roast (4 pounds)

1/4 teaspoon salt

1/4 teaspoon pepper

CRANBERRY WINE SAUCE:

2 shallots, chopped

2 tablespoons butter, divided

3/4 cup cranberry juice

3/4 cup dry red wine or beef broth

1/2 cup beef broth

1/2 teaspoon minced fresh thyme

In a large saucepan, combine the cranberries, wine, shallots and butter. Cook over medium heat until the cranberries pop, about 15 minutes.

Cut a lengthwise slit down the center of the tenderloin to within 1/2 in. of bottom. Open tenderloin so it lies flat. On each half, make another lengthwise slit down the center to within 1/2 in. of bottom; open roast and cover with plastic wrap. Flatten to 1/2-in. thickness. Remove plastic.

Sprinkle beef with salt and pepper; spread cranberry mixture over meat. Roll up jelly-roll style, starting with a long side. Tie tenderloin at 2-in. intervals with kitchen string. Place on a rack in a shallow roasting pan.

Bake at 425° for 40-50 minutes or until meat reaches desired doneness (for medium-rare, a meat thermometer should read 145°; medium, 160°; well-done, 170°). Let the roast stand for 10 minutes before slicing.

Meanwhile, saute shallots in 1 tablespoon butter until tender. Add the juice, wine, broth and thyme. Bring to a boil; cook until liquid is reduced by half, about 20 minutes. Remove from the heat; stir in remaining butter. Serve with beef. YIELD: 12 servings (1 cup sauce).

phyllo-wrapped pesto chicken

Chicken breasts can be a little too plain for special suppers. I decided to dress them up by topping them with pesto and cheese and then wrapping in phyllo dough. There's nothing ordinary about them!

Gail Humfeld | NEWARK, DE

12 sheets phyllo dough (14 inches x 9 inches)

1/2 cup butter, melted, divided

6 boneless skinless chicken breast halves (7 ounces each)

Pepper to taste

1 jar (10 ounces) basil pesto

6 slices Monterey Jack cheese

Brush two phyllo sheets with butter; stack one sheet on the other. Brush top with butter. Form five additional stacks.

Flatten chicken; place one piece of chicken on each phyllo stack, with the long side of chicken 1 in. from the long side of the phyllo. Sprinkle with pepper. Place 2 tablespoons pesto on each; top each with a slice of cheese. Fold bottom edge of phyllo over chicken; fold in short sides and roll up.

Place seam side down in a greased 15-in. x 10-in. x 1-in. baking pan. Brush with remaining butter. Bake, uncovered, at 375° for 45-50 minutes or until chicken juices run clear and pastry is golden brown. YIELD: 6 servings.

herb-crusted rack of lamb with mushroom sauce

(PICTURED AT RIGHT)

With this easy, surefire recipe, you don't have to be too intimidated to prepare rack of lamb for a holiday dinner. Rice pilaf and roasted asparagus are a lovely way to round out the meal.

Mary Kay LaBrie | CLERMONT, FL

2 frenched racks of lamb (1-1/2 pounds each)

1 tablespoon steak seasoning

4-1/2 teaspoons olive oil

1 tablespoon Dijon mustard

1/3 cup panko (Japanese) bread crumbs

1 tablespoon minced fresh thyme
or 1 teaspoon dried thyme

1 tablespoon minced fresh mint
or 1 teaspoon dried mint

1 teaspoon Worcestershire sauce

1/2 teaspoon dried rosemary, crushed

MUSHROOM SAUCE:

3/4 pound sliced fresh mushrooms

2 tablespoons olive oil

1/4 cup butter, divided

4 garlic cloves, minced

1/2 cup dry red wine or beef broth

1/4 cup beef broth

1/2 teaspoon honey

2 tablespoons minced chives, optional

Sprinkle lamb with steak seasoning. In a large skillet over medium-high heat, cook lamb in oil for 2 minutes on each side. Brush with mustard.

In a small bowl, combine the panko, thyme, mint, Worcestershire sauce and rosemary; press onto lamb. Transfer to a greased 15-in. x 10-in. baking pan. Bake, uncovered, at 375° for 15-20 minutes or until meat reaches desired doneness (for medium-rare, a meat thermometer should read 145°; medium, 160°; well-done, 170°).

In a large skillet, saute mushrooms in oil and 2 tablespoons butter until tender. Add garlic; cook 1 minute longer. Stir in wine. Bring to a boil; cook until liquid is reduced by half. Remove from the heat. Stir in the broth, honey, remaining butter and chives if desired.

Remove lamb from oven and loosely cover with foil. Let stand for 5 minutes before slicing. Serve with sauce. **YIELD:** 4 servings (1 cup sauce).

EDITOR'S NOTE: This recipe was tested with McCormick's Montreal Steak Seasoning. Look for it in the spice aisle.

mozzarella-stuffed meatballs

*Three kinds of meat infuse these meatballs with authentic Italian flavor.
The surprise of fresh mozzarella cheese inside is always a hit.*
Cyndy Gerken | NAPLES, FL

2 eggs, lightly beaten

1 tablespoon Worcestershire sauce

2 large onions, finely chopped

2/3 cup seasoned bread crumbs

1/3 cup grated Parmesan cheese

3 tablespoons minced fresh parsley

2 tablespoons minced fresh basil

1 tablespoon minced fresh oregano

8 garlic cloves, minced

1/2 teaspoon kosher salt

1/4 teaspoon pepper

1/8 teaspoon crushed red pepper flakes

1 pound lean ground beef (90% lean)

1/2 pound ground pork

1/2 pound ground veal

16 fresh mozzarella cheese balls, drained and patted dry

Hot cooked spaghetti

Marinara or spaghetti sauce, warmed

In a large bowl, combine eggs and Worcestershire sauce. Add the onions, bread crumbs, Parmesan cheese, parsley, basil, oregano, garlic, salt, pepper and red pepper flakes. Crumble the beef, pork and veal over mixture; mix well.

Divide the mixture into 16 portions. Shape each portion around a mozzarella ball.

Place meatballs on a greased rack in a shallow baking pan. Bake at 400° for 25-30 minutes or until no longer pink. Drain on paper towels. Serve with spaghetti and marinara sauce. **YIELD:** 8 servings.

fish in rosemary broth

*Tender mahi mahi fillets swim in this beautiful broth infused with tomatoes,
asparagus, white kidney beans and rosemary. The addition of gnocchi makes it a hearty meal.*
Mary Cannataro | CHICAGO, IL

4 mahi mahi fillets (6 ounces each)

1/2 teaspoon salt

1/2 teaspoon pepper

2 tablespoons olive oil, divided

2 garlic cloves, minced

3 cups chicken broth

1-1/2 cups white wine or additional chicken broth

5 plum tomatoes, seeded and chopped

1 pound fresh asparagus, trimmed and cut into 1-inch pieces

1 can (15 ounces) white kidney or cannellini beans, rinsed and drained

1/2 pound potato gnocchi (about 1-1/2 cups)

1 tablespoon minced fresh rosemary or 1 teaspoon dried rosemary, crushed

Sprinkle fish with salt and pepper. In a large ovenproof skillet, brown fish in 4-1/2 teaspoons oil for 2 minutes on each side. Bake, uncovered, at 425° for 6-8 minutes or until fish just turns opaque.

In a large saucepan, saute garlic in remaining oil for 1 minute. Add the broth, wine and tomatoes; bring just to a boil. Carefully add the asparagus, beans, gnocchi and rosemary. Cook, stirring occasionally, for 3-5 minutes or until asparagus is tender. Place fish in four serving bowls; spoon broth mixture over the top. **YIELD:** 4 servings.

EDITOR'S NOTE: Look for potato gnocchi in the pasta or frozen foods section.

braised
short ribs

(PICTURED AT RIGHT)

I've been relying on this recipe ever since I bought my first slow cooker some 20 years ago. The fall-off-the-bone-tender entree is much appreciated on busy days.

Peggy Edwards | HEBER CITY, UT

1/2 cup all-purpose flour

1-1/2 teaspoons salt

1-1/2 teaspoons paprika

1/2 teaspoon ground mustard

4 pounds bone-in beef short ribs

2 tablespoons canola oil

2 medium onions, sliced

1 cup beer or beef broth

1 garlic clove, minced

GRAVY:

2 teaspoons all-purpose flour

1 tablespoon cold water

In a large resealable plastic bag, combine the flour, salt, paprika and mustard. Add ribs in batches and shake to coat. In a large skillet, brown ribs in oil; drain.

Place onions in a 5-qt. slow cooker; add ribs. Top with beer and garlic. Cover and cook on low for 6-7 hours or until meat is tender.

Remove ribs and onions to a serving platter; keep warm. Skim fat from cooking juices; transfer to a small saucepan. Bring to a boil. Combine flour and water until smooth; gradually stir into the pan. Bring to a boil; cook and stir for 2 minutes or until thickened. Serve with ribs. **YIELD:** 7 servings.

pork scallopini with caper sauce

Pork Scallopini offers the true taste of Italy. Tender medallions are quickly browned, topped with prosciutto and cheese and then crowned with an amazing thyme sauce.

Jeff Olney | SEATTLE, WA

2 pork tenderloins (1 pound each)

1 cup all-purpose flour

4-1/2 teaspoons salt

3 teaspoons pepper

1 tablespoon butter

4 thin slices prosciutto or deli ham, halved

4 ounces fresh mozzarella cheese, cut into eight slices

SAUCE:

1/4 cup white wine or chicken broth

2 tablespoons white wine vinegar

1 tablespoon finely chopped shallot

1 tablespoon lemon juice

2 teaspoons minced fresh thyme or 1/2 teaspoon dried thyme

2 teaspoons heavy whipping cream

1/2 cup butter, cut into four pieces

4-1/2 teaspoons capers, drained

Cut each tenderloin into eight slices; flatten to 1/4-in. thickness. In a large resealable plastic bag, combine the flour, salt and pepper. Add pork, one piece at a time, and shake to coat.

In a large skillet, brown pork in butter in batches. Place eight pork slices in a greased 15-in. x 10-in. x 1-in baking pan. Layer with prosciutto and mozzarella; top with remaining pork.

Bake at 450° for 15-20 minutes or until a meat thermometer reads 160°.

Meanwhile, in a small saucepan, combine the wine, vinegar, shallot, lemon juice and thyme. Bring to a boil; cook until liquid is reduced by half. Reduce heat to low; stir in cream. Gradually whisk in butter until butter is melted. Remove from the heat; strain. Stir in capers. Serve with scallopini. **YIELD:** 8 servings.

WHAT ARE CAPERS?

Capers are the immature buds from a small bush native to the Middle East and Mediterranean regions. They are either brined in vinegar or packed in coarse salt to preserve. It is best to rinse capers before using.

four-pepper ribeye roast

Our home economists suggest you consider the grill next time you serve prime rib for a special meal. For the most robust flavor, marinate the seasoned roast overnight.

1 tablespoon paprika

1 tablespoon coarsely ground pepper

1 teaspoon kosher salt

1 teaspoon fennel seed, crushed

1/2 teaspoon white pepper

1/4 teaspoon cayenne pepper

1 beef ribeye roast (4 to 5 pounds)

2 tablespoons olive oil

2 cups soaked wood chips, optional

In a small bowl, combine the first six ingredients. Tie the roast at 1-1/2-in. to 2-in. intervals with kitchen string. Rub with seasonings; cover and refrigerate 8 hours or overnight.

Remove roast from refrigerator 30 minutes before grilling; brush with oil. Prepare grill for indirect heat, using a drip pan. Add wood chips to grill according to manufacturer's directions if desired.

Place roast over drip pan and grill, covered, over indirect medium-low heat for 2 to 2-1/2 hours or until meat reaches desired doneness (for medium-rare, a meat thermometer should read 145°; medium, 160°; well-done, 170°). Let stand for 15 minutes before slicing. **YIELD:** 12 servings.

pistachio-crusted chicken breasts

(PICTURED AT RIGHT)

As a salesperson in the medical field, I'm often in hospitals during the lunch hour. One day, I was fortunate to sample this great dish. The chef wouldn't share the recipe, so I came up with my own version.

Bibi Gromling | FLAGLER BEACH, FL

6 boneless skinless chicken breast halves (6 ounces each)

1/4 teaspoon salt

1/4 teaspoon pepper

2 cups pistachios, finely chopped

1 tablespoon minced fresh tarragon or 1 teaspoon dried tarragon

3/4 cup all-purpose flour

3 eggs, beaten

1/3 cup butter, cubed

SAUCE:

2 tablespoons all-purpose flour

1-1/2 cups white wine or chicken broth

1-1/2 cups heavy whipping cream

2 tablespoons minced fresh tarragon or 2 teaspoons dried tarragon

1/8 teaspoon salt

1/8 teaspoon pepper

Flatten chicken breasts to 1/2-in. thickness. Sprinkle with salt and pepper.

In a shallow bowl, combine pistachios and tarragon. Place the flour and eggs in separate bowls. Coat chicken with flour, then dip in eggs and coat with pistachio mixture.

In a large skillet, cook chicken in butter in batches over medium heat for 5-7 minutes on each side or until juices run clear. Remove and keep warm.

In the same skillet, stir in flour until blended. Gradually add the wine, cream, tarragon, salt and pepper. Bring to a boil; cook and stir for 2 minutes or until thickened. Serve with chicken. **YIELD:** 6 servings.

seared salmon with pomegranate-thyme butter

Salmon has such fantastic flavor on its own that you don't need much to make it taste better. My family likes when I top cooked fillets with a butter prepared with pomegranate juice, balsamic vinegar and thyme.

De'Lawrence Reed | DURHAM, NC

1/2 cup pomegranate juice

1/4 cup balsamic vinegar

1 shallot, finely chopped

1/4 cup butter, softened

3/4 teaspoon minced fresh thyme
or 1/4 teaspoon dried thyme

4 salmon fillets (6 ounces each)

1/4 teaspoon salt

1/4 teaspoon coarsely ground pepper

1 tablespoon olive oil

In a small saucepan, combine the pomegranate juice, vinegar and shallot. Bring to a boil; cook until liquid is reduced by half, about 8-10 minutes. Transfer to a small bowl; let cool. Beat in the butter and thyme.

Shape into a log; wrap in plastic wrap. Refrigerate for 30 minutes or until firm.

Sprinkle fillets with salt and pepper. In a large nonstick skillet, cook fillets in oil over medium heat for 4-5 minutes on each side or until fish flakes easily with a fork.

Unwrap pomegranate butter; cut into four slices. Place a slice on each fillet. **YIELD:** 4 servings.

hazelnut & lemon-crusted turkey breast

This recipe is proof that simple recipes can still be special. Placing the turkey breast over lemon slices before roasting results in a moist and tender main course.

Lorraine Caland | THUNDER BAY, ON

1/2 cup hazelnuts, toasted

1/4 cup olive oil

3 tablespoons minced fresh rosemary
or 1 tablespoon dried rosemary, crushed

3 tablespoons lemon juice

2 tablespoons butter, softened

2 garlic cloves, minced

2 teaspoons grated lemon peel

1/4 teaspoon salt

1/4 teaspoon pepper

1 boneless skinless turkey breast half (2 pounds)

1 medium lemon, thinly sliced

Place the first nine ingredients in a food processor; cover and process until finely chopped. Rub mixture over turkey.

Arrange lemon slices in a foil-lined 13-in. x 9-in. baking pan; top with turkey.

Bake, uncovered, at 325° for 1-1/4 to 1-1/2 hours or until a meat thermometer reads 170°. Let stand for 10 minutes before slicing. **YIELD:** 6 servings.

pasta and white bean soup with sun-dried tomatoes

(PICTURED AT RIGHT)

The Christmas season often means indulging in lots of rich foods. So I like to prepare a vegetarian soup that's hot and hearty but not heavy.

Mary Swartz | PALM DESERT, CA

1 cup dried great northern beans

2 cups finely chopped onions

2 medium carrots, chopped

1/2 cup sliced fennel bulb or celery

1/4 cup olive oil

4 garlic cloves, minced

3/4 teaspoon crushed red pepper flakes

2 bay leaves

4 cans (14-1/2 ounces each) chicken or vegetable broth

2 cups uncooked bow tie pasta

1/2 cup oil-packed sun-dried tomatoes, chopped

1/4 cup minced fresh parsley

1/2 teaspoon salt

Shredded Parmesan cheese, optional

Soak beans according to package directions. Drain and rinse beans; discard liquid and set beans aside.

In a Dutch oven, saute the onions, carrots and fennel in oil until tender. Add the garlic, pepper flakes and bay leaves; cook 1 minute longer. Add broth and beans.

Bring to a boil. Reduce heat; cover and simmer until beans are almost tender, about 1 hour. Stir in pasta, tomatoes, parsley and salt. Bring to a boil. Reduce heat; cover and simmer 15 minutes longer or until beans and pasta are tender. Discard bay leaves. Serve with cheese if desired. **YIELD:** 6 servings (2 quarts).

After indulging in a heavy holiday meal, nothing satisfies quite like a lovely dessert brimming with minty flavor.

You don't need to work the day away in the kitchen to create a decadent, delicious bite. Layered Peppermint Icebox Cake, for instance, calls for only four ingredients. Best of all, the tempting treat comes together in 20 minutes and then simply sits in the refrigerator overnight.

We're willing to bet that such convenience certainly comes as a refreshing change compared to the time it took you to make the rest of the holiday meal!

Let guests ooh and aah over the impressive dessert displayed on your table...only you need to know just how easy it really was!

COOL & CREAMY
(PICTURED AT RIGHT)

Layered Peppermint Icebox Cake (p. 60)

dazzling
MINT DESSERTS

layered peppermint icebox cake

(PICTURED ON PAGE 59)

*Our home economists take four ingredients and turn them into
an impressive no-bake cake. Do-ahead desserts don't get any better!*

3 cups heavy whipping cream

3 tablespoons sugar

1 teaspoon peppermint extract

2 packages (9 ounces each) chocolate wafers

Edible flowers of your choice, chocolate curls
and crushed candy canes, optional

In a large bowl, beat the cream, sugar and extract on high until stiff peaks form. Cut a small hole in the corner of a pastry or plastic bag. Fill with whipped cream.

On a serving plate, arrange seven cookies in a circle, using one cookie in the center. Pipe 2/3 cup whipped cream over cookies. Repeat layers nine times. Refrigerate overnight.

Garnish with flowers, chocolate curls and crushed candy if desired. **YIELD:** 8 servings.

peppermint red velvet cupcakes

*I dress up a boxed cake mix by stirring in sour cream, red food coloring and chocolate chips.
A white chocolate and cream cheese frosting sprinkled with crushed mints is the crowning touch.*

Donna Bardocz | HOWELL, MI

1 package (18-1/4 ounces) German chocolate
cake mix

1 cup (8 ounces) sour cream

3 eggs

1/4 cup water

1/3 cup canola oil

1 bottle (1 ounce) red food coloring

1 cup (6 ounces) miniature semisweet
chocolate chips

FROSTING:

1/2 cup butter, softened

1 package (8 ounces) reduced-fat cream cheese

12 ounces white baking chocolate, melted

2 teaspoons peppermint extract

7 cups confectioners' sugar

White chocolate curls and crushed
peppermint candies, optional

In a large bowl, combine the cake mix, sour cream, eggs, water, oil and food coloring; beat on low speed for 30 seconds. Beat on medium for 2 minutes. Fold in chocolate chips.

Fill paper-lined muffin cups two-thirds full. Bake at 350° for 18-22 minutes or until a toothpick inserted near the center comes out clean. Cool for 10 minutes before removing from pans to wire racks to cool completely.

For frosting, in a large bowl, beat butter and cream cheese until fluffy. Beat in the melted white chocolate and extract. Beat in confectioners' sugar until smooth.

Frost cupcakes. Sprinkle with chocolate curls and peppermint candies if desired. Store in the refrigerator. **YIELD:** 2 dozen.

CRUSHING PEPPERMINT CANDY

To easily crush peppermint candy, put the candy in a heavy-duty resealable plastic bag and seal. Using a hammer or flat side of a meat mallet, pound the candy on a sturdy countertop.

For 1 cup crushed candies, begin with about 40 miniature or 12 full-size candy canes.

meringue torte with peppermint cream

(PICTURED AT RIGHT)

The mother of my brother-in-law Bill often made this melt-in-your-mouth torte. A few years after she passed away, I surprised him by serving it at Christmas. He was delighted.

Christine Venzon | PEORIA, IL

3 egg whites

1 teaspoon water

1 teaspoon white vinegar

1 teaspoon vanilla extract

Dash salt

2 drops red food coloring, optional

1 cup sugar

1/2 cup semisweet chocolate chips

1 teaspoon shortening

1 cup heavy whipping cream

2/3 cup crushed soft peppermint candies

Chocolate curls and additional crushed soft peppermint candies

Place egg whites in a large bowl; let stand at room temperature for 30 minutes. Add the water, vinegar, vanilla, salt and food coloring if desired; beat on medium speed until soft peaks form. Gradually beat in the sugar, 1 tablespoon at a time, on high until stiff glossy peaks form and sugar is dissolved.

With a pencil, draw three 5-in. x 8-in. rectangles on a sheet of parchment paper. Place paper, pencil mark down, on baking sheets. Spread the meringue evenly over each rectangle.

Bake at 300° for 20 minutes. Turn oven off; leave meringues in oven for 1-1/2 hours. Remove from the oven and cool on baking sheets. When cooled completely, remove meringues from paper.

In a microwave, melt chocolate and shortening; stir until smooth. Spread over tops of meringues. In a large bowl, beat cream until stiff peaks form; fold in peppermint candies.

Place a meringue shell on a serving plate; top with 2/3 cup peppermint cream. Repeat layers twice. Garnish with chocolate curls and additional crushed candies. **YIELD:** 8 servings.

EDITOR'S NOTE: This recipe was tested with Bob's Sweet Stripes peppermint candies.

candy cane fudge

(PICTURED AT FAR RIGHT)

*Everyone enjoys fudge, especially around the holidays, so I created this
refreshing recipe. Store it in the refrigerator for a fast treat.*

Vicki Van Valkenburg | DEMOREST, GA

1 teaspoon plus 4 tablespoons butter, divided

39 miniature candy canes, crushed
(about 1 cup)

1-1/2 cups semisweet chocolate chips

1 can (14 ounces) sweetened condensed milk,
divided

4 ounces white baking chocolate, chopped

1 teaspoon cream of tartar

Line an 8-in. square pan with foil and
grease the foil with 1 teaspoon butter.
Sprinkle pan with half of the crushed candy;
set aside.

In a microwave-safe bowl, combine the chocolate chips and
2 tablespoons of butter. Microwave on high for 1 minute; stir.
Microwave at additional 15-second intervals, stirring until smooth.
Stir in 2/3 cup milk. Carefully pour over candy layer in prepared
pan. Refrigerate for 10 minutes.

Meanwhile, in a microwave-safe bowl, combine white baking
chocolate and the remaining butter. Microwave on high for
40-50 seconds and stir until smooth. Stir in the cream of tartar,
remaining milk and candy. Spread over chocolate layer.

Refrigerate for 2 hours or until firm. Using foil, remove fudge
from pan. Invert onto a cutting board; remove foil. Cut into 1-in.
squares. **YIELD:** about 1-3/4 pounds.

EDITOR'S NOTE: This recipe tested in a 1,100-watt microwave.

holiday baked alaska

*With a gingersnap crust, minty ice cream filling and airy meringue topping,
this treat is deliciously different. Chill for a day, and bake just before serving.*

Carole Halling | BATAVIA, IL

1-1/2 cups crushed gingersnap cookies
(about 25 cookies)

1/4 cup butter, melted

3 tablespoons brown sugar

1/2 teaspoon ground cinnamon

6 cups peppermint ice cream, softened

2 tablespoons peppermint schnapps liqueur

5 egg whites

2/3 cup sugar

1/2 teaspoon cream of tartar

In a small bowl, combine the cookie crumbs, butter, brown sugar
and cinnamon; set aside 1/3 cup. Press remaining crumb mixture
onto the bottom and up the sides of a greased 9-in. deep-dish pie
plate. Refrigerate for 30 minutes.

Meanwhile, combine ice cream, schnapps and reserved crumbs;
spoon into crust. Freeze overnight or until firm.

In a large heavy saucepan, combine the egg whites, sugar and
cream of tartar. With a hand mixer, beat on low speed for 1 minute.
Continue beating over low heat until egg mixture reaches 160°,
about 10 minutes. Transfer to a bowl; beat until stiff glossy peaks
form and sugar is dissolved. Spread meringue over ice cream,
sealing to edges of crust.

Bake at 400° for 2-5 minutes or until meringue is lightly browned.
Serve immediately. **YIELD:** 8 servings.

candy cane souffle

(PICTURED AT RIGHT)

I came up with this recipe by modifying one of my mom's gelatin-based desserts. The pretty pink sweet is a welcome sight on the table.

Joni Hilton | ROCKLIN, CA

2 envelopes unflavored gelatin

1 cup cold water

12 candy canes, crushed (about 1 cup)

2 teaspoons peppermint extract

6 egg whites

1/2 cup sugar

Dash salt

3 cups heavy whipping cream

Whipped cream and additional crushed candy canes, optional

In a small saucepan, sprinkle gelatin over cold water; let stand for 1 minute. Add crushed candy canes. Heat over low heat, stirring until gelatin is completely dissolved. Stir in extract; set aside.

In a large heavy saucepan, combine the egg whites and sugar. With a hand mixer, beat on low speed for 1 minute. Continue beating over low heat until egg mixture reaches 160°, about 15 minutes. Transfer to a bowl. Add salt; beat until stiff glossy peaks form and sugar is dissolved.

Meanwhile, in a large bowl, beat cream until it begins to thicken. Add reserved candy cane mixture; beat until slightly thickened. Fold in egg white mixture.

Pour into a large glass dessert bowl or ten 6-ounce dessert dishes. Refrigerate for 6 hours or overnight. Garnish with whipped cream and crushed candy cane if desired. YIELD: 10 servings.

white chocolate peppermint cheesecake

Bits of pretty mint candies dot every slice of this velvety cheesecake. You'll turn to this classic dessert time and again.

Grenville Samson | OSWEGO, NY

1-1/2 cups graham cracker crumbs

1 tablespoon sugar

1/2 cup butter, melted

FILLING:

3 packages (8 ounces each) cream cheese, softened

1 cup sugar

1 tablespoon brown sugar

1 cup (8 ounces) sour cream

3 tablespoons all-purpose flour

1 teaspoon vanilla extract

1 teaspoon peppermint extract

6 eggs, lightly beaten

1 cup white baking chips

1 cup crushed peppermint candies, divided

Place a greased 10-in. springform pan on a double thickness of heavy-duty foil (about 18 in. square). Securely wrap foil around pan. In a large bowl, combine the cracker crumbs, sugar and butter. Press onto the bottom and 1 in. up the sides of prepared pan. Bake at 325° for 10 minutes. Cool on a wire rack.

In a large bowl, beat cream cheese and sugars until smooth. Beat in the sour cream, flour and extracts. Add eggs; beat on low speed just until combined. Fold in chips and 3/4 cup crushed candies. Pour into crust. Sprinkle with remaining candies. Place springform pan in a large baking pan; add 1 in. of hot water to larger pan.

Bake at 325° for 1-1/4 hours or until center is just set and top appears dull. Remove springform pan from water bath. Cool on a wire rack for 10 minutes. Carefully run a knife around edge of pan to loosen; cool 1 hour longer. Refrigerate overnight. Remove sides of pan. **YIELD:** 16 servings.

chocolate mint truffle tart

Indulging in a slice of this decadent dessert is like biting into a smooth truffle candy. You can vary the taste by using raspberry-flavored baking chocolate chips.

Sally Sibthorpe | SHELBY TOWNSHIP, MI

2 cups cream-filled chocolate sandwich cookie crumbs

3/4 cup butter, softened, divided

1 package (10 ounces) mint chocolate chips

1/2 cup sugar

2 teaspoons vanilla extract

1 cup heavy whipping cream

3 eggs, lightly beaten

Whipped cream, additional mint chocolate chips and mint sprigs, optional

In a small bowl, combine cookie crumbs and 1/4 cup butter; press onto the bottom and up the sides of an ungreased 9-in. tart pan. Refrigerate for 15 minutes.

Meanwhile, in a food processor, combine the chips, sugar and vanilla; cover and process for 20 seconds or until chips are chopped. In a small heavy saucepan, heat cream and remaining butter until bubbles form around sides of pan. Drizzle over chopped chocolate while processing. Whisk a small amount of chocolate mixture into eggs; return all to food processor and process until smooth.

Pour into tart shell. Bake at 350° for 25-30 minutes or until center is just set (mixture will jiggle). Cool completely on a wire rack. Store in the refrigerator. Garnish with whipped cream, additional mint chips and mint sprigs if desired. **YIELD:** 16 servings.

EDITOR'S NOTE: If mint chocolate chips are not available, place 2 cups (12 ounces) semisweet chocolate chips and 1/4 teaspoon peppermint extract in a plastic bag; seal and toss to coat. Allow chips to stand for 24-48 hours.

mint angel cake

(PICTURED AT RIGHT)

One sight of this lovely cake will have guests saving room for dessert! For an easy garnish, sprinkle with crushed mint candies.

Agnes Ward | STRATFORD, ON

12 egg whites (about 1-1/2 cups)

1 cup cake flour

1 teaspoon cream of tartar

1 teaspoon almond extract

1/4 teaspoon salt

1-1/4 cups sugar

1/4 cup plus 2 tablespoons crushed peppermint candies, divided

1/4 cup water

1-3/4 cups heavy whipping cream

Fresh mint leaves and peppermint candies

Place egg whites in a large bowl; let stand at room temperature for 30 minutes. Sift flour twice; set aside.

Add the cream of tartar, almond extract and salt to egg whites; beat on medium speed until soft peaks form. Gradually add sugar, about 2 tablespoons at a time, beating on high until stiff peaks form. Gradually fold in flour, about 1/2 cup at a time.

Gently spoon into an ungreased 10-in. tube pan. Cut through batter with a knife to remove air pockets. Bake on the lowest oven rack at 350° for 40-50 minutes or until lightly browned and entire top appears dry. Immediately invert the pan; cool completely, about 1 hour.

In a small saucepan, combine 1/4 cup crushed candies and water. Cook and stir over medium heat until candies are melted. In a large bowl, beat cream until stiff peaks form.

Run a knife around side and center tube of pan. Remove cake to a serving plate. Cut cake horizontally into three layers. Place bottom layer on a serving plate; drizzle with 2 tablespoons mint syrup. Spread with 1/2 cup whipped cream; sprinkle with 1 tablespoon crushed candies. Repeat layers.

Top with third cake layer. Frost top and sides of cake with remaining whipped cream. Garnish with mint leaves and candies. Store in the refrigerator. **YIELD:** 16 servings.

Are you unable to give your true love five golden rings, four calling birds, three French hens, two turtle doves and a partridge in a pear tree this Christmas season?

You can still display your sweet adoration during the yuletide by making and sharing batches of tasty cookies and mouthwatering candies.

For confections everyone will adore, Orange-Almond Chocolate Logs surely fit the bill. No candy thermometer is required, so it's a great recipe for experienced and beginning candy makers alike.

Similarly, when Lemon Pistachio Wreaths and Coconut Cranberry Yummies are the featured delicacies, there won't be any crumbs left on the cookie platters at your parties!

TRUE LOVE TREATS
(PICTURED AT RIGHT)

Orange-Almond Chocolate Logs (p. 68)
Coconut Cranberry Yummies (p. 68)
Lemon Pistachio Wreaths (p. 74)

12 days of
COOKIES AND CANDY

orange-almond chocolate logs

(PICTURED ON PAGE 66)

A sure hit for the holidays, these lovely logs from our Test Kitchen staff feature the can't-beat combination of almond, orange and chocolate.

1/3 cup butter, softened

1/4 cup almond paste

2 teaspoons grated orange peel, divided

9 ounces white baking chocolate, chopped

2 tablespoons orange juice

3 tablespoons coarse sugar

1-1/2 cups dark chocolate chips

1-1/2 teaspoons shortening

In a small bowl, cream the butter, almond paste and 1/2 teaspoon orange peel until light and fluffy. In a microwave, melt white baking chocolate; stir until smooth. Gradually add to creamed mixture. Slowly stir in orange juice. Beat until smooth. Cover and refrigerate for 20 minutes or until easy to handle, stirring occasionally.

Shape into 2-in. logs; place on waxed paper-lined baking sheets. Loosely cover and refrigerate for 30 minutes or until firm. Combine coarse sugar and remaining orange peel; set aside.

In a microwave, melt chocolate chips and shortening; stir until smooth. Dip logs in chocolate, allowing excess to drip off. Place on waxed paper-lined baking sheets. Sprinkle with sugar mixture. Let stand until firm. **YIELD:** 2 dozen.

coconut cranberry yummies

(PICTURED ON PAGE 67)

When my husband came home from the grocery store with six bags of fresh cranberries, I launched a full-scale effort to creatively use them all. Bursting with tart cranberry and sweet coconut flavor, these tasty bites are my favorite result from that experiment.

Amy Alberts | APPLETON, WI

1 can (14 ounces) sweetened condensed milk

1 package (14 ounces) flaked coconut

1 cup white baking chips

1/4 cup ground almonds

1 teaspoon almond extract

1 cup chopped fresh or frozen cranberries

2 to 4 tablespoons confectioners' sugar

In a large bowl, combine the first five ingredients; mix well. Stir in the cranberries. Drop by tablespoonfuls 3 in. apart onto parchment paper-lined baking sheets; gently shape into mounds.

Bake at 325° for 10-12 minutes or until edges are lightly browned. Cool for 3 minutes before removing from pans to wire racks to cool completely. Dust with confectioners' sugar. **YIELD:** 5 dozen.

pistachio brittle

(PICTURED AT RIGHT)

Here's a fun twist on traditional brittle. Pistachios not only add wonderful taste to the rich, buttery candy, but delicious texture.

Valonda Seward | HANFORD, CA

1-1/4 cups sugar

1/3 cup water

1/3 cup light corn syrup

1 teaspoon salt

1/2 cup butter, cubed

2 cups pistachios, toasted

1/2 teaspoon baking soda

1/2 teaspoon vanilla extract

Butter a 15-in. x 10-in. x 1-in. pan, set aside. In a large saucepan, combine the sugar, water, corn syrup and salt. Cook over medium heat until a candy thermometer reads 240° (soft-ball stage). Carefully add butter and pistachios; cook and stir until mixture reaches 284° (soft-crack stage).

Remove from the heat; stir in baking soda and vanilla. Immediately pour into prepared pan. Spread to 1/4-in. thickness.

Cool before breaking into pieces. Store in an airtight container. **YIELD:** about 1-1/2 pounds.

EDITOR'S NOTE: We recommend that you test your candy thermometer before each use by bringing water to a boil; the thermometer should read 212°. Adjust your recipe temperature up or down based on your test.

USING A CANDY THERMOMETER

Always use a thermometer designed for candy making. It must have a movable clip that's used to secure it to the side of the pan and to keep the end of the thermometer off the bottom of the pan. Be sure to read the thermometer at eye level.

Check your candy thermometer for accuracy each time you make candy. Place the thermometer in a saucepan of boiling water for several minutes before reading. If the thermometer reads 212° in boiling water, it is accurate. If it rises above or does not reach 212°, add or subtract the difference to the temperature called for in the recipe.

A candy mixture will cook very slowly when boiling until it reaches 220°, then it will cook quickly. It's important to closely watch the thermometer at this point.

To avoid breakage, allow the thermometer to cool before washing it.

macadamia peanut butter cups

(PICTURED AT FAR RIGHT)

A little goes a long way when it comes to these rich morsels.
One bite and store-bought peanut butter cups will be a distant memory.

Joyce Guth | MOHNTON, PA

1 cup macadamia nuts, divided

1/4 cup creamy peanut butter

3 tablespoons confectioners' sugar

3 tablespoons sour cream

1/4 teaspoon vanilla extract

1-1/2 pounds bittersweet chocolate, chopped

Set aside 36 macadamia nuts for garnish. Finely chop the remaining nuts; set aside.

In a small bowl, combine the peanut butter, confectioners' sugar, sour cream, vanilla and the reserved chopped nuts. Cover and refrigerate for 15 minutes.

Meanwhile, in a microwave, melt chocolate; stir until smooth. Pipe about 1 teaspoon chocolate into each of 36 foil-lined miniature muffin cups. Chill for 10 minutes or until firm.

Spoon 1/2 teaspoon peanut butter mixture into each cup. Pipe enough additional chocolate into each cup to cover peanut butter filling. Top each with a macadamia nut. Chill for 10 minutes or until firm. Store the candies in an airtight container in the refrigerator. **YIELD:** 3 dozen.

lace cookies with chocolate middles

Melted chocolate sandwiched between two golden and slightly crisp oatmeal cookies
makes for a delicious spin on traditional oatmeal chocolate chip cookies.

Lynn Shafer | MINOOKA, IL

1/2 cup butter, softened

1 cup sugar

1 egg

1 teaspoon vanilla extract

1 cup quick-cooking oats

3 tablespoons all-purpose flour

1/2 teaspoon salt

2 cups (12 ounces) semisweet chocolate chips, melted

In a large bowl, cream butter and sugar until light and fluffy. Beat in egg and vanilla. Combine the oats, flour and salt; gradually add to creamed mixture and mix well.

Drop by teaspoonfuls 3 in. apart onto parchment paper-lined baking sheets.

Bake at 350° for 8-10 minutes or until golden brown. Cool completely on pans before carefully removing to wire racks.

Spread melted chocolate on the bottoms of half of the cookies; top with the remaining cookies. Store in an airtight container. **YIELD:** 2 dozen sandwich cookies.

linzer tarts

(PICTURED AT RIGHT)

With a creamy chocolate and hazelnut filling, these decadent Christmas cookies look and taste amazing. Guests will never guess how relatively easy they are to make.

Mary Askin | BELLMORE, NY

1 cup butter, softened

1 cup confectioners' sugar

1 egg

3 cups all-purpose flour

1/4 teaspoon salt

1/2 cup chocolate hazelnut spread

Additional confectioners' sugar

In a large bowl, cream the butter and confectioners' sugar until light and fluffy. Beat in egg. Combine flour and salt; gradually add to creamed mixture and mix well. Divide dough in thirds. Shape each into a ball, then flatten into a disk. Wrap in plastic wrap; refrigerate for 30 minutes.

On a lightly floured surface, roll one portion of dough to 1/8-in. thickness. Cut with floured 2-1/2-in. holiday-shaped cookie cutters. Using floured 1-in. shaped cookie cutters, cut out the centers of half of the cookies.

Place solid and cutout cookies 1 in. apart on greased baking sheets. Repeat with the remaining portions of dough. Bake at 350° for 8-10 minutes or until set. Remove to wire racks to cool completely.

Sprinkle the cutout cookies with additional confectioners' sugar. Spread 1 teaspoon chocolate filling on the bottom of each solid cookie; place the cookies with cutout centers over filling. **YIELD:** 2 dozen.

EDITOR'S NOTE: Look for chocolate hazelnut spread in the peanut butter section.

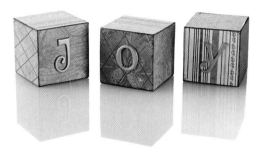

mayan chocolate biscotti

Those who enjoy Mexican hot chocolate will also like the subtle sweetness and slight heat found in every bite of this perked-up biscotti.

Chris Michalowski | DALLAS, TX

1/2 cup butter, softened

3/4 cup sugar

2 eggs

1-1/2 teaspoons coffee liqueur

1-1/2 teaspoons vanilla extract

2 cups all-purpose flour

1-1/2 teaspoons ground ancho chili pepper

1/2 teaspoon baking soda

1/2 teaspoon baking powder

1/2 teaspoon ground cinnamon

1/8 teaspoon salt

1-1/2 cups chopped pecans

1 cup (6 ounces) semisweet chocolate chips

1 ounce 53% cacao dark baking chocolate, grated

In a large bowl, cream the butter and sugar until light and fluffy. Add eggs, one at a time, beating well after each addition. Stir in coffee liqueur and vanilla. Combine the flour, chili pepper, baking soda, baking powder, cinnamon and salt; gradually add to creamed mixture and mix well. Stir in the pecans, chocolate chips and grated chocolate.

Divide dough in half. On an ungreased baking sheet, shape each half into a 10-in. x 2-in. rectangle. Bake at 350° for 20-25 minutes or until set and lightly browned.

Place pans on wire racks. When cool enough to handle, transfer to a cutting board; cut diagonally with a serrated knife into 3/4-in. slices. Place cut side down on ungreased baking sheets.

Bake for 8-10 minutes on each side or until golden brown. Remove to wire racks to cool completely. Store in an airtight container. **YIELD:** 2 dozen.

ginger shortbread cookies

The traditional holiday flavor of gingerbread meets the buttery goodness of shortbread in this irresistible cookie. Pretty flecks of candied ginger make the treats a lovely addition to any cookie platter.

Raymonde Bourgeois | SWASTIKA, ON

1 cup butter, softened

1/3 cup confectioners' sugar

2 cups all-purpose flour

1 teaspoon ground ginger

3/4 teaspoon baking powder

1/4 teaspoon salt

1/3 cup finely chopped walnuts

1/4 cup crystallized ginger, finely chopped

In a large bowl, cream butter and confectioners' sugar until light and fluffy. Combine the flour, ground ginger, baking powder and salt; gradually add to creamed mixture and mix well. Stir in walnuts and crystallized ginger.

Shape into two 10-in. rolls; wrap each in plastic wrap. Refrigerate for 2 hours or until firm. Cut into 1/4-in. slices. Place 2 in. apart on ungreased baking sheets.

Bake at 350° for 12-15 minutes or until lightly browned. Remove to wire racks to cool. Store in an airtight container. **YIELD:** 5 dozen.

chocolate caramels

(PICTURED AT RIGHT)

When I was growing up, my mom made these delicious candies every Christmas. They were my favorite then...and still are today!

Sue Gronholz | BEAVER DAM, WI

1 teaspoon butter, softened

1 cup sugar

3/4 cup light corn syrup

2 ounces unsweetened chocolate, chopped

1-1/2 cups heavy whipping cream, divided

Line a 9-in. x 5-in. loaf pan with foil and grease the foil with butter; set aside.

In a large heavy saucepan, bring the sugar, corn syrup and chocolate to a boil over medium heat; stir until smooth. Add 1/2 cup cream; cook, stirring constantly, until a candy thermometer reads 234°. Add another 1/2 cup cream; return mixture to 234°. Add the remaining cream; cook to 248°.

Immediately pour into prepared pan (do not scrape saucepan). Let stand until firm, about 5 hours or overnight. Using foil, lift candy out of pan. Discard foil; cut candy into 1-in. squares using a buttered knife. Wrap individually in waxed paper; twist ends. **YIELD:** 1-1/4 pounds.

EDITOR'S NOTE: We recommend that you test your candy thermometer before each use by bringing water to a boil; the thermometer should read 212°. Adjust your recipe temperature up or down based on your test.

STORING HOMEMADE CANDY

Stored in an airtight container in a cool dry place, most homemade candy will keep for about 2 to 3 weeks. Fudge and caramels can be wrapped tightly and frozen for up to 1 year.

To prevent candies from exchanging flavors, always store different types of candy in separate containers and use waxed paper between the layers.

Also keep hard candy and soft candy in different containers; otherwise, the moisture from the soft candy will cause the hard candy to become sticky.

lemon pistachio wreaths

(PICTURED ON PAGE 67)

I have made these fun and festive wreaths for the past few years. The zest from the lemon and crunch from the pistachios create a hard-to-resist sweet.

Jauneen Hosking | WIND LAKE, WI

1/2 cup plus 2 tablespoons butter

1/2 cup plus 1 tablespoon sugar

2 egg yolks

5 teaspoons grated lemon peel

1 teaspoon vanilla extract

1 cup all-purpose flour

3/4 cup plus 1 tablespoon cornstarch

1 teaspoon baking powder

1/4 teaspoon salt

1-3/4 cups confectioners' sugar

6 to 8 teaspoons lemon juice

1-1/4 cups pistachios, toasted and finely chopped

In a small bowl, cream butter and sugar until light and fluffy. Beat in the egg yolks, lemon peel and vanilla. Combine the flour, cornstarch, baking powder and salt; gradually add to creamed mixture and mix well.

Shape into a ball, then flatten into a disk. Wrap in plastic wrap; refrigerate for 1 hour.

On a lightly floured surface, roll dough to 1/8-in. thickness. Cut with a floured 2-1/2-in. doughnut cutter. Place 2 in. apart on greased baking sheets.

Bake at 350° for 10-12 minutes or until lightly browned. Remove to wire racks to cool.

In a small bowl, beat confectioners' sugar and enough lemon juice to achieve desired consistency. Spread over cookies. Sprinkle with pistachios. Let stand until set. Store in an airtight container. **YIELD:** 1-1/2 dozen.

candy cane truffle lollipops

Let these too-cute truffle "lollipops" from our staff double as a festive treat and a table topper. Refreshing peppermint and smooth chocolate make the perfect pair.

84 miniature candy canes, divided

3 cups (18 ounces) semisweet chocolate chips, divided

3/4 cup heavy whipping cream

1/4 teaspoon peppermint extract

1 tablespoon shortening

Remove hooks from 24 candy canes; set aside sticks. Crush hooks and remaining candy canes.

Place 2 cups chocolate chips in a small bowl. In a small saucepan, bring cream and 3/4 cup crushed candy canes to a boil; cook and stir until candy canes are melted. Remove from the heat; stir in extract. Pour over chocolate; whisk until smooth. Cool to room temperature, stirring occasionally. Refrigerate until firm.

Shape chocolate mixture into 24 balls; insert a candy cane stick into each truffle. In a microwave, melt shortening and remaining chocolate chips; stir until smooth. Dip truffles in chocolate; allow excess to drip off. Roll in remaining crushed candy canes. Place on waxed paper; let stand until set. **YIELD:** 2 dozen.

nanaimo bars

(PICTURED AT RIGHT)

I originally created these rich bars for my coworkers. Everyone raved about the shortbread crust, creamy middle layer and orange and chocolate flavor combination. They were such a hit, they're now a staple for many gatherings.

Del Mason | MARTENSVILLE, SK

1/3 cup butter, cubed

1/4 cup sugar

1 dark chocolate candy bar (3-1/4 ounces), chopped

1 egg, beaten

17 shortbread cookies, crushed

1/2 cup flaked coconut

1/2 cup finely chopped pecans

1 teaspoon grated orange peel

FILLING:

1/2 cup butter, softened

2 tablespoons instant vanilla pudding mix

2 cups confectioners' sugar

2 tablespoons orange juice

1 teaspoon grated orange peel

1 to 2 drops orange paste food coloring, optional

GLAZE:

1 dark chocolate candy bar (3-1/4 ounces), chopped

1 teaspoon butter

In a large heavy saucepan, combine the butter, sugar and candy bar. Cook and stir over medium-low heat until melted. Whisk a small amount of hot mixture into egg.

Return all to the pan, whisking constantly. Cook and stir over medium-low heat until mixture reaches 160°.

In a large bowl, combine the cookie crumbs, coconut, pecans and orange peel. Stir in chocolate mixture until blended. Press into a greased 9-in. square baking pan. Refrigerate for 30 minutes or until set.

For filling, in a large bowl, cream butter and pudding mix. Beat in the confectioners' sugar, orange juice, peel and food coloring if desired. Spread over crust.

For glaze, melt the candy bar and butter in a microwave; stir until smooth. Spread over the top. Refrigerate until set. Cut into bars.
YIELD: 3 dozen.

Dinner parties during the holiday season call for foods that are a little more elegant than those offered throughout the rest of the year.

Perfect for your immediate family on Christmas Day or for close friends on New Year's Eve, this from-the-sea menu will lure guests to your table.

Alongside zesty Lemon Spaghetti, Pan-Fried Scallops with White Wine Reduction are so satisfying without being overly filling.

Oven-roasting mellows the flavor of Three-Cheese Stuffed Onions, so they'll please all palates. And ordinary butter simply cannot compare to Parmesan Butter, especially when it is spread on fresh-from-the-oven Rosemary-Garlic Dinner Rolls.

SEAFOOD FARE
(PICTURED AT RIGHT)

Pan-Fried Scallops with
White Wine Reduction (p. 82)
Lemon Spaghetti (p. 80)
Three-Cheese Stuffed Onions (p. 80)
Rosemary-Garlic Dinner Rolls (p. 84)
Parmesan Butter (p. 79)

sparkling
MIDNIGHT SUPPER

Holiday Dinner
Planner

A Few Weeks Before:

- Prepare two grocery lists: one for nonperishable items to purchase now and one for perishable items to purchase a few days before the party.
- Bake Rosemary-Garlic Dinner Rolls. Let cool; place in a heavy-duty resealable plastic bag and freeze.

Two Days Before:

- Buy remaining grocery items.
- For the Brie Toasts with Cranberry Compote, make the compote. Cover and chill.

The Day Before:

- Set the table.
- Assemble the Heavenly Illuminated Centerpieces on page 85.
- Prepare the dressing for the Poached Egg Salads with Pancetta Vinaigrette; refrigerate in a covered container.
- Prepare Parmesan Butter; store covered in the refrigerator.
- Bake Cappuccino Cheesecake; chill.
- Peel and core onions for Three-Cheese

Stuffed Onions; cover tightly and store in the refrigerator.
- Prepare the vanilla syrup for Vanilla Bean Fizz; cover and chill.

The Day of the Party:

- In the morning, thaw Rosemary-Garlic Dinner Rolls at room temperature.
- Assemble Goat Cheese and Spinach Stuffed Mushrooms; cover with a damp paper towel and refrigerate.
- Just before guests arrive, bake the Brie Toasts with Cranberry Compote and the Goat Cheese and Spinach Stuffed Mushrooms.
- Bake Three-Cheese Stuffed Onions.
- As the first course, serve Poached Egg Salads with Pancetta Vinaigrette.
- If desired, wrap Rosemary-Garlic Dinner Rolls in foil and reheat in the oven. Serve with Parmesan Butter.
- Prepare the Lemon Spaghetti and the Pan-Fried Scallops with White Wine Reduction.
- Serve the Cappuccino Cheesecake for dessert, and offer each guest a Vanilla Bean Fizz.

brie toasts with cranberry compote

(PICTURED AT RIGHT)

Just six ingredients are all I need to create an elegant appetizer perfect for entertaining. The tart cranberry compote pairs well with creamy Brie cheese.

Katherine Watson | OMAHA, NE

1 cup dried cranberries

1 cup balsamic vinegar

1/2 cup jellied cranberry sauce

1 tablespoon sugar

1 loaf (1 pound) French bread, cut into 1/2-in. slices

3 tablespoons butter, melted

1/2 pound Brie cheese, thinly sliced

In a small saucepan, combine the dried cranberries, vinegar, cranberry sauce and sugar. Cook and stir over medium heat until thickened, about 12 minutes.

Brush bottoms of bread with butter; place on ungreased baking sheets. Bake at 350° for 1-2 minutes or until lightly toasted.

Top bread with Brie. Bake for 4-6 minutes or until cheese is melted. Spoon cranberry mixture over cheese, about 1 tablespoon on each. **YIELD:** about 2 dozen.

parmesan butter

(PICTURED ON PAGE 77)

Basic butter is fine for everyday dining. But when I want to serve guests something a little nicer, I reach for this recipe.

Gail Garcelon | BEAVERTON, OR

1/2 cup butter, softened

1/4 cup grated Parmesan cheese

1 garlic clove, minced

1 teaspoon dried thyme

1/2 teaspoon coarsely ground pepper

1/4 teaspoon salt

In a small bowl, combine all ingredients. Store in the refrigerator. **YIELD:** 3/4 cup.

three-cheese stuffed onions

(PICTURED ON PAGE 76)

Rich and decadent describe my deliciously different vegetable side dish featuring three kinds of cheese.
Sonya Labbe | LOS ANGELES, CA

8 medium onions

1 cup crumbled Gorgonzola cheese

4 ounces cream cheese, cubed

1 tablespoon olive oil

1/2 cup grated Romano cheese

1/2 teaspoon salt

1/2 teaspoon pepper

1 can (14-1/2 ounces) vegetable broth

Peel onions. Cut a 1/2-in. slice from top of each onion; remove centers with a melon baller, leaving 1/2-in. shells.

Combine Gorgonzola cheese and cream cheese; stuff into onion shells. Place in an ungreased 13-in. x 9-in. baking dish. Drizzle with oil; sprinkle with Romano cheese, salt and pepper. Pour broth around onions.

Bake, uncovered, at 375° for 50-60 minutes or until tender. **YIELD:** 8 servings.

lemon spaghetti

(PICTURED ON PAGE 77)

*My family loves everything lemon and everything pasta. So when I came across this recipe,
it was an instant favorite. The refreshing flavor is especially good with seafood.*
Cori Cooper | BOISE, ID

1 package (16 ounces) spaghetti

2/3 cup grated Parmesan cheese

1/3 cup lemon juice

1/3 cup olive oil

5 fresh basil leaves, thinly sliced

3 teaspoons grated lemon peel

Cook spaghetti according to package directions.

In a small bowl, combine the cheese, lemon juice and oil. Drain spaghetti and transfer to a large bowl. Pour cheese mixture over spaghetti; toss to coat. Sprinkle with the basil and lemon peel. **YIELD:** 10 servings.

SIMPLE SPAGHETTI

Carefully hold spaghetti in boiling water and ease it down into the water as it softens, pushing it around the edge of the pan. When fully immersed in the water, gently stir the spaghetti to separate the strands.

poached egg salads with pancetta vinaigrette

(PICTURED AT RIGHT)

My husband and I think the best way to eat an egg is to poach it. Nothing is better than when the yolk breaks and combines with this salad's rustic flavors of shiitake mushrooms, pancetta and arugula.

Cindie Haras | JUPITER, FL

1 can (14 ounces) water-packed quartered artichoke hearts, rinsed and drained

1-1/2 cups whole fresh shiitake mushrooms

2 tablespoons olive oil

1 teaspoon minced fresh rosemary

1/2 teaspoon salt

1/4 teaspoon coarsely ground pepper

DRESSING:

2 ounces pancetta or bacon strips, chopped

1 shallot, finely chopped

1/4 cup sherry vinegar

1 tablespoon Dijon mustard

1 teaspoon sugar

1/4 cup olive oil

SALADS:

1 tablespoon white vinegar

8 eggs

2 cups fresh arugula

In a large bowl, combine the artichokes, mushrooms, oil, rosemary, salt and pepper; transfer to an ungreased baking sheet. Bake at 425° for 10-15 minutes or until the mushrooms are tender.

Meanwhile, in a large skillet, cook pancetta and shallot over medium heat until pancetta is crisp. Stir in the sherry vinegar, mustard and sugar; heat through. Transfer to a small bowl; gradually whisk in oil. Set aside.

Place 2-3 in. of water in a large skillet with high sides; add white vinegar. Bring to a boil; reduce heat and simmer gently. Break cold eggs, one at a time, into a custard cup or saucer; holding the cup close to the surface of the water, slip each egg into water.

Cook, uncovered, until whites are completely set and yolks are still soft, about 4 minutes. With a slotted spoon, lift eggs out of water.

Divide arugula among eight salad plates. Top each with artichoke mixture and a poached egg; drizzle with vinaigrette. YIELD: 8 servings.

vanilla bean fizz

(PICTURED AT FAR RIGHT)

A homemade vanilla bean syrup from our Test Kitchen infuses Champagne with a terrific taste. The bubbly beverage is ideal for holidays throughout the year.

2 cups water

1 cup sugar

4 vanilla beans, split

4 cups Champagne, chilled

In a small saucepan, bring water and sugar to a boil. Add vanilla beans. Reduce heat; simmer, uncovered, for 10 minutes. Remove from the heat; cool to room temperature. Discard beans.

For each serving, pour 1/4 cup vanilla syrup into a Champagne flute; add 1/2 cup Champagne. YIELD: 8 servings.

pan-fried scallops with white wine reduction

(PICTURED ON PAGE 76)

I learned the art of reduction from a cooking class...the flavor is fabulous! Despite the fancy title, this special-occasion entree is easy to prepare.

Katherine Robinson | GLENWOOD SPRINGS, CO

2 pounds sea scallops

1 teaspoon salt

1/4 teaspoon pepper

2 tablespoons olive oil

1/2 cup white wine or chicken broth

1/3 cup orange juice

1/4 cup finely chopped onion

1 teaspoon dried oregano

1 teaspoon Dijon mustard

1 garlic clove, minced

3 tablespoons cold butter, cubed

Sprinkle scallops with salt and pepper. In a large skillet, saute scallops in oil until firm and opaque. Remove and keep warm.

Add wine to the skillet, stirring to loosen browned bits from pan. Stir in the orange juice, onion, oregano, mustard and garlic. Bring to a boil; cook and stir for 2-3 minutes or until reduced by half. Remove from the heat; stir in butter until melted. Serve with scallops. YIELD: 8 servings.

cappuccino cheesecake

(PICTURED AT RIGHT)

Instead of pouring the decadent ganache over the top of this coffee-flavored cheesecake, I use most of it to cover the chocolate crust.

Linda Stemen | MONROEVILLE, IN

24 cream-filled chocolate sandwich cookies

1/3 cup butter, melted

GANACHE:

1 package (11-1/2 ounces) 60% cacao bittersweet chocolate baking chips

1 cup heavy whipping cream

1/3 cup coffee liqueur

FILLING:

1 tablespoon instant coffee granules

2 tablespoons dark rum

4 packages (8 ounces each) cream cheese, softened

1-1/3 cups sugar

2 tablespoons all-purpose flour

2 tablespoons ground coffee

3 teaspoons vanilla extract

2 teaspoons molasses

4 eggs, lightly beaten

TOPPING:

1-1/2 cups (12 ounces) sour cream

1/3 cup sugar

2 teaspoons vanilla extract

Place cookies in a food processor. Cover and pulse until fine crumbs form. Transfer to a bowl and stir in butter. Press onto the bottom of a greased 10-in. springform pan; set aside.

Place chocolate in a small bowl. In a small saucepan, bring cream just to a boil. Pour over chocolate; whisk until smooth. Stir in liqueur. Pour 1-3/4 cups over crust. Freeze for 30 minutes or until firm. For garnishes, drop remaining ganache by teaspoonfuls onto waxed paper-lined sheets; cover and refrigerate.

Dissolve coffee granules in rum. In a large bowl, beat cream cheese and sugar until smooth. Beat in the flour, ground coffee, vanilla, molasses and rum mixture. Add the eggs; beat on low speed just until combined. Pour over the ganache. Place pan on a baking sheet.

Bake at 350° for 1 to 1-1/4 hours or until center is almost set. Let stand for 5 minutes. Combine the sour cream, sugar and vanilla; spread over top of cheesecake. Bake 5 minutes longer. Cool on a wire rack for 10 minutes. Carefully run a knife around edge of pan to loosen; cool 1 hour longer. Refrigerate overnight.

Remove sides of pan. Just before serving, arrange garnishes over top. **YIELD:** 16 servings.

rosemary-garlic dinner rolls

(PICTURED ON PAGE 77)

These rolls are so soft and have such wonderful flavor.
What a nice touch to bring to both holiday dinners and family meals.

Linda Crawford | ELM GROVE, WI

1 cup water (70° to 80°)

2 tablespoons butter, softened

1 egg, lightly beaten

3 tablespoons sugar

1 tablespoon dried rosemary, crushed

2 teaspoons dried minced garlic

1 teaspoon salt

3-1/4 cups bread flour

1 package (1/4 ounce) active dry yeast

In bread machine pan, place all ingredients in order suggested by manufacturer. Select dough setting (check dough after 5 minutes of mixing; add 1 to 2 tablespoons of water or flour if needed).

When cycle is completed, turn dough onto a lightly floured surface. Divide into 16 portions; shape into balls. Divide between two greased 9-in. round baking pans. Cover and let rise until doubled, about 30 minutes. Bake at 375° for 12-15 minutes or until golden brown. Remove from pans to wire racks. YIELD: 16 rolls.

goat cheese and spinach stuffed mushrooms

I take stuffed mushrooms to new heights by using a flavorful filling of walnuts,
spinach and goat cheese. They're not only tasty but pretty as well.

Amanda Reed | NASHVILLE, TN

24 medium fresh mushrooms

2 tablespoons olive oil

1/2 cup finely chopped walnuts

1/3 cup chopped onion

2 tablespoons butter

1 garlic clove, minced

1 package (10 ounces) frozen chopped spinach, thawed and squeezed dry

1-1/4 cups crumbled goat cheese

1/4 teaspoon pepper

1/8 teaspoon salt

Remove stems from mushrooms; place mushroom caps in a large bowl. Add oil and toss to coat. Finely chop stems.

In a large skillet, saute the chopped mushrooms, walnuts and onion in butter until tender. Add garlic; cook 1 minute longer. Stir in the spinach, cheese, pepper and salt; cook and stir until cheese is melted. Stuff into mushroom caps.

Place on greased baking sheets. Bake at 375° for 12-14 minutes or until mushrooms are tender. YIELD: 2 dozen.

heavenly illuminated centerpieces

(PICTURED AT RIGHT)

Add a little bit of sparkle to your enchanting table decor with a set of easy yet elegant centerpieces that light up the night!

Turn on the charm with these impressive luminaries that take advantage of battery-operated "candles." Not only do these centerpieces cast a romantic glow, but they come together without much fuss.

To begin, simply gather a variety of your favorite fresh or artificial flowers. We chose blooms in shades of white and cream, but pick flowers that best match your tableware, party theme or color scheme of the room.

Next, choose a few identical clear vases in whatever size you desire. Remember, however, that you'll want to keep the height of the centerpieces to a minimum so guests can easily converse with one another across the table and over the flowers.

Using either a small foam base or floral tape, create three similar bouquets with the flowers. If your vases aren't already frosted, use a glass frosted spray paint to coat each vase's exterior and let them dry thoroughly.

Insert one or two small battery-operated flameless candles into the bottom of each vase. Top each with a flower bouquet.

The tradition of gathering with others to sing Christmas carols around the neighborhood may no longer be popular, but karaoke is a fad that's not fading away!

This yuletide season, invite friends over for a night of caroling, karaoke-style, in the comfort of your home.

Set the tone for the casual party by offering a melody of kettle creations. Beef & Barley Soup has staple ingredients that blend together beautifully. With tomato juice, cream, shrimp and lobster, Seafood Bisque is a rich accompaniment, while Creamy Chicken Gnocchi Soup is a spin on the chicken noodle classic that's sure to be a hit.

Serve the soups in homemade Mini Cheddar Bread Bowls and guests will be singing your praises!

With this chapter's great appetizers, beverages, desserts and more, it's easy to orchestrate an evening of fun and laughter with friends and family.

SYMPHONY OF SOUPS
(PICTURED AT RIGHT)

Mini Cheddar Bread Bowls (p. 88)
Creamy Chicken Gnocchi Soup (p. 91)
Beef & Barley Soup (p. 88)
Seafood Bisque (p. 90)

not so silent night
KARAOKE PARTY

beef & barley soup

(PICTURED ON PAGE 86)

With a medley of barley, beef and vegetables, this thick, stew-like soup is brimming
with flavor and texture. Every spoonful will warm you from head to toe on a cold winter night.

Rachel Kohnen | POMEROY, IA

4 bacon strips, diced

2 pounds beef stew meat, cut into 1-inch cubes

2 medium onions, chopped

4 medium carrots, chopped

1/2 pound sliced baby portobello mushrooms

1 cup dry red wine or beef broth

8 cups beef broth, divided

4 teaspoons spicy brown mustard

1 teaspoon dried thyme or 4 fresh thyme sprigs, chopped

1 bay leaf

1 cup medium pearl barley

1/4 teaspoon salt

1/4 teaspoon pepper

In a Dutch oven, cook bacon over medium heat until crisp. Using a slotted spoon, remove to paper towels. Brown beef in drippings. Remove and set aside.

In the same pan, saute the onions, carrots and mushrooms until tender. Add wine, stirring to loosen browned bits from pan. Stir in 4 cups broth, mustard, thyme, bay leaf and beef. Bring to a boil. Reduce heat; cover and simmer for 1 hour or until beef is tender.

Stir in the barley, salt, pepper and remaining broth. Return to a boil. Reduce heat; cover and simmer for 1 hour or until barley is tender. Discard bay leaf. Stir in the bacon. **YIELD:** 8 servings (2-1/2 quarts).

mini cheddar bread bowls

(PICTURED ON PAGE 86)

These golden, cheesy bread bowls are a fun and delicious way
to serve homemade soup. Try toasting the bread before ladling soup into the bowls.

Angela Carlisle | DE MOSSVILLE, KY

2 packages (1/4 ounce each) active dry yeast

2 cups warm water (110° to 115°), divided

2 teaspoons sugar

1 teaspoon salt

4-1/2 to 5-1/2 cups all-purpose flour

1 cup (4 ounces) shredded cheddar cheese

1 teaspoon dried oregano

In a large bowl, dissolve yeast in 1/2 cup warm water. Add the sugar, salt, 3 cups flour and remaining water. Beat on medium speed for 3 minutes. Stir in enough remaining flour to form a soft dough (dough will be sticky).

Turn onto a floured surface; knead until smooth and elastic, about 6-8 minutes, while slowly adding cheese and oregano. Place in a greased bowl, turning once to grease the top. Cover and let rise in a warm place until doubled, about 1 hour.

Punch dough down. Turn onto a lightly floured surface. Divide into 10 pieces; shape each into a ball. Place balls 3 in. apart on two greased baking sheets. Cover and let rise until doubled, about 30 minutes. Bake at 350° for 20-25 minutes or until golden brown. Remove from pans to wire racks to cool.

Cut a thin slice off the top of bread. Hollow out bottom of loaf, leaving a 1/4-in. shell (discard removed bread or save for another use). Return to oven for 5 minutes to toast bread bowl before filling. **YIELD:** 10 mini bread bowls.

artichoke, spinach & sun-dried tomato dip

(PICTURED AT RIGHT)

This creamy, robust artichoke dip boasts the colorful addition of sun-dried tomatoes. It's great served with tortilla, pita or bagel chips.

Lorilyn Tenney | BOISE, ID

2 packages (8 ounces each) cream cheese, softened

1/2 cup mayonnaise

2 shallots, finely chopped

3 garlic cloves, minced

1 package (10 ounces) frozen chopped spinach, thawed and squeezed dry

1 jar (7-1/2 ounces) marinated quartered artichoke hearts, drained and chopped

1 cup sun-dried tomatoes (not packed in oil), chopped

3/4 cup grated Asiago cheese

Tortilla chips

In a large bowl, combine the cream cheese, mayonnaise, shallots and garlic. Stir in the spinach, artichokes, tomatoes and Asiago cheese. Transfer to a greased 11-in. x 7-in. baking dish.

Bake at 350° for 30-35 minutes or until golden brown. Serve with tortilla chips. **YIELD:** 5 cups.

SQUEEZING SPINACH DRY

Before using frozen chopped spinach in recipes, it's important to remove all liquid so the dish doesn't become watery.

Remove the spinach from its packaging and place in a colander in a shallow bowl. Thaw in the refrigerator. When completely thawed, squeeze out the water with clean hands.

rosemary-parmesan biscotti

(PICTURED AT FAR RIGHT)

*With its flaky texture and heavenly rosemary and Parmesan flavor,
this savory biscotti from our Test Kitchen is delicious served alongside a bowl of soup or a salad.*

3 cups all-purpose flour

1 cup whole wheat flour

3 tablespoons minced fresh rosemary or
1 tablespoon dried rosemary, crushed

2 teaspoons baking powder

1 teaspoon salt

1/2 teaspoon coarsely ground pepper

2-1/4 cups grated Parmesan cheese, divided

3/4 cup cold butter

3 eggs

1-1/4 cups whole milk

In a large bowl, combine the flours, rosemary, baking powder, salt, pepper and 2 cups cheese. Cut in butter until mixture resembles coarse crumbs. Whisk eggs and milk; stir into crumb mixture just until moistened.

Divide dough into four portions. On an ungreased baking sheet, shape each portion into a 12-in. x 2-in. rectangle. Sprinkle each portion with remaining cheese. Bake at 350° for 30-35 minutes or until golden brown.

Place pans on wire racks. When cool enough to handle, transfer to a cutting board; cut diagonally with a serrated knife into 1-in. slices. Place cut side down on ungreased baking sheets.

Bake for 25-30 minutes or until golden brown. Remove to wire racks to cool completely. Store in an airtight container. **YIELD:** 4 dozen.

seafood bisque

(PICTURED ON PAGE 87)

Creamy bisque is elegant enough for sit-down dinners yet hearty and easy enough for casual gatherings.

Mike Payne | HIXSON, TN

1 small onion, chopped

1 garlic clove, minced

5 tablespoons olive oil, divided

1/2 cup all-purpose flour

3 cups chicken broth

1 teaspoon chicken bouillon granules

2 cans (15 ounces each) tomato sauce

2 cups tomato juice

1 cup white wine or additional broth

1/2 cup chopped fresh basil

1/2 teaspoon salt

Dash white pepper

1 cup heavy whipping cream

1 cup uncooked medium shrimp, peeled and deveined

1 cup frozen uncooked lobster chunks, thawed

Additional chopped basil

In a Dutch oven, saute onion and garlic in 3 tablespoons oil until tender. Stir in flour until blended; cook and stir for 2 minutes or until golden brown. Stir in broth and bouillon. Bring to a boil. Cook and stir for 2 minutes or until thickened.

Stir in the tomato sauce, juice, wine, basil, salt and pepper. Return to a boil. Reduce heat; simmer, uncovered, for 10 minutes. Add cream; heat through (do not boil).

Meanwhile, in a small skillet, cook shrimp and lobster in the remaining oil until the shrimp turn pink, about 5 minutes. Add to the soup. Garnish individual servings with the additional basil. **YIELD:** 10 servings (2-1/2 quarts).

creamy chicken gnocchi soup

(PICTURED AT RIGHT AND ON PAGE 87)

Warm up on a snowy eve by enjoying a bowl of my chicken and pasta soup. It's quick to fix and loved by all who try it.

Jaclynn Robinson | SHINGLETOWN, CA

1 pound boneless skinless chicken breasts, cut into 1/2-inch pieces

1/3 cup butter, divided

1 small onion, chopped

1 medium carrot, shredded

1 celery rib, chopped

2 garlic cloves, minced

1/3 cup all-purpose flour

3-1/2 cups 2% milk

1-1/2 cups heavy whipping cream

1 tablespoon reduced-sodium chicken bouillon granules

1/4 teaspoon coarsely ground pepper

1 package (16 ounces) potato gnocchi

1/2 cup fresh spinach, chopped

In a Dutch oven, brown the chicken in 2 tablespoons butter. Remove and keep warm. In the same pan, saute the onion, carrot, celery and garlic in remaining butter until tender.

Whisk in flour until blended; gradually stir in the milk, cream, bouillon and pepper. Bring to a boil. Reduce heat; cook and stir for 2 minutes or until thickened.

Add the gnocchi and spinach; cook for 3-4 minutes or until the spinach is wilted. Add the chicken. Cover and simmer for 10 minutes or until heated through (do not boil). **YIELD:** 8 servings (2 quarts).

EDITOR'S NOTE: Look for potato gnocchi in the pasta or frozen foods section.

hot apple pie sipper

(PICTURED AT FAR RIGHT)

If you love apple pie, this tasty beverage was created just for you. The ice cream batter gives the sweet cider a smooth, creamy texture. Make it an adult drink by stirring in a little brandy.

Connie Young | PONY, MT

1/4 cup butter, softened

1/3 cup packed brown sugar

2 teaspoons ground cinnamon

1 teaspoon ground nutmeg

1/4 teaspoon ground cloves

1 pint vanilla ice cream, softened

4 cups hot apple cider
or unsweetened apple juice

Brandy, optional

In a large bowl, cream the butter, brown sugar, cinnamon, nutmeg and cloves until light and fluffy. Beat in ice cream. Cover and freeze until firm.

For each serving, place 1/3 cup ice cream mixture in a mug; add 2/3 cup cider. Stir in brandy if desired. **YIELD:** 6 servings.

gingerbread fizz

(PICTURED AT FAR RIGHT)

Here's a sweet treat that blends the seasonal flavor of gingerbread with a fun fizz. Garnish with a dollop of whipped cream, a sprinkling of cookie crumbs and a gingersnap cookie.

Randie Scott | SALT LAKE CITY, UT

1 cup water

1 cup molasses

1 tablespoon minced fresh gingerroot

6 whole cloves

1 cinnamon stick (3 inches), crushed

6 cups lemon-lime soda, chilled

Whipped cream and crushed gingersnap cookies

In a small saucepan, combine the first five ingredients. Bring to a boil; cook until liquid is reduced by half, about 15 minutes. Strain and cool.

In a large pitcher, combine molasses mixture and soda. Pour into glasses. Garnish with whipped cream and cookie crumbs. **YIELD:** 8 servings.

FRESH GINGERROOT FACTS

Fresh gingerroot is available in your grocer's produce section. It should have a smooth skin. If wrinkled and cracked, the root is dry and past its prime.

If stored in a heavy-duty resealable plastic bag, unpeeled gingerroot can be frozen for up to 1 year. When needed, simply peel and grate.

coconut-caramel hot cocoa

(PICTURED AT RIGHT)

You'll think you're drinking your dessert when you indulge in this homemade hot cocoa. The decadent beverage features rich chocolate, peanut butter, caramel and coconut.

Roxanne Chan | ALBANY, CA

1 can (13.66 ounces) coconut milk

1-1/2 cups 2% milk

1/2 cup semisweet chocolate chips, melted

1/4 cup creamy peanut butter

1/4 cup hot caramel ice cream topping

Coconut rum, optional

Whipped cream and toasted flaked coconut, optional

Place the first five ingredients in a blender; cover and process until smooth. Transfer to a large saucepan. Cook and stir over medium heat until heated through. Remove from the heat; stir in rum if desired. Pour into mugs. Garnish with whipped cream and coconut if desired. YIELD: 6 servings.

sweet & spicy kettle corn

A crispy, sugary coating and a slight kick from ancho chili powder make this popcorn simply addicting. You might want to prepare a double batch—it's guaranteed to go fast!

Phyllis Schmalz | KANSAS CITY, KS

1/2 cup popcorn kernels

3 tablespoons canola oil

3 tablespoons sugar

2 tablespoons ground ancho chili pepper

2 teaspoons salt

In a Dutch oven over medium heat, heat the popcorn, oil and sugar until oil begins to sizzle. Cover and shake for 2-3 minutes or until popcorn stops popping.

Transfer to a large bowl. Add chili pepper and salt; toss to coat. YIELD: 4 quarts.

maple sausage cheesecake

Don't be fooled by the name of this truly tempting appetizer. The savory-sweet starter has the consistency of a cheeseball, making it well received at any kind of get-together.

Paula Marchesi | LENHARTSVILLE, PA

1 pound bulk maple pork sausage

4 cups cubed Italian bread, toasted

1/2 cup pine nuts, toasted

1/2 cup butter, melted

3 packages (8 ounces each) plus 1 package (3 ounces) cream cheese, softened

1/2 cup sour cream

1/2 cup heavy whipping cream

4 eggs, lightly beaten

1/2 cup grated Asiago cheese

2 green onions, finely chopped

1/4 teaspoon crushed red pepper flakes

1/4 teaspoon pepper

1/8 teaspoon salt

Assorted crackers

Place a greased 9-in. springform pan on a double thickness of heavy-duty foil (about 18 in. square). Securely wrap foil around pan.

In a large heavy skillet over medium heat, cook sausage until no longer pink; drain and set aside.

In a food processor, combine bread cubes and pine nuts; cover and process until crumbly. Transfer to a small bowl; add butter. Press onto the bottom and 1 in. up the sides of prepared pan; set aside.

In a large bowl, beat the cream cheese, sour cream and cream until smooth. Add eggs; beat on low speed just until combined. Stir in the Asiago cheese, onions, pepper flakes, pepper and salt. Pour into crust. Place springform pan in a large baking pan; add 1 in. of hot water to larger pan.

Bake at 350° for 55-65 minutes or until center is almost set. Remove springform pan from water bath. Cool on a wire rack for 10 minutes. Carefully run a knife around edge of pan to loosen; cool 1 hour longer. Refrigerate overnight. Remove sides of pan. Serve with crackers. YIELD: 24 servings.

peppery herb flatbread

Dress up a prebaked pizza crust for a quick and easy snack. Seasoned with a blend of Parmesan cheese, garlic powder, oregano, pepper and salt, the toasty wedges are perfect for dipping in marinara sauce.

Mark Piskorski | FLEETWOOD, PA

1 prebaked 12-inch pizza crust

2 tablespoons olive oil

1/2 cup shredded Parmesan cheese

1 teaspoon garlic powder

3/4 teaspoon coarsely ground pepper

1/2 teaspoon dried oregano

1/4 teaspoon coarse salt

Place crust on an ungreased baking sheet; brush with oil. Combine the remaining ingredients; sprinkle over crust.

Bake at 450° for 12-15 minutes or until edges are lightly browned. YIELD: 6 servings.

layered gingerbread bars

(PICTURED AT RIGHT)

For a truly special dessert that celebrates the season, bake a batch of these bars. The bottom layer tastes like a cookie, the middle layer features smooth buttercream and the top layer is a luscious frosting.

Patti Ann Christian | ARARAT, NC

1/2 cup butter, softened

2/3 cup packed brown sugar

1 egg

1/3 cup molasses

1-2/3 cups all-purpose flour

1-1/8 teaspoons ground ginger

1/2 teaspoon salt

1/2 teaspoon baking soda

1/2 teaspoon ground cinnamon

1/2 teaspoon ground allspice

1/4 teaspoon ground nutmeg

1/8 teaspoon ground cloves

BUTTERCREAM LAYER:

1/2 cup sugar

3 tablespoons all-purpose flour

1/2 cup 2% milk

3/4 cup butter, softened

1 teaspoon lemon extract

ICING:

1/2 cup packed brown sugar

1/3 cup heavy whipping cream

1/4 cup butter, cubed

2 tablespoons molasses

1/4 teaspoon ground allspice

1/4 teaspoon ground ginger

1/8 teaspoon salt

2-1/2 cups confectioners' sugar

2 tablespoons minced crystallized ginger

In a large bowl, cream butter and brown sugar. Beat in egg and molasses. Combine the flour, ginger, salt, baking soda, cinnamon, allspice, nutmeg and cloves; add to creamed mixture. Pour into a greased 13-in. x 9-in. baking dish. Bake at 350° for 20-25 minutes or until a toothpick comes out clean. Cool on a wire rack.

Meanwhile, in a small saucepan, combine sugar and flour. Whisk in milk until smooth. Cook and stir over medium heat until mixture comes to a boil. Reduce heat; cook and stir for 2 minutes or until thickened. Remove from the heat. Transfer to a small bowl; cover and refrigerate until chilled, about 1 hour.

Beat in butter and extract until light and fluffy. Spread over cooled gingerbread. Cover and freeze for 15 minutes.

For icing, in a small saucepan, combine the brown sugar, cream and butter; bring to a boil. Remove from the heat; whisk in the molasses, allspice, ginger and salt. Transfer to a large bowl; add the confectioners' sugar and beat until smooth. Spread over the buttercream layer. Sprinkle with crystallized ginger. Refrigerate leftovers. **YIELD:** 3 dozen.

Three Kings Day (also known as the Epiphany) falls on January 6 each year and signals the end of the 12 days of Christmas. It commemorates the day when the three kings, or three wise men, brought gifts to the Christ child after following the star to Bethlehem.

Although celebrated throughout the world, Three Kings Day is especially valued in the Puerto Rican culture. The festivities vary from family to family but often include attending mass and enjoying plays, music and dance performances.

Needless to say, no celebration is complete without a menu of fantastic foods, such as Family-Favorite Pina Coladas, Pollo Guisado—a Puerto Rican chicken stew—and Arroz Con Gandules (Rice with Pigeon Peas).

FIT FOR A KING
(PICTURED AT RIGHT)

Pollo Guisado (Chicken Stew) (p. 100)
Arroz Con Gandules
(Rice with Pigeon Peas) (p. 102)
Family-Favorite Pina Coladas (p. 98)

feast of
THE THREE KINGS

family-favorite pina coladas

(PICTURED AT FAR RIGHT, BOTTOM, AND ON PAGE 97)

*A family-friendly version of the classic adult beverage adds tropical fun
and flair to any gathering. Garnish individual glasses with fresh pineapple slices.*

Susan Marshall | COLORADO SPRINGS, CO

6 cups ice cubes

1-1/3 cups unsweetened pineapple juice

2/3 cup cream of coconut

1/8 teaspoon salt

2/3 cup club soda

Fresh pineapple slices, optional

In a blender, combine the ice cubes, juice, cream of coconut and salt; cover and process until smooth. Stir in club soda. Pour into chilled glasses; garnish with pineapple if desired. Serve immediately. **YIELD:** 5 servings.

vanilla flan

*Sweet, creamy and comforting, flan is a universally known Spanish dessert. The rich treat
is the perfect finale to any spicy meal, especially when served with a cup of strong coffee.*

Aura Rivera | ST. FRANCIS, WI

1 cup sugar

1 cup water

5 eggs

1 can (14 ounces) sweetened condensed milk

1 can (12 ounces) evaporated milk

1-1/2 teaspoons vanilla extract

In a large heavy saucepan over medium heat, combine the sugar and water. Cook, stirring occasionally, until the sugar begins to melt.

Using a pastry brush dipped in cold water, wash down the sides of the pan to eliminate the sugar crystals. Cook, without stirring, until amber brown, about 25 minutes.

Quickly pour into an ungreased 9-in. round baking pan, tilting to coat bottom of pan. Place pan in a large baking pan; let stand for 10 minutes.

In a blender, combine the eggs, condensed milk, evaporated milk, and vanilla. Cover and process for 1 minute or until well blended. Slowly pour into prepared baking pan.

Add 1 in. of hot water to larger pan. Bake, uncovered, at 325° for 35-40 minutes or until center is just set (mixture will jiggle). Remove baking pan from water bath; cool for 1 hour. Cover and refrigerate overnight.

To serve flan, run a knife around edge of pan; quickly invert onto a rimmed serving dish. **YIELD:** 8 servings.

coquito

(PICTURED AT RIGHT, TOP)

An all-time family favorite, this smooth, frosty adult beverage features cream of coconut blended with cloves, cinnamon, vanilla and rum.

Evelyn Robles | OAK CREEK, WI

1 can (15 ounces) cream of coconut

1 can (14 ounces) sweetened condensed milk

1 can (12 ounces) evaporated milk

1/2 cup water

1 teaspoon vanilla extract

1/2 teaspoon ground cinnamon

1/4 teaspoon ground cloves

1 cup rum

Place the first seven ingredients in a blender; cover and process until blended. Refrigerate until chilled. Stir in rum before serving. **YIELD:** 8 servings.

MAKING A WATER BATH

To ensure even cooking, the recipe for Vanilla Flan (recipe on opposite page) requires you to bake it in a water bath.

Do so by placing the baking dish in a larger baking pan or dish, then placing them on a rack in the oven. Using a kettle or large measuring cup, carefully pour hot or boiling water into the larger pan or dish. Fill to a depth of 1 in., and bake as the recipe directs.

When done baking, carefully remove the pan from the water. Let the flan cool on a wire rack for 1 hour before covering and refrigerating overnight.

tostones

(PICTURED AT FAR RIGHT)

My parents lived in Puerto Rico for two years while my dad taught English. I grew up eating many dishes from there, but tostones have always been my favorite. I still make the fried snacks when I miss my family.

Leah Martin | GILBERTSVILLE, PA

3 garlic cloves, minced

1 tablespoon garlic salt

1/2 teaspoon onion powder

6 green plantains, peeled and cut into 1-inch slices

Oil for deep-fat frying

SEASONING MIX:

1 tablespoon garlic powder

1-1/2 teaspoons garlic salt

1/2 teaspoon onion powder

1/2 teaspoon kosher salt

In a large bowl, combine the garlic, garlic salt and onion powder. Add plantains; cover with cold water. Soak for 30 minutes.

Drain plantains; place on paper towels and pat dry. In an electric skillet or deep fryer, heat oil to 375°. Add plantains, a few at a time, and cook for 30-60 seconds or until lightly browned. Remove with a slotted spoon; drain on paper towels.

Place plantain pieces between two sheets of aluminum foil. With the bottom of a glass, flatten to 1/2-in. thickness. Fry 2-3 minutes longer or until golden brown.

Combine the seasoning mix ingredients; sprinkle over tostones. **YIELD:** 3 dozen.

pollo guisado (chicken stew)

(PICTURED ON PAGE 97)

Featuring a pretty golden-red color and comforting flavor, this chicken stew will be a welcome entree at any celebration. It's perfect for pairing with red beans and rice.

Susana Crespo | MILWAUKEE, WI

1/2 cup Sofrito (recipe on page 104)

2 bay leaves

1 envelope Goya sazon with coriander and annatto

1 teaspoon adobo seasoning

1 broiler/fryer chicken (3 to 4 pounds), cut up

3 tablespoons canola oil

2 medium potatoes, peeled and cubed

1/2 cup water

1/2 cup tomato sauce

In a large resealable plastic bag, combine the first four ingredients. Add the chicken; seal bag and turn to coat. Refrigerate for at least 8 hours or overnight.

In a large nonstick skillet, brown chicken in oil. Stir in the potatoes, water and tomato sauce. Bring to a boil; cover and simmer for 45-60 minutes or until chicken is tender. Add additional water if necessary. Discard bay leaves before serving. **YIELD:** 6 servings.

EDITOR'S NOTE: Look for Sazon Goya, a seasoning blend, in the international foods section.

shrimp salsa

(PICTURED AT RIGHT)

For a salsa with lots of texture, color and mouthwatering taste, look no further! A medley of chopped shrimp, avocado, tomato, cucumber, onion and cilantro are tossed in lime juice and perked up with a blend of mild spices.

Eliza Novoa-Gonzalez | HENDERSON, NV

1 pound peeled and deveined cooked medium shrimp, chopped

5 medium tomatoes, seeded and chopped

2 medium ripe avocados, peeled and chopped

1 medium cucumber, peeled and chopped

1 cup minced fresh cilantro

1/3 cup chopped sweet onion

1/3 cup orange juice

1/4 cup key lime juice

2 tablespoons lime juice

1 teaspoon salt

1 teaspoon garlic powder

1 teaspoon garlic salt

1 teaspoon coarsely ground pepper

Tostones or tortilla chips

In a large bowl, combine the first 13 ingredients. Serve salsa immediately with Tostones. **YIELD:** 8 cups.

spanish smashed potatoes with cilantro sauce

(PICTURED AT FAR RIGHT)

*I was inspired to create this after visiting a great Latin restaurant.
The salty potatoes and the bright herbs are great together.*

Libby Walp | CHICAGO, IL

1 pound fingerling potatoes

1 cup fresh cilantro leaves

4 garlic cloves, peeled

3/4 teaspoon kosher salt

1/4 cup water

2 teaspoons sherry vinegar

1/2 cup olive oil

Place potatoes in a large saucepan and cover with water. Bring to a boil. Reduce heat; cover and simmer for 15-20 minutes or until tender. Drain and transfer to a small bowl.

Place the cilantro, garlic and salt in a small food processor; cover and pulse until chopped. Add the water and vinegar; cover and process until blended. While processing, gradually add the oil in a steady stream.

Using a fork, flatten potatoes slightly; pour sauce over the top. **YIELD:** 4 servings.

arroz con gandules (rice with pigeon peas)

(PICTURED ON PAGE 97)

*Feed a crowd with this authentic rice dish that was handed down
to me from my mom. It's a staple with the "familia" at all our gatherings.*

Evelyn Robles | OAK CREEK, WI

1/2 cup Sofrito (recipe on page 104)

2 tablespoons canola oil

4 cups uncooked long grain rice

1 envelope Goya sazon with coriander and annatto

7 cups water

1 can (15 ounces) pigeon peas, drained

2 cans (5 ounces each) Vienna sausage, drained and chopped

1/2 cup tomato sauce

1-1/4 teaspoons salt

1 envelope Goya ham-flavored concentrate

1/2 teaspoon chicken bouillon granules

1/4 teaspoon pepper

In a Dutch oven, cook Sofrito in oil over medium-low heat for 5 minutes, stirring occasionally. Add rice and sazon; cook and stir for 3-4 minutes or until rice is lightly toasted. Add the remaining ingredients. Bring to a boil. Reduce heat; cover and simmer for 15-20 minutes or until rice is tender. Fluff with a fork. **YIELD:** 18 servings (3/4 cup each).

EDITOR'S NOTE: Look for Sazon Goya, a seasoning blend, in the international foods section.

roasted pork shoulder

(PICTURED AT RIGHT)

*When I discovered Puerto Rican food,
I was hooked. I've made this recipe
my very own through trial and error and
by researching ingredients and adding
more or less of them to suit my taste.
I think the results in this dish are just right.*

Joanne Morgan | KANSAS CITY, MO

1/2 cup white wine vinegar

1/2 cup olive oil

12 garlic cloves, peeled

1/4 cup minced fresh cilantro

3 tablespoons kosher salt

3 tablespoons chili powder

2 tablespoons dried oregano

2 tablespoons whole peppercorns

1 boneless pork shoulder butt roast
(3 to 4 pounds)

10 cups water

In a food processor, combine the first eight ingredients. Cover and process until combined. Pour into a large resealable plastic bag; add pork. Seal bag; turn to coat. Refrigerate for 8 hours or overnight.

Drain and discard marinade. Place roast on a rack in a roasting pan; pour 2 cups water into pan.

Bake, uncovered, at 450° for 1 hour. Reduce heat to 400°. Bake 1-1/2 to 2 hours longer or until meat is tender, adding more water to the pan as needed. Let stand for 15 minutes before slicing. **YIELD:** 8 servings.

HOW MUCH PORK TO PURCHASE

The amount of pork you need varies with the cut selected. Follow these guidelines:
  2 to 2-1/2 servings per 1 pound of bone-in chops and roasts;
  3 to 4 servings per 1 pound of boneless chops and roasts;
  1 to 1-1/4 servings per 1 pound of spareribs.

habichuelas (red beans)

My grandmother gave me the recipe for this traditional red bean dish. It's been a tried-and-true standby in my family for years. It's best served as a side, usually with white rice, and goes well with any entree.

Linda Robles | MILWAUKEE, WI

2 tablespoons Sofrito (recipe below)

1 tablespoon olive oil

2 cups water

1 can (16 ounces) kidney beans, rinsed and drained

2 medium potatoes, peeled and cubed

1 can (8 ounces) tomato sauce

1 envelope Goya sazon with coriander and annatto

1/4 teaspoon salt

1/4 teaspoon pepper

Hot cooked rice, optional

In a large skillet, cook Sofrito in oil over medium-low heat for 5 minutes, stirring occasionally.

Add the water, beans, potatoes, tomato sauce, sazon, salt and pepper; bring to a boil. Reduce the heat; cover and simmer for 30-35 minutes or until the potatoes are tender. Serve with rice if desired. **YIELD:** 4 servings.

EDITOR'S NOTE: Look for Sazon Goya, a seasoning blend, in the international foods section.

SO WHAT IS SAZON?

Sazon is a Spanish-style seasoned salt. Typical ingredients include cilantro, achiote, garlic and salt. Goya brand offers several Sazon varieties, including coriander and annatto, tomato and coriander, and garlic and onion.

sofrito

Sofrito is a base frequently used in many Puerto Rican recipes to add bold flavor. Its texture and appearance is similar to a green salsa. You can also try it on chilies, enchiladas and tacos.

Evelyn Robles | OAK CREEK, WI

1 whole garlic bulb

1 medium green pepper, quartered

1 medium onion, quartered

1/2 cup fresh cilantro leaves

1 plum tomato, quartered

Separate and peel the garlic cloves. Place the garlic and remaining four ingredients in a food processor; cover and process until finely chopped.

Use immediately or refrigerate for up to 1 week. May also be frozen in small portions in resealable freezer bags for up to 1 month. **YIELD:** 2 cups.

puerto rican coconut pudding

(PICTURED AT RIGHT)

Tembleque, or coconut pudding, brings back so many memories of the days my family would vacation in Puerto Rico to see my relatives. It was one of my favorite things to eat.

Linette Serenil | UPLAND, CA

2/3 cup sugar

1/2 cup cornstarch

1/2 teaspoon salt

2 cans (13.66 ounces each) coconut milk

1/2 teaspoon ground cinnamon

In a small saucepan, combine the sugar, cornstarch and salt. Add milk; stir until smooth. Cook and stir over medium heat until mixture comes to a boil. Cook and stir 1-2 minutes longer or until thickened.

Remove from the heat; pour into dessert dishes. Cool slightly. Cover and refrigerate for 2 hours. Just before serving, sprinkle with cinnamon. **YIELD:** 8 servings.

GIVING *thanks*

Few holidays center around the dinner table like Thanksgiving. An appreciation for those you hold dear and a heartwarming menu are all it takes to make your Thanksgiving memorable. Turn to this comforting section for traditional favorites, new takes on autumnal classics and luscious menu finales that are sure to become requested at your home year after year.

$\mathcal{E}$ver notice how serving dishes make their way around and around the Thanksgiving table? Our dinner plates just aren't big enough to hold all of the tasty trimmings at once.

Thanksgiving is one time of year family cooks go all out and prepare a cornucopia of irresistible recipes.

Roasted Sweet Potato Soup... Pumpkin with Walnuts and Blue Cheese...Sizzling Green Beans...Pearl Onion, Cherry & Pear Chutney. Such spectacular sides will take center stage on your table and certainly prompt requests for seconds.

And, because Thanksgiving dinner simply would not be complete without a golden turkey, showcase a beautiful bird this year by preparing Rosemary Roasted Turkey.

FABULOUS FIXINGS
(PICTURED AT RIGHT)

Rosemary Roasted Turkey (p. 115)
Pearl Onion, Cherry & Pear Chutney (p. 114)
Sizzling Green Beans (p. 112)
Pumpkin with Walnuts and Blue Cheese (p. 111)
Roasted Sweet Potato Soup (p. 112)

traditional
THANKSGIVING DINNER

Thanksgiving Day
Timeline

A Few Weeks Before:

- Prepare two grocery lists: one for nonperishable items to purchase now and one for perishable items to purchase a few days before Thanksgiving Day.

- Order a fresh turkey or buy and freeze a frozen turkey.

- Bake Cranberry Focaccia. Let cool; place in a heavy-duty resealable plastic bag and freeze.

Four to Three Days Before:

- Thaw the frozen turkey in a pan in the refrigerator. (Allow 24 hours of thawing for every 5 pounds. A thawed turkey can be refrigerated for 1 to 2 days.)

- Buy the remaining grocery items, including the fresh turkey if ordered.

The Day Before:

- Set the table.

- Make the Pearl Onion, Cherry & Pear Chutney. Once cooked, cover saucepan and refrigerate.

- Assemble Pecan Sausage Stuffing; cover and chill.

- Prepare Roasted Sweet Potato Soup; cover Dutch oven and chill.

- Peel and cube the pumpkin for Pumpkin with Walnuts and Blue Cheese; refrigerate in a covered container.

- For Sizzling Green Beans, clean and trim beans; refrigerate in a resealable plastic bag. Toast almonds; store in a covered container at room temperature.

- Prepare the Gorgonzola mixture for the Gorgonzola Baked Apples with Balsamic Syrup; cover and chill.

- Bake Brown Sugar & Almond Pumpkin Custard Pie; refrigerate.

Thanksgiving Day:

- In the morning, peel and cube the potatoes and turnips for Gruyere-Turnip Mashed Potatoes. Cover with cold water; refrigerate.

- Thaw Cranberry Focaccia at room temperature.

- Prepare Rosemary Roasted Turkey; bake as directed.

- Assemble and bake Gorgonzola Baked Apples with Balsamic Syrup.

- Roast Sizzling Green Beans.

- Reheat Roasted Sweet Potato Soup and Pearl Onion, Cherry & Pear Chutney.

- Let the cooked turkey stand 15 minutes before carving. Meanwhile, make gravy.

- Bake Pumpkin with Walnuts and Blue Cheese and Pecan Sausage Stuffing.

- If desired, wrap Cranberry Focaccia in foil and reheat in the oven.

- For dessert, serve the Brown Sugar & Almond Pumpkin Custard Pie.

cranberry focaccia

(PICTURED AT RIGHT)

This slightly sweet version stars dried cranberries and pumpkin pie spice.

Veronica Gantley | NORFOLK, VA

2 teaspoons active dry yeast

1 cup warm water (110° to 115°)

5 tablespoons sugar

3 tablespoons butter, softened

2 tablespoons nonfat dry milk powder

1 teaspoon salt

1 teaspoon pumpkin pie spice

3 cups all-purpose flour

3/4 cup dried cranberries

1/2 cup packed brown sugar

In a large bowl, dissolve yeast in warm water. Add the sugar, butter, milk powder, salt, pie spice and 2 cups flour. Beat until smooth. Stir in enough remaining flour to form a soft dough (dough will be sticky).

Turn onto a floured surface; knead until smooth and elastic, about 6-8 minutes. Place dough in a greased bowl, turning once to grease the top. Cover and let rise in a warm place until doubled, about 1 hour.

Punch dough down. Cover and let rest for 10 minutes. Shape into a 14-in. x 10-in. rectangle and place on a greased baking sheet. Cover and let rise until doubled, about 30 minutes. With fingertips, make several dimples over top of dough.

Sprinkle with dried cranberries and brown sugar. Bake at 400° for 10-15 minutes or until golden brown. Remove to a wire rack. **YIELD:** 1 loaf (12 pieces).

pumpkin with walnuts and blue cheese

(PICTURED ON PAGE 109)

Don't hold off on serving pumpkin as the dinner finale. Bring it to the forefront with this unique side dish.

Laurie Bock | LYNDEN, WA

5 pounds pie pumpkins, seeded, peeled and cut into 1-inch cubes

1/4 cup olive oil, divided

2 teaspoons salt

1 teaspoon pepper

2 medium onions, chopped

2/3 cup chopped walnuts

2/3 cup crumbled blue cheese

20 fresh sage leaves, thinly sliced

Place pumpkin in a greased 15-in. x 1-in. x 1-in. baking pan. Drizzle with 2 tablespoons oil; sprinkle with salt and pepper. Bake at 375° for 30-35 minutes or until tender.

In a large skillet, saute onions in remaining oil until tender. Add walnuts; cook 3-5 minutes or until toasted. Place pumpkin on a serving platter. Top with onion mixture. Sprinkle with blue cheese and sage. **YIELD:** 12 servings.

roasted sweet potato soup

(PICTURED ON PAGE 109)

*My great-grandmother passed down the recipe for this golden soup. Not only is it
a great first course, it's also a satisfying meal for my vegetarian friends.*

Trisha Kruse | EAGLE, ID

3 pounds medium sweet potatoes, peeled and cut into 1-inch cubes

2 large sweet onions, coarsely chopped

1 can (49-1/2 ounces) chicken broth, divided

2 tablespoons reduced-sodium soy sauce

2 tablespoons maple syrup

1 garlic clove, minced

1/4 teaspoon pepper

Salted pumpkin seeds and/or pepitas, optional

Place the sweet potatoes and onions in separate greased 15-in. x 10-in. x 1-in. baking pans. Bake, uncovered, at 425° for 15 minutes, stirring once.

Meanwhile, combine 1/2 cup broth, soy sauce, maple syrup and garlic; drizzle over onions and toss to coat. Bake potatoes and onions 15-20 minutes longer or until tender.

In a blender, cover and process potatoes and remaining broth in batches until smooth. Transfer mixture to a Dutch oven; add onion mixture and pepper. Heat through. Garnish with pumpkin seeds if desired. **YIELD:** 12 servings (about 2 quarts).

sizzling green beans

(PICTURED ON PAGE 109)

*I've loved green beans ever since I started eating them off the vine in my grandmother's garden.
To add a little heat to these baked beauties, I sometimes sprinkle them with crushed red pepper flakes.*

Kristin Schultz | MANOR, TX

2 pounds fresh green beans, trimmed

16 shallots, quartered

1/4 cup olive oil

1/4 cup minced fresh basil or 4 teaspoons dried basil

2 teaspoons minced fresh thyme or 1/2 teaspoon dried thyme

2 tablespoons minced fresh oregano or 2 teaspoons dried oregano

4 garlic cloves, minced

1 teaspoon salt

1/2 teaspoon coarsely ground pepper

1/4 cup lemon juice

1/4 cup balsamic vinegar

1/2 cup slivered almonds, toasted

In a large bowl, toss the first nine ingredients; transfer to two greased 15-in. x 10-in. x 1-in. baking pans. Bake, uncovered, at 400° for 25-30 minutes or until crisp-tender.

Transfer to a serving bowl. Drizzle with lemon juice and vinegar; toss to coat. Sprinkle with almonds. **YIELD:** 10 servings.

TRIM GREEN BEANS IN NO TIME

When you buy fresh green beans, be sure to select beans with slender green pods free of bruises or brown spots. Wash just before using.

Trimming fresh beans for Sizzling Green Beans can be done simply and quickly. Just line up the ends of the beans, and, using a chef's knife, slice several at a time.

gorgonzola baked apples with balsamic syrup

(PICTURED AT RIGHT)

Gorgonzola cheese and a balsamic vinegar reduction sauce are pleasing partners to sweet apples. Serve this fruity favorite alongside any entree.

Crystal Holsinger | SURPRISE, AZ

1/3 cup chopped hazelnuts

1/4 cup butter, chopped

3 tablespoons crumbled Gorgonzola cheese

1 tablespoon brown sugar

1/4 teaspoon ground cinnamon

1/8 teaspoon salt

1/8 teaspoon onion powder

6 medium tart apples, cored

1 cup balsamic vinegar

In a small bowl, combine the first seven ingredients. Stuff apples with mixture and place in a greased 11-in. x 7-in. baking dish. Bake, uncovered, at 325° for 40-45 minutes or until apples are tender.

Meanwhile, in a small saucepan, bring the vinegar to a boil; cook until liquid is reduced to 1/3 cup. Drizzle the syrup over apples. **YIELD:** 6 servings.

gruyere-turnip mashed potatoes

I pep up plain potatoes by cooking and mashing them with turnips and fresh garlic. Family and friends often request this dish for holiday dinners.

Sonya Labbe | LOS ANGELES, CA

3 medium potatoes, peeled and cut into 1/2-inch cubes

3 medium turnips, peeled and cut into 1/2-inch cubes

6 garlic cloves, halved

1/3 cup whole milk

2 tablespoons butter

1 cup (4 ounces) shredded Gruyere cheese

2 green onions, chopped

1/2 teaspoon salt

1/2 teaspoon pepper

Place the potatoes, turnips and garlic in a large saucepan and cover with water. Bring to a boil. Reduce heat; cover and cook for 15-20 minutes or until tender.

Meanwhile, in a small saucepan, heat milk and butter until butter is melted. Drain potato mixture; mash with milk mixture. Stir in the cheese, onions, salt and pepper. **YIELD:** 6 servings.

pearl onion, cherry & pear chutney

(PICTURED ON PAGE 109)

When I first saw this chutney's interesting combination of pearl onions and dried cherries, I knew I had to give the recipe a try. It tastes even better than I imagined!
Cheryl Neely | MARKHAM, ON

1 pound pearl onions

2-1/2 cups dried cherries

2 cups water

1 cup sugar

1 cup red wine vinegar

1 teaspoon salt

1/4 teaspoon ground cloves

4 medium pears, peeled and chopped

1/4 cup lemon juice

In a Dutch oven, bring 6 cups water to a boil. Add pearl onions; boil for 3 minutes. Drain and rinse in cold water; peel, cut in half and place in a large saucepan. Stir in the cherries, water, sugar, vinegar, salt and cloves.

Toss pears with lemon juice; stir 2 cups into saucepan. Bring to a boil. Reduce heat; simmer, uncovered, for 1 hour or until desired consistency is achieved. Stir in remaining pears; heat through. **YIELD:** 6 cups.

pecan sausage stuffing

Apples and sausage keep every bite of this stuffing moist and delicious, while toasted pecans add a bit of crunch. Fresh herbs are a tasty touch, too.
Linda Burk | MONROE, GA

1-1/2 pounds bulk pork sausage

3 cups chopped onions

2 cups chopped celery

1/2 cup butter, cubed

6 garlic cloves, minced

1 loaf (1 pound) French bread, cubed and toasted

3 medium apples, peeled and chopped

1-1/2 cups chopped pecans, toasted

1/4 cup chopped fresh sage or 4 teaspoons dried sage leaves

1 tablespoon dried thyme

1-1/4 teaspoons salt

1-1/4 teaspoons pepper

2 to 3 cups reduced-sodium chicken broth

In a large skillet, cook sausage over medium heat until no longer pink; drain. Transfer to a large bowl. In the same skillet, saute onions and celery in butter until tender. Add the garlic and cook 1 minute longer.

Add the bread cubes, apples, pecans, sage, thyme, salt, pepper and onion mixture to the sausage. Stir in enough broth to reach desired moistness. Transfer to a greased 13-in. x 9-in. baking dish (dish will be full). Bake, uncovered, at 375° for 25-30 minutes or until lightly browned. **YIELD:** 21 servings (3/4 cup each).

EDITOR'S NOTE: This recipe makes enough stuffing to stuff a 21-pound turkey. Bake until a meat thermometer reads 180° for turkey and 165° for stuffing.

rosemary roasted turkey

(PICTURED AT RIGHT AND ON PAGE 109)

Our Test Kitchen staff perched a turkey on top of whole onions, which can be served alongside the carved bird. The pairing of white wine and rosemary creates a mouthwatering gravy.

3 whole garlic bulbs

6 large onions, halved

5 fresh rosemary sprigs

1 turkey (14 to 16 pounds)

2 cups white wine

3 tablespoons olive oil

1 tablespoon minced fresh rosemary

3/4 teaspoon salt

3/4 teaspoon pepper

1/4 cup butter, cubed

1/4 cup all-purpose flour

Remove papery outer skin from garlic (do not peel or separate cloves). Cut tops off of garlic bulbs. Place the garlic, onions and rosemary sprigs in a shallow roasting pan. Pat turkey dry. Tuck wings under turkey; tie drumsticks together. Place breast side up over onion mixture. Pour wine into pan.

Brush turkey with oil and sprinkle with rosemary, salt and pepper. Bake, uncovered, at 325° for 3-1/2 to 4 hours or until a meat thermometer reads 180°, basting occasionally with pan drippings. Cover loosely with foil if turkey browns too quickly. Cover and let stand for 20 minutes before slicing.

For gravy, strain drippings into a small bowl. In a small saucepan, melt butter. Stir in flour until smooth; gradually add drippings. Bring to a boil; cook and stir for 2 minutes or until thickened. Serve with turkey. YIELD: 14 servings (2-1/2 cups gravy).

brown sugar & almond pumpkin custard pie

Plain old pumpkin pie is fine, but for special occasions, I reach for this recipe!
A tender homemade crust is topped with a crunchy brown sugar layer and creamy pumpkin custard.

Michaela Rosenthal | WOODLAND HILLS, CA

1-2/3 cups all-purpose flour

2/3 cup shortening

3/4 teaspoon salt

2 tablespoons plus 1-1/2 teaspoons cold water

2 tablespoons plus 1-1/2 teaspoons cider vinegar

BROWN SUGAR LAYER:

1 cup finely chopped almonds

1/2 cup packed brown sugar

2 tablespoons almond paste

2 tablespoons finely chopped crystallized ginger

2 teaspoons all-purpose flour

1 teaspoon grated lemon peel

1/4 teaspoon almond extract

3 tablespoons cold butter

CUSTARD LAYER:

3 ounces cream cheese, softened

1 cup packed brown sugar

1/3 cup sour cream

1-1/3 cups canned pumpkin

1/2 cup evaporated milk

2 tablespoons molasses

2 teaspoons pumpkin pie spice

2 eggs plus 1 egg yolk, lightly beaten

In a food processor, combine the flour, shortening and salt; cover and pulse until mixture resembles coarse crumbs. While processing, gradually add water and vinegar until dough forms a ball. Wrap in plastic wrap. Refrigerate for 30 minutes or until easy to handle.

Roll out pastry to fit a 9-in. deep-dish pie plate. Transfer pastry to pie plate. Trim the pastry to 1/2 in. beyond edge of plate; flute the edges.

In a small bowl, combine the almonds, brown sugar, almond paste, ginger, flour, lemon peel and extract; cut in butter until crumbly. Spread over bottom of crust.

In a large bowl, beat the cream cheese, brown sugar and sour cream until smooth. Beat in the pumpkin, milk, molasses and pie spice until blended. Add eggs and egg yolk; beat on low speed just until combined. Pour filling over almond layer. Cover edges of pie loosely with foil.

Bake at 425° for 10 minutes. Reduce the heat to 375°; bake for 45-55 minutes or until set. Cool pie on a wire rack. Refrigerate leftovers. **YIELD:** 8 servings.

FLUTED EDGES ARE AS EASY AS PIE

A fluted edge adds elegant flair to a homemade pie crust. To achieve the look, position your index finger on the edge of the crust, pointing out. Place the thumb and index finger of your other hand on the outside edge and pinch dough around the index finger to form a V shape. Continue around the edge.

stunning squash vase

(PICTURED AT RIGHT)

Bring the beauty of the outdoors to your Thanksgiving table with a gourd-geous, natural centerpiece featuring squash.

Start by looking at farmers markets or garden centers for a medium-sized, round winter squash that sits upright.

In the photo at right, we used a buttercup squash, but feel free to get creative and try another variety. There are many shape and color options available, including calabaza, hubbard, kabocha and pumpkin.

With a sharp knife, hollow out the center of the squash, leaving about a 2-in. shell at the bottom.

Insert floral foam into the squash; add water. Cut stems of various fall flowers, berries and greens. Arrange in the floral foam, making sure to cover the hole in the top of the squash.

If desired, make two more squash vases. Set them on a wooden plank down the length of your dinner table. (Protect the table with a cloth runner.) Add candles of varying heights, small gourds and fresh grapes to accent the display.

To make the arrangement even easier, simply gather an assortment of winter squash, gourds and candles, assemble them on a wooden plank and finish with a few candles and fall leaves.

It's an annual debate. What do people look forward to more: Thanksgiving dinner or all of the yummy extras the next day? It seems Thanksgiving leftovers are as much a holiday tradition as the feast itself.

This year, break the turkey sandwich routine. Satisfy post-holiday shopping hunger with a hearty assortment of tasty main dishes, sandwiches, soups and small bites...featuring Thanksgiving extras.

Surplus stuffing and jellied cranberry take on new character as savory Meatballs with Cranberry Sauce, while extra mashed potatoes become creamy Potato Chive Soup.

Got turkey? Then enjoy a slice of melty Bistro Turkey Calzone alongside a bowl of Curried Turkey Soup.

NEXT DAY DISHES
(PICTURED AT RIGHT)

Potato Chive Soup (p. 122)
Curried Turkey Soup (p. 120)
Meatballs with Cranberry Sauce (p. 120)
Bistro Turkey Calzone (p. 121)

turkey day
LEFTOVERS

meatballs with cranberry sauce

(PICTURED ON PAGE 119)

*With their cranberry dipping sauce, these no-fuss appetizer meatballs make use of traditional
Thanksgiving ingredients, so they're ideal around the holiday or anytime you're craving those favorite seasonal tastes.*

Ann Baker | TEXARKANA, TX

3 cups leftover cooked stuffing

1 pound ground turkey

1 pound bulk pork sausage

1 cup jellied cranberry sauce

1/2 cup chili sauce

1/4 cup orange juice

3 tablespoons brown sugar

1 teaspoon soy sauce

1/2 teaspoon grated orange peel

Place the stuffing in a large bowl. Crumble the ground turkey and pork sausage over stuffing and mix well. Shape into 2-in. balls. Place on a greased rack in a shallow baking pan. Bake at 375° for 15-20 minutes or until no longer pink. Drain on paper towels.

Meanwhile, in a small saucepan, combine the remaining ingredients; heat through. Serve with meatballs. **YIELD:** 3 dozen (1-1/2 cups sauce).

curried turkey soup

(PICTURED ON PAGE 119)

*This colorful soup is a delight to serve the day after Thanksgiving. Best of all, it comes together
in the slow cooker, allowing you some time to get a head start on your holiday shopping.*

Holly Bauer | WEST BEND, WI

4-1/2 cups chicken broth

1 can (14-1/2 ounces) diced tomatoes, undrained

2 medium carrots, chopped

2 celery ribs, chopped

1 medium onion, chopped

1 medium green pepper, chopped

1 medium tart apple, peeled and chopped

1 tablespoon curry powder

1/2 teaspoon salt

1/2 teaspoon pepper

1/4 cup all-purpose flour

1/2 cup unsweetened apple juice or additional chicken broth

3 cups cubed cooked turkey

3 cups hot cooked rice

Combine the first ten ingredients in a 4- or 5-qt. slow cooker. Cover and cook on low for 7-8 hours or until vegetables are tender. Mix flour and apple juice until smooth; stir into soup. Cover and cook on high for 30 minutes or until soup is thickened.

Stir in turkey; heat through. Serve with rice. **YIELD:** 6 servings (2-1/2 quarts).

SAFELY STORING LEFTOVERS

Leftover turkey, stuffing and pumpkin pie can be refrigerated for 3 to 4 days. Meat combined with gravy and gravy by itself should be used within 1 to 2 days. Cranberry sauce and relish can be stored in the refrigerator for 5 to 7 days. Cooked vegetables should be eaten within 3 to 5 days.

Freeze any leftovers you won't eat within 3 days. Use frozen cooked meat and gravy within 2 to 3 months.

pumpkin gnocchi in sage butter

(PICTURED AT RIGHT)

For a delicious autumn spin on an Italian classic, try this hearty dish.
Donna Mosca Kahler | JUPITER, FL

1-1/2 cups all-purpose flour

1/4 teaspoon salt

1/4 teaspoon pepper

1/8 teaspoon ground nutmeg

1 cup canned pumpkin

6 quarts water

1/2 cup butter, cubed

4 fresh sage leaves, thinly sliced

1 garlic clove, minced

In a small bowl, combine the flour, salt, pepper and nutmeg. Stir in pumpkin until blended. On a lightly floured surface, knead 10-12 times, forming a soft dough. Let dough rest for 10 minutes.

Divide dough into four portions. On a lightly floured surface, roll each portion into a 1/2-in.-thick rope; cut into 3/4-in. pieces. Press and roll each piece with a lightly floured fork.

In a Dutch oven, bring water to a boil. Cook gnocchi in batches for 1 to 1-1/2 minutes or until they float. Remove with a slotted spoon; keep warm.

In a large heavy saucepan, melt butter over medium heat. Add the sage, garlic and gnocchi; stir to coat. **YIELD:** 4 servings.

bistro turkey calzone

(PICTURED ON PAGE 118)

Turkey, cheddar and bacon harmonize well with the apple in this family-friendly fare.
Donna Marie Ryan | TOPSFIELD, MA

1 tablespoon cornmeal

1 loaf (1 pound) frozen pizza dough, thawed

3/4 pound thinly sliced cooked turkey

8 slices cheddar cheese

5 bacon strips, cooked and crumbled

1 small tart apple, peeled and thinly sliced

1 egg, beaten

1/2 teaspoon Italian seasoning

Sprinkle cornmeal over a greased baking sheet. On a lightly floured surface, roll dough into a 15-in. circle. Transfer to prepared pan. Arrange half of turkey over half of the dough; top with cheese, bacon, apple and remaining turkey. Fold dough over filling and pinch edges to seal.

With a sharp knife, cut three slashes in the top. Brush with egg and sprinkle with Italian seasoning. Bake at 400° for 20-25 minutes or until golden brown. Let stand for 5 minutes before cutting into wedges. **YIELD:** 6 servings.

potato chive soup

(PICTURED ON PAGE 118)

The homespun flavor in every spoonful of this delicate cream soup disguises its easy preparation. Based on a favorite restaurant soup, this version comes in handy when there are extra mashed potatoes from a holiday meal.

Linda Harrington | HUDSON, NH

1/2 cup butter, cubed

1 medium onion, chopped

1/2 cup minced fresh chives

1 carton (32 ounces) chicken broth

2-1/2 cups mashed potatoes (with added milk and butter)

1 cup heavy whipping cream
or half-and-half cream

Oyster crackers, optional

In a large saucepan over medium heat, melt butter. Add onion; cook and stir until crisp-tender. Add chives; cook 2 minutes longer. Remove from the heat; stir in broth and potatoes.

In a blender or food processor, process mixture in batches until smooth. Return to the pan; stir in cream. Heat through (do not boil). Serve with crackers if desired. **YIELD:** 8 servings (2 quarts).

turkey & rice tostadas

These yummy bites make a great snack during the big game or a light lunch after an afternoon of shopping. Starring turkey, rice, beans and a zesty sauce, the tostadas are a tasty alternative to the usual turkey sandwiches.

Dawn Onuffer | CRESTVIEW, FL

1 can (15 ounces) tomato sauce

2 tablespoons dried minced onion

2 teaspoons dried minced garlic

2 teaspoons chili powder

1/8 teaspoon ground cumin

8 corn tortillas (6 inches)

Cooking spray

2 cups shredded cooked turkey breast

1/2 cup cooked brown rice

1 can (16 ounces) refried beans

Optional toppings: shredded lettuce, chopped tomato and shredded Mexican cheese blend

In a small saucepan, combine the tomato sauce, onion, garlic, chili powder and cumin. Bring to a boil. Reduce heat; simmer, uncovered, for 10 minutes or until slightly thickened.

Place tortillas on an ungreased baking sheet; spritz on both sides with cooking spray. Bake tortillas at 400° for 5-7 minutes on each side or until edges are crisp.

Meanwhile, in a large microwave-safe bowl, combine turkey and rice. Microwave on high for 3 minutes or until heated through. Place refried beans in a small microwave-safe bowl; heat through.

Spread beans over tortillas. Top with turkey mixture and sauce. Serve with toppings of your choice. **YIELD:** 4 servings.

EDITOR'S NOTE: This recipe was tested in a 1,100-watt microwave.

breakfast sausage & sweet potato muffins

(PICTURED AT RIGHT)

What do you do with the leftover sweet potatoes from Thanksgiving dinner? Turn them into breakfast the next morning in these slightly savory, slightly sweet muffins! The sausage adds interest, and the mashed sweet potato lends delightful texture to every bite.

Diane Roark | CONWAY, AR

3/4 cup sugar

3/4 cup all-purpose flour

1/2 cup old-fashioned oats

1-1/2 teaspoons ground allspice

1/2 teaspoon salt

1/2 teaspoon baking soda

1 cup leftover mashed sweet potatoes

2 eggs

1/4 cup butter, melted

1/4 cup canola oil

1/4 cup maple syrup

1 pound bulk pork sausage, cooked and drained

In a large bowl, combine the sugar, flour, oats, allspice, salt and baking soda. In another bowl, combine the sweet potatoes, eggs, butter, oil and syrup. Stir into dry ingredients just until moistened. Fold in sausage.

Fill greased or paper-lined muffin cups three-fourths full. Bake at 350° for 25-30 minutes or until a toothpick inserted in muffin comes out clean. Cool for 5 minutes before removing from pan to a wire rack. Serve warm. Refrigerate leftovers. YIELD: 1 dozen.

cranberry ice cream pie

(PICTURED AT FAR RIGHT)

Vanilla ice cream and vanilla pudding make a creamy, delicious duo in this festive pie.
Cranberry sauce adds the right balance of tartness and sweetness for a flavor combination that's sure to wow.

Mary Lajoie | GLENOMA, WA

Pastry for single-crust pie (9 inches)

1-1/4 cups jellied cranberry sauce

2 cups vanilla ice cream, softened

1/4 cup thawed orange juice concentrate

1 package (3.4 ounces) instant vanilla pudding mix

1/2 cup heavy whipping cream

Ground nutmeg

Line a 9-in. pie plate with pastry; trim and flute edges. Line unpricked pastry with a double thickness of heavy-duty foil. Bake at 450° for 8 minutes. Remove foil; bake 5-7 minutes longer or until lightly browned. Cool on a wire rack.

Spread cranberry sauce over bottom of pie crust; set aside. In a large bowl, combine the ice cream, juice concentrate and pudding mix. In a small bowl, beat cream until soft peaks form; fold into ice cream mixture. Pour over cranberry sauce; sprinkle with nutmeg. Freeze until firm. Remove from the freezer 15 minutes before slicing. **YIELD:** 8 servings.

day-after-thanksgiving turkey stir-fry

I work for a priest, Fr. Leo, who loves to cook. He shared this recipe with me.
Perfect for the day after Thanksgiving, this dish encompasses the holiday spirit with an added twist.

Stefen Lovelace | MARRIOTTSVILLE, MD

1 cup cut fresh green beans

1 small red onion, chopped

1 tablespoon peanut or canola oil

1 garlic clove, minced

2 tablespoons whole-berry cranberry sauce

1 tablespoon soy sauce

1 teaspoon white vinegar

1/8 teaspoon salt

1/8 teaspoon pepper

1-1/2 cups cubed cooked turkey breast

2 tablespoons chopped cashews

1 tablespoon minced fresh cilantro

Hot cooked rice

In a large skillet, saute beans and onion in oil until tender. Add garlic; cook 1 minute longer.

Meanwhile, in a small bowl, combine the cranberry sauce, soy sauce, vinegar, salt and pepper; pour over bean mixture. Add turkey; simmer, uncovered, for 4-6 minutes or until heated through. Sprinkle with the cashews and cilantro. Serve with hot cooked rice. **YIELD:** 2 servings.

STIR-FRY SECRET

Select a wok or skillet large enough to accommodate the volume of food you'll be stir-frying. If the food is crowded in the pan, it will steam and could become soggy. If necessary, stir-fry the food in batches.

choco-tato truffles

(PICTURED AT RIGHT)

Who knew yesterday's mashed potatoes could become a decadent truffle dessert? Dark chocolate and a hint of Irish cream make these luscious treats a must.

Kathy Keleher | OAK CREEK, WI

1 cup (6 ounces) semisweet chocolate chips

2 ounces unsweetened chocolate, chopped

2 tablespoons butter

1 egg yolk, beaten

1 cup confectioners' sugar

1/2 cup ground pecans

1/3 cup mashed potatoes (with added milk)

2 tablespoons Irish cream liqueur, Kahlua or strong brewed coffee

Baking cocoa or additional ground pecans

In a double boiler or metal bowl over simmering water, heat the chocolate chips, unsweetened chocolate and butter until melted, whisking frequently. Whisk a small amount of mixture into egg yolk. Return all to the heat, whisking constantly. Cook and stir until mixture is thickened and coats the back of a spoon.

Remove from the heat; stir in the sugar, pecans, mashed potatoes and Irish cream. Refrigerate for 1 hour or until easy to handle. Shape into 1-in. balls.

Roll the truffles in cocoa or additional pecans. Refrigerate for 2 hours or until firm. Store in the refrigerator. YIELD: 3 dozen.

It's hard to believe that after eating more than a fair share of turkey, stuffing, mashed potatoes and all the other fixings, people still have room for dessert!

But after a savory meal, a little something sweet sure tantalizes the taste buds—particularly when cool autumn winds begin to blow.

If you can't decide what treat to try first, we suggest that you start with Butternut Cheesecake. It brings the comforting flavor of pumpkin pie to a classic, crowd-pleasing dessert.

For several additional dinner finales that feature items such as fresh fruits, seasonal sweet potatoes, crunchy nuts and, of course, decadent chocolate, simply turn the page!

IT TAKES TWO
(PICTURED AT RIGHT)

Butternut Cheesecake (p. 128)

awesome
AUTUMN DESSERTS

butternut cheesecake

(PICTURED ON PAGE 127)

Why settle for a single dessert when you can have both squash pie and cheesecake in one delectable bite? I appreciate this recipe's do-ahead convenience.

Ellen Miller | MILLERSBURG, OH

2 cups graham cracker crumbs

1 tablespoon sugar

1/2 cup butter, melted

CHEESECAKE:

2 packages (8 ounces each) cream cheese, softened

1/2 cup sugar

1/2 cup sour cream

1 tablespoon cornstarch

1 teaspoon vanilla extract

2 eggs, lightly beaten

SQUASH:

2 cups mashed cooked butternut squash or canned pumpkin

1-1/4 cups sugar

3 eggs

3 tablespoons all-purpose flour

1-1/2 teaspoons vanilla extract

1/4 teaspoon ground cinnamon

Place a greased 9-in. springform pan on a double thickness of heavy-duty foil (about 18 in. square). Securely wrap foil around pan. Combine the cracker crumbs, sugar and butter; press onto the bottom and 1-1/2 in. up sides of pan. Set aside.

In a large bowl, beat cream cheese and sugar until smooth. Beat in the sour cream, cornstarch and vanilla. Add eggs; beat on low speed just until combined. Spread into prepared pan. In a food processor, combine ingredients for the squash layer. Gently spread over cheesecake layer. Place springform pan in a large baking pan; add 1 in. of hot water to larger pan.

Bake at 325° for 1-1/2 hours or until center is just set. Remove springform pan from water bath. Cool on a wire rack for 10 minutes. Carefully run a knife around edge of pan to loosen; cool 1 hour longer. Refrigerate cheesecake overnight. Remove sides of pan. **YIELD:** 16 servings.

ABOUT BUTTERNUT SQUASH

Butternut squash is a bell-shaped winter squash with a pale tan shell. The orange flesh is sweet and flavorful, making it perfect for using in desserts.

Select a squash that feels heavy for its size. The shells should be hard and be free of cracks and soft spots. Store in a cool, dry well-ventilated area for up to 1 month.

To cook a butternut squash for Butternut Cheesecake, cut it in half lengthwise; scoop out the seeds and discard. Place two halves cut side down in a 13-in x 9-in. baking pan. Add 1 in. water to the pan. Bake at 350° for about 1 hour or until tender. When cool enough to handle, scoop out the pulp and mash.

A 2-pound butternut squash will yield about 2 cups cooked, mashed squash.

pear pie with cardamom cream

(PICTURED AT RIGHT)

My fondness of pears inspired me to develop this pie. The addition of wine and Brie in the filling gives it a lovely custard-like texture.

Rosemary Johnson | IRONDALE, AL

1-1/4 cups sugar, divided

1/4 cup all-purpose flour

1/2 teaspoon ground ginger, divided

1/2 teaspoon ground cardamom, divided

3 medium pears, peeled and chopped

1/2 cup white wine or pear nectar

4 ounces Brie cheese, rind removed, cubed

2 tablespoons butter

1 teaspoon lemon juice

Pastry for double-crust pie (9 inches)

2 tablespoons water

CREAM:

1 cup heavy whipping cream

2 tablespoons honey

1/4 teaspoon ground ginger

1/4 teaspoon ground cardamom

In a large saucepan, combine 1 cup sugar, flour, 1/4 teaspoon ginger and 1/4 teaspoon cardamom; add pears and wine. Cook over medium heat for 15 minutes or until thickened, stirring occasionally. Stir in the cheese, butter and lemon juice until cheese is melted. Combine the remaining sugar, ginger and cardamom; set aside.

Line a 9-in. pie plate with bottom pastry; trim to 1 in. beyond edge of plate. Spoon filling into crust. Roll out remaining pastry to fit top of pie; place over filling. Trim, seal and flute edges. Cut slits in pastry. Brush with water; sprinkle with the sugar mixture.

Bake at 375° for 40-45 minutes or until crust is golden brown. Cover edges with foil during the last 15 minutes to prevent overbrowning if necessary. Cool on a wire rack.

In a large bowl, beat the cream, honey, ginger and cardamom until stiff peaks form. Serve with pie. YIELD: 8 servings.

cranberry sherbet

(PICTURED AT FAR RIGHT)

*Heavy holiday dinners call for a refreshing dessert such as
my colorful sherbet. Lemonade and orange juice add a pleasant citrus taste.*

Mary Ann Bostic | SINKS GROVE, WV

4 cups fresh or frozen cranberries

4 cups water

2-3/4 cups sugar

1 can (12 ounces) frozen lemonade concentrate, thawed

1 can (12 ounces) frozen orange juice concentrate, thawed

1 cup 2% milk

1 teaspoon lemon juice

1/4 teaspoon salt

In a large saucepan, combine cranberries and water. Cook over medium heat until berries pop, about 15 minutes. Remove from the heat. Stir in sugar until dissolved.

Transfer the cranberry mixture to a food processor. Add the lemonade concentrate, orange juice concentrate, milk, lemon juice and salt; cover and process until smooth.

Fill cylinder of ice cream freezer two-thirds full; freeze according to the manufacturer's directions. Refrigerate remaining mixture until ready to freeze. Transfer to a freezer container; freeze for 4 hours or until firm. **YIELD:** 2-1/2 quarts.

triple nut tart

*A tender cream cheese crust serves as the rich base for a buttery filling
featuring cashews, almonds and macadamia nuts. One slice goes a long way.*

Nancy Piano | NEVADA CITY, CA

1 cup all-purpose flour

1/2 cup cold butter, cubed

1 package (3 ounces) cream cheese, cubed

FILLING:

1/3 cup packed brown sugar

1/3 cup butter, cubed

3 tablespoons honey

4 teaspoons sugar

1-1/3 cups salted cashews

1 jar (3 ounces) macadamia nuts, coarsely chopped

1/2 cup slivered almonds

2 tablespoons plus 1 cup heavy whipping cream, divided

Place flour in a food processor. Add butter and cream cheese; cover and pulse just until mixture forms a ball. Cover and refrigerate for 1 hour or until easy to handle.

On a lightly floured surface, roll out pastry. Press onto the bottom and up the sides of an ungreased 11-in. fluted tart pan with removable bottom; trim edges. Line unpricked pastry with a double thickness of heavy-duty foil. Bake at 450° for 10 minutes. Cool on a wire rack. Reduce heat to 400°.

In a large saucepan, combine the brown sugar, butter, honey and sugar. Cook and stir over medium heat until butter is melted. Bring to a boil; cook and stir 1 minute longer.

Remove from the heat; stir in nuts and 2 tablespoons cream. Pour into crust. Bake at 400° for 10-12 minutes or until bubbly. Cool on a wire rack.

In a small bowl, beat remaining cream until stiff peaks form; serve with tart. **YIELD:** 16 servings.

grand marnier cranberry pound cake

(PICTURED AT RIGHT)

The combination of cranberries and orange liqueur makes this luscious treat a bit different from the usual pound cake.

Kathy Hunter | WOODLAND, WA

2 cups dried cranberries

1/2 cup Grand Marnier (orange liqueur)

1/2 cup butter, softened

1 package (8 ounces) cream cheese, softened

2 cups sugar

4 eggs

2 teaspoons vanilla extract

3 cups all-purpose flour

1 teaspoon baking powder

1/2 teaspoon salt

1/2 teaspoon baking soda

3/4 cup (6 ounces) orange yogurt

GLAZE:

1-1/4 to 1-1/2 cups confectioners' sugar

2 tablespoons Grand Marnier (orange liqueur)

In a microwave, heat the cranberries and orange liqueur just until heated through. Set aside.

In a large bowl, cream the butter, cream cheese and sugar until light and fluffy. Add eggs, one at a time, beating well after each addition. Beat in vanilla. Combine the flour, baking powder, salt and baking soda; add to batter alternately with yogurt. Drain cranberries; fold into batter.

Transfer batter to a greased 10-in. fluted tube pan. Bake at 350° for 55-65 minutes or until a toothpick inserted near the center comes out clean. Cool for 10 minutes before removing from pan to a wire rack to cool completely. Combine confectioners' sugar and liqueur; drizzle over cake. **YIELD:** 12 servings.

cranberry meringue pie

Guests who favor the tartness of cranberries will fall for this pretty pie.
The crimson berries look so beautiful under the airy meringue topping.

Marie Rizzio | INTERLOCHEN, MI

Pastry for single-crust pie (9 inches)

4 cups fresh or frozen cranberries, thawed

2 cups sugar

3/4 cup water

4 egg yolks

2 tablespoons all-purpose flour

1/4 teaspoon salt

2 tablespoons butter

1/2 teaspoon almond extract

MERINGUE:

3 egg whites

1/4 teaspoon cream of tartar

1/2 teaspoon vanilla extract

6 tablespoons sugar

Unroll pastry into a 9-in. deep-dish pie plate; flute edges. Line unpricked pastry with a double thickness of heavy-duty foil. Bake at 450° for 8 minutes. Remove foil; bake 5 minutes longer. Cool on a wire rack.

Meanwhile, in a large saucepan, combine the cranberries, sugar and water. Cook, stirring occasionally, over medium heat until berries pop, about 15 minutes. In a small bowl, combine the egg yolks, flour and salt. Remove cranberry mixture from the heat; stir a small amount into egg mixture. Return all to the pan, stirring constantly. Stir in butter and extract. Pour into crust.

For meringue, in a large bowl, beat the egg whites, cream of tartar and vanilla on medium speed until soft peaks form. Gradually beat in sugar, 1 tablespoon at a time, on high until stiff peaks form. Spread over hot filling, sealing edges to crust.

Bake at 350° for 18-22 minutes or until golden brown. Cool pie on a wire rack for 1 hour; refrigerate for 1-2 hours before serving. **YIELD:** 8 servings.

stuffed apples with honey creme fraiche

This is an apple treat that I've served for breakfast as well as dessert. Lemon, cherries and honey add awesome flavor.

Diane Halferty | CORPUS CHRISTI, TX

1/4 cup dried cherries

1/4 cup plus 2 tablespoons honey, divided

1 teaspoon minced fresh gingerroot

1 teaspoon grated lemon peel

4 medium apples

4 teaspoons butter

1/2 cup unsweetened apple juice

1/2 teaspoon ground cinnamon

TOPPING:

1/2 cup creme fraiche or sour cream

1/2 cup heavy whipping cream

2 tablespoons honey

In a small bowl, combine the cherries, 1/4 cup honey, ginger and lemon peel; set aside.

Core apples, leaving bottoms intact. Peel top half of each apple; place apples in an ungreased 8-in. square baking dish. Fill with cherry mixture; dot with butter. Combine the apple juice, cinnamon and remaining honey; pour over apples. Bake, uncovered, at 350° for 55-65 minutes or until tender, basting occasionally with pan juices.

In a small bowl, beat the creme fraiche, cream and honey until soft peaks form. Serve with warm apples. **YIELD:** 4 servings.

apple-cinnamon shortcakes

(PICTURED AT RIGHT)

Putting a spin on a summertime favorite, our Test Kitchen staff decided to top tender shortcakes with delightful sauteed apples. The humble dessert is true comfort!

2 cups all-purpose flour

2 tablespoons plus 2 teaspoons sugar, divided

3 teaspoons baking powder

1 teaspoon ground cinnamon

1/2 teaspoon salt

1 cup heavy whipping cream

1/2 cup plus 4 teaspoons melted butter, divided

FILLING:

1/4 cup butter, cubed

4 large tart apples, peeled and sliced

1/2 cup packed brown sugar

1/2 teaspoon ground cinnamon

1/8 teaspoon ground nutmeg

In a large bowl, combine the all-purpose flour, 2 tablespoons sugar, baking powder, cinnamon and salt. In a small bowl, combine cream and 1/2 cup butter; stir into dry ingredients just until moistened.

Drop dough by 1/4 cupfuls 2 in. apart onto a greased baking sheet. Brush with remaining butter; sprinkle with remaining sugar. Bake at 375° for 18-20 minutes or until golden brown. Cool shortcakes slightly.

In a large skillet, melt butter. Add apples; saute until tender. Stir in the brown sugar, cinnamon and nutmeg. Gently split warm shortcakes in half horizontally. Top bottom halves with apple mixture; replace tops. Serve immediately. **YIELD:** 8 servings.

big sweet potato flan

*My family is always delighted to see this creamy custard on the dessert table
at holiday dinners. I've used squash instead with equally outstanding results.*

Deirdre Dee Cox | MILWAUKEE, WI

1 large sweet potato, peeled and cubed

1-1/4 cups sugar, divided

2-1/2 cups evaporated milk

5 eggs

2 egg yolks

1 teaspoon ground cinnamon

1/4 teaspoon salt

1-1/2 teaspoons vanilla extract

TOPPING:

1/2 cup heavy whipping cream

1 tablespoon sugar

1/4 teaspoon grated orange peel

Place sweet potato in a small saucepan and cover with water. Bring to a boil. Reduce heat; cover and simmer for 15-20 minutes or until tender. Drain. Place potato in a food processor; cover and process until smooth. Set aside.

Grease a 9-in. cake pan; set aside. In a small heavy skillet over medium-low heat, cook 1/2 cup sugar until it begins to melt. Gently drag melted sugar to the center of pan so sugar melts evenly. Cook, without stirring, until the sugar is dark reddish brown, about 15 minutes. Quickly pour into prepared pan.

In a small saucepan, heat milk until bubbles form around sides of pan. In a small bowl, whisk eggs, egg yolks, cinnamon, salt, pureed sweet potato and remaining sugar. Remove milk from heat; stir a small amount of hot milk into egg mixture. Return all to pan; stir constantly. Stir in vanilla. Pour over caramelized sugar.

Place cake pan in a large baking pan; add 1 in. of boiling water to larger pan. Bake, uncovered, at 350° for 40-45 minutes or until center is just set (mixture will jiggle). Remove cake pan from water bath; cool for 1 hour. Cover and refrigerate overnight.

In a small bowl, beat cream until soft peaks form. Add sugar and orange peel; beat until stiff peaks form. To serve flan, run knife around edge of pan. Invert flan onto a serving plate; serve with whipped cream. **YIELD:** 8 servings.

white chocolate panna cotta with espresso syrup

White chocolate puts a delicious spin on traditional panna cotta. A coffee syrup draped over the top is simply fantastic.

Mariam Ishaq | BUFFALO, NY

2-1/2 cups heavy whipping cream

2/3 cup sugar

2/3 cup 2% milk

1 envelope unflavored gelatin

6 ounces white baking chocolate, chopped

ESPRESSO SYRUP:

3/4 cup brewed espresso

1/4 cup sugar

In a small saucepan, combine the cream, sugar and milk. Sprinkle with gelatin; let stand for 1 minute. Heat over low heat, stirring until sugar and gelatin are completely dissolved. Stir in chocolate until melted.

Pour into eight 4-oz. ramekins or custard cups coated with cooking spray. Cover and refrigerate for at least 5 hours or until set.

In a small saucepan, combine espresso and sugar. Bring to a boil; cook until liquid is thickened to a syrup consistency and reduced to about 1/4 cup. Unmold panna cotta onto dessert plates; drizzle each serving with 1-1/2 teaspoons syrup. **YIELD:** 8 servings.

bourbon chocolate pecan pie

(PICTURED AT RIGHT)

*When my fiance first made this for me,
I declared it to be the best pie ever!
Creamy chocolate combines with
crunchy nuts in a sinful, gooey filling.*

Tanya Taylor | CARY, NC

1 cup all-purpose flour

1 tablespoon sugar

1/2 teaspoon salt

6 tablespoons cold butter

2 to 3 tablespoons cold water

FILLING:

3 eggs

1 cup packed dark brown sugar

1/2 cup light corn syrup

1/2 cup dark corn syrup

1/4 cup bourbon

2 tablespoons butter, melted

1/2 teaspoon salt

1-1/2 cups pecan halves, divided

3/4 cup 60% cacao bittersweet chocolate baking chips, divided

In a small bowl, combine the flour, sugar and salt. Cut in butter until mixture resembles coarse crumbs. Add water; toss with a fork until mixture forms a ball. Flatten into a disk. Wrap dough in plastic wrap and refrigerate for 30 minutes or until easy to handle.

On a floured surface, roll out dough to fit a 9-in. deep-dish pie plate. Transfer pastry to pie plate; trim to 1/2 in. beyond edge of plate and flute edges.

In a large bowl, beat the eggs, brown sugar, corn syrups, bourbon, butter and salt until blended. Stir in 1 cup pecans and 1/2 cup chocolate chips. Pour filling into crust; sprinkle with remaining pecans and chocolate chips. Bake at 325° for 50-60 minutes or until crust is golden brown and filling is puffed. Cool completely on a wire rack. **YIELD:** 8 servings.

EASTER
gatherings

Greet the arrival of the Easter season with a basketful of springtime cooking, baking and entertaining ideas. The simple elegance of an outdoor Easter dinner...the fresh garden flavors captured in a buffet of side dishes...sweet and savory breads fresh from the oven—the bounty of seasonal delights featured here will round out menus for an Easter celebration to remember.

Spring is full of natural beauty and new beginnings. The trees begin to bud, the birds start to sing and the landscape comes to life with a splash of color. Celebrate this season of renewal and growth with a lovely garden-themed Easter dinner.

A wide assortment of colorful and delectable dishes serves up tempting spring flavors while bringing simple elegance to your outdoor celebration.

With its pretty color and fresh herb garnish, Carrot Soup with Orange & Tarragon pleases the eyes as well as the palate.

Pair the soup with the robust flavors of Italian Fennel Salad and tender Rosemary Roasted Lamb, and this becomes a meal that makes guests think they are truly enjoying outdoor dining at a five-star restaurant.

EASTER DINNER
(PICTURED AT RIGHT)

Carrot Soup with Orange & Tarragon (p. 142)
Italian Fennel Salad (p. 141)
Rosemary Roasted Lamb (p. 142)

elegant easter
GARDEN PARTY

Easter Dinner
Agenda

A Few Weeks Before:

- Prepare two grocery lists: one for nonperishable items to purchase now and one for the perishable items to purchase a few days before Easter.

- Order a leg of lamb from your butcher.

Two Days Before:

- Buy remaining grocery items, including the lamb.

- If desired, put together the Glass Jar Chandelier on page 147.

The Day Before:

- Set the table.

- Assemble Spinach and Artichoke Bread Pudding. Cover; refrigerate overnight.

- Make the Carrot Soup with Orange & Tarragon. Cover Dutch oven and chill.

- Prepare and apply the rub for the Rosemary Roasted Lamb. Cover and set in the refrigerator.

- Shell peas for Herb-Crusted Tomatoes & Sweet Peas. Store in an airtight container in the refrigerator.

- Trim and cut asparagus for Spring Brunch Bruschetta and Springtime Asparagus Pizza. Store separately in airtight containers; chill.

- Make aioli for Shrimp & Artichoke Spring Rolls with Lemon Aioli. Cover and refrigerate. Chop the shrimp and artichoke hearts. Chill separately in airtight containers.

- Make the Lemon and Honey Mustard Vinaigrette. Store in an airtight container in the refrigerator.

- Bake cakes for Coconut Chiffon Cake. Wrap each cake tightly in plastic wrap; store in a large resealable plastic bag.

Easter Day:

- In the morning, assemble Italian Fennel Salad; cover and chill.

- Prepare frosting for Coconut Chiffon Cake and toast coconut. Assemble cake; refrigerate until serving.

- An hour before guests arrive, make Shrimp & Artichoke Spring Rolls. Cover with damp towels until ready to serve with the Lemon Aioli.

- Thirty minutes before guests arrive, bake Springtime Asparagus Pizza.

- Bake the leg of lamb.

- Assemble and serve Spring Brunch Bruschetta.

- Remove Spinach and Artichoke Bread Pudding from the refrigerator 30 minutes before baking according to recipe directions.

- Prepare Herb-Crusted Tomatoes & Sweet Peas.

- Reheat Carrot Soup with Orange & Tarragon over low heat.

- Toss a green salad with Lemon and Honey Mustard Vinaigrette.

spinach and artichoke bread pudding

(PICTURED AT RIGHT)

Bread pudding is usually considered a dessert. But this rich and savory version packed with spinach, artichokes and cheese is a perfect side for both dinner or brunch.

Kathleen Fraher | FLORISSANT, MO

2 packages (9 ounces each) fresh spinach

2 cans (14 ounces each) water-packed artichoke hearts, rinsed, drained and quartered

9 eggs

2-3/4 cups heavy whipping cream

1 cup (4 ounces) shredded Monterey Jack cheese

1 cup (4 ounces) shredded cheddar cheese

1/2 cup shredded Parmesan cheese

1/2 cup shredded Romano cheese

Dash salt

8 cups day-old cubed French bread

In a large saucepan, bring 1/2 in. of water to a boil. Add spinach; cover and boil for 3-5 minutes or until wilted. Drain.

In a large bowl, combine the artichokes, eggs, cream, cheeses and salt. Gently stir in bread cubes and spinach. Transfer to a greased 13-in. x 9-in. baking dish. Cover and refrigerate overnight.

Remove from the refrigerator 30 minutes before baking. Bake, uncovered, at 350° for 35-40 minutes or until a knife inserted near the center comes out clean. Let stand 10 minutes before cutting. **YIELD:** 15 servings.

italian fennel salad

(PICTURED ON PAGE 139)

Not familiar with fennel? Crunchy and slightly sweet, it's a refreshing contribution to any spring side dish. Give this effortless recipe a try; it's sure to become one of your favorites.

Lily Julow | GAINESVILLE, FL

3 large fennel bulbs, sliced

1 small red onion, halved and thinly sliced

2 tablespoons olive oil

2 tablespoons lemon juice

1-1/2 teaspoons salt

1/2 teaspoon pepper

Trim fennel bulbs and cut into thin wedges. Snip feathery fronds; reserve 1 tablespoon.

In a large bowl, combine onion and fennel wedges. In a small bowl, whisk the oil, lemon juice, salt and pepper. Drizzle over salad; toss to coat. Refrigerate for at least 1 hour. Sprinkle with snipped fronds before serving. **YIELD:** 8 servings.

rosemary roasted lamb

(PICTURED AT FAR RIGHT AND ON PAGE 139)

*Who knew so few ingredients could result in such an elegant and savory entree?
One bite will make this no-fuss main dish memorable.*

Matthew Lawrence | VASHON, WA

1/2 cup olive oil

3 garlic cloves, minced

1 tablespoon kosher salt

1 tablespoon minced fresh rosemary

1 leg of lamb (7 to 9 pounds)

In a small bowl, combine the oil, garlic, salt and rosemary; rub over lamb. Cover and refrigerate overnight. Place lamb, fat side up, on a rack in a shallow roasting pan.

Bake, uncovered, at 425° for 20 minutes. Reduce heat to 350°; bake 1-3/4 to 2-1/4 hours longer or until meat reaches desired doneness (for medium-rare, a meat thermometer should read 145°; medium, 160°; well-done, 170°), basting occasionally with the pan juices. Let stand for 15 minutes before slicing. **YIELD:** 10 servings.

carrot soup with orange & tarragon

(PICTURED ON PAGE 138)

A pretty orange color, delicious hint of citrus and garden-fresh flavor make this soup a requested dish at my many celebrations. Try sprinkling individual bowls with fresh tarragon before serving.

Phyllis Schmalz | KANSAS CITY, KS

2 pounds fresh carrots, sliced

2 medium onions, chopped

2 tablespoons butter

6 cups reduced-sodium chicken broth

1 cup orange juice

2 tablespoons brandy

4 teaspoons minced fresh tarragon
or 1/2 teaspoon dried tarragon

1 teaspoon salt

1 teaspoon pepper

8 tarragon sprigs

In a Dutch oven, saute carrots and onions in butter for 8-10 minutes or until onion is tender. Add the broth; bring to a boil. Reduce heat; simmer, uncovered, for 10-12 minutes or until carrots are very tender. Cool slightly.

In a blender, process soup in batches until smooth. Return all to pan; stir in the orange juice, brandy and minced tarragon. Bring to a boil. Reduce heat; simmer, uncovered, for 5 minutes to allow flavors to blend. Season with salt and pepper. Garnish with tarragon sprigs before serving. **YIELD:** 8 servings (2 quarts).

herb-crusted tomatoes & sweet peas

(PICTURED AT RIGHT)

Brighten up your spring meals with this fabulously fresh and easy side dish. Vibrant green peas and bold red cherry tomatoes are tossed in a mouthwatering bread crumb and herb mixture before being baked and topped with chives.

Marie Rizzio | INTERLOCHEN, MI

1 pound fresh peas, shelled (about 1 cup)

1 pound cherry tomatoes

1/3 cup soft bread crumbs

2 tablespoons grated Parmesan cheese

4 teaspoons minced fresh parsley

2-1/2 teaspoons olive oil

2 teaspoons minced fresh thyme
or 1/2 teaspoon dried thyme

1 teaspoon minced fresh oregano
or 1/2 teaspoon dried oregano

1/4 teaspoon salt

1/8 teaspoon ground mustard

1 tablespoon minced chives

In a large saucepan, bring 8 cups water to a boil. Add peas. Cover; cook for 4 minutes. Drain and immediately place peas in ice water. Drain and pat dry.

Place peas and tomatoes in an ungreased 9-in. pie plate. In a small bowl, combine the bread crumbs, cheese, parsley, oil, thyme, oregano, salt and mustard; sprinkle over top.

Bake, uncovered, at 400° for 20-25 minutes or until top is lightly browned. Sprinkle with chives. **YIELD:** 6 servings.

EDITOR'S NOTE: Recipe may be prepared substituting 1 cup thawed frozen peas for fresh peas. Omit blanching. Proceed as directed.

lemon and honey mustard vinaigrette

A bit of honey helps balance the lemon juice and mustard in this delightful homemade dressing. I use it on salads, as a topping for steamed veggies and as a marinade for chicken.

Greg Fontenot | THE WOODLANDS, TX

1/4 cup lemon juice

2 tablespoons honey

1 tablespoon yellow mustard

2 teaspoons balsamic vinegar

1 teaspoon grated lemon peel

1/2 teaspoon dried basil

1/4 teaspoon salt

1/8 teaspoon pepper

1/3 cup olive oil

Place the first eight ingredients in a blender; cover and process until blended. While processing, gradually add oil in a steady stream. Refrigerate until serving. **YIELD:** 3/4 cup.

spring brunch bruschetta

My kids and husband can't get enough of these veggie-topped bites. Sometimes I use miniature bagel halves, Melba toasts or split English muffins in place of French baguette slices.

Laura Fall-Sutton | BUHL, ID

1 pound fresh asparagus, trimmed and cut into 1/2-inch pieces

2 teaspoons plus 1 tablespoon olive oil, divided

1 French bread baguette (10-1/2 ounces), cut into 1/2-inch slices

1 garlic clove, peeled and halved

4 eggs

1 tablespoon 2% milk

1/4 teaspoon pepper

1/8 teaspoon salt

2 tablespoons butter

1/4 cup Manchego cheese, grated, divided

Caviar, capers and/or paprika

Place asparagus in an ungreased 15-in. x 10-in. x 1-in. baking pan; drizzle with 2 teaspoons oil. Bake, uncovered, at 400° for 20-25 minutes or until crisp-tender, stirring occasionally.

Brush baguette slices with remaining oil. Place on ungreased baking sheets. Bake at 400° for 6-8 minutes or until toasted. Rub garlic clove over each slice; discard garlic.

In a small bowl, whisk the eggs, milk, pepper and salt. In a large skillet, melt butter over medium-high heat. Add egg mixture; cook and stir until almost set. Stir in asparagus and 2 tablespoons cheese. Cook and stir until completely set.

Spoon egg mixture over the baguette slices; sprinkle with the remaining cheese. Garnish with caviar, capers and/or paprika. Serve immediately. **YIELD:** 3 dozen.

PREPARING ASPARAGUS

To prepare asparagus, rinse stalks well in cold water. Snap off the tough white portion. If stalks are large, use a vegetable peeler to gently peel the tough area of the stalk from the end to just below the tip. If the tips are large, scrape off the scales with a knife.

coconut chiffon cake

(PICTURED AT RIGHT)

Toasted coconut adds visual appeal to this tall and impressive cake. With an airy texture and heavenly hint-of-ginger flavor, it's a lovely way to end meals throughout the year.

Fern Hancock | PUEBLO, CO

5 eggs, separated

3 tablespoons crystallized ginger

1-1/2 cups sugar, divided

2-1/4 cups cake flour

2 teaspoons baking powder

1/2 teaspoon salt

2 eggs

1/2 cup canola oil

1/4 cup water

2 teaspoons coconut extract

1 teaspoon cream of tartar

FROSTING:

1 cup butter, softened

8 cups confectioners' sugar

1/2 cup evaporated milk

2 teaspoons coconut extract

1/2 teaspoon salt

2-1/2 cups flaked coconut, toasted

Candied orange and lime peel

Place egg whites in a large bowl; let stand at room temperature for 30 minutes.

Meanwhile, place the ginger and 2 tablespoons sugar in a small food processor; cover and process until finely chopped.

In a large bowl, combine the flour, 1-1/4 cups sugar, baking powder, salt and ginger mixture. In another bowl, whisk the egg yolks, eggs, oil, water and extract. Add to dry ingredients; beat until well blended.

Add cream of tartar and remaining sugar to egg whites; beat with clean beaters until stiff peaks form. Fold into batter.

Gently spoon into three ungreased 9-in. round baking pans. Cut through batter with a knife to remove air pockets. Bake on the lowest oven rack at 325° for 22-26 minutes or until cake springs back when lightly touched.

Cool for 10 minutes before removing from pans to wire racks to cool completely.

In a large bowl, beat butter until fluffy. Add the confectioners' sugar, milk, extract and salt; beat until smooth.

Place bottom cake layer on a serving plate; spread with 1 cup frosting. Repeat layers twice. Frost sides of cake with remaining frosting. Press coconut over top and sides of cake. Garnish with orange and lime peel. Refrigerate until serving. **YIELD:** 16 servings.

shrimp & artichoke spring rolls with lemon aioli

These spring rolls are stuffed with an assortment of fixings, such as spinach, carrots, artichokes and cilantro. Even those who don't usually care for shrimp can't get enough of these fun snacks.

Jennifer Fisher | AUSTIN, TX

1/2 cup mayonnaise

2 tablespoons minced fresh cilantro

2 tablespoons lemon juice

1 garlic clove, minced

1/2 teaspoon grated lemon peel

1/4 teaspoon salt

SPRING ROLLS:

1-1/2 cups chopped cooked peeled shrimp

1 can (14 ounces) water-packed artichoke hearts, rinsed, drained and coarsely chopped

1 tablespoon lemon juice

1/4 teaspoon grated fresh gingerroot

1/4 teaspoon sriracha Asian hot chili sauce or hot pepper sauce

4 cups fresh spinach, shredded

1/2 cup shredded carrot

1/4 cup minced fresh cilantro

8 spring roll wrappers or rice papers (8 inches)

In a small bowl, combine the first six ingredients. Cover and refrigerate until serving.

In a large bowl, combine the shrimp, artichokes, lemon juice, ginger and chili sauce. In another bowl, combine the spinach, carrots and cilantro; set aside.

Soak each spring roll wrapper in cool water for 1 minute; place spring roll wrapper on a flat surface. Place 1/3 cup shrimp mixture and 1/2 cup spinach mixture down the center of each wrapper to within 1-1/2 in. of ends.

Fold both ends over filling; fold one long side over the filling, then carefully roll up tightly. Place seam side down on a serving plate. Cover with damp paper towels until serving. Serve with aioli. **YIELD:** 8 servings.

springtime asparagus pizza

Here's a pizza that celebrates spring's best. A chewy crust is topped with a blend of mozzarella and feta cheeses, fresh asparagus spears and even anchovy fillets, if you like.

Deena Prichep | PORTLAND, OR

1 teaspoon cornmeal

1 pound prepared pizza dough, room temperature

1 cup (4 ounces) shredded part-skim mozzarella cheese

1/2 cup crumbled feta cheese

3/4 pound fresh asparagus, trimmed and cut into 2-inch pieces

2 teaspoons grated lemon peel

1/4 teaspoon crushed red pepper flakes

8 anchovy fillets, optional

Grease a large baking sheet; sprinkle with cornmeal. Roll out dough into a 15-in. circle; transfer to prepared baking sheet.

Sprinkle crust with mozzarella and feta cheeses; top with asparagus. Bake at 450° for 10-15 minutes or until crust is golden and cheese is melted. Sprinkle with lemon peel and red pepper flakes. Top with anchovy fillets if desired. **YIELD:** 8 servings.

glass jar chandelier

(PICTURED AT RIGHT)

Add shabby-chic charm to your garden-themed Easter dinner with this easy-to-make upcycled glass jar chandelier. All you need are a few items you probably have around the house. First, find a metal cooling rack with a square grid. Next, gather some twine, thin gauge wire, scissors, wire cutters and an assortment of small jars (we used glass baby food containers). Clean the jars thoroughly and remove any labels.

Once you've rounded up all the right materials, begin by adding a wire handle to each small jar. Loop thin gauge wire around the rim's base two times. Use wire cutters to snip the wire, leaving about 1 inch at each end. Twist the ends tightly to secure in place, pressing excess wire against the jar rim. Repeat for each jar.

Next, cut several 6- to 8-inch sections of wire for the handles. On each jar, place one end of a wire section under the wrapped rim wire. Twist a small portion of wire around the rest to secure in place. Insert the other end of the wire on the opposite side and wrap the remaining small portion around the newly formed handle. Repeat to add handles to each jar.

Prepare your cooling rack by securely tying several different lengths of twine randomly onto the grid. Then, cut four long, equal lengths of twine. Tie one at each corner of the cooling rack on the opposite side of the other lengths of twine. Gather the four equal lengths of twine centered above the rack's top, and make a square knot to secure in place. Leave a few inches

of room between the knot and the rack. Now, you can place a hook or other hanging device under the knot. To attach your miniature jar lanterns, tie each of the different lengths of twine to a wire handle.

Fill each little jar about 1/3 full of clean sand, and place a tea light candle into the sand base of each. (Be sure to press the candles firmly into the base so they don't move around!) Finally, hang your newly created chandelier from a tree limb or sturdy structure, and light the candles using a long-handled lighter or matchstick.

eaturing lovely arrays of flavors and textures, Easter breads are always delicious ways to round out your brunch or dinner menu.

If you're welcoming morning guests, offer Mom's Almond-Filled Coffee Rings. The almond- and cinnamon-filled treats make any morning—particularly a holiday—seem extra special, especially with all of that sweet icing!

From traditional favorites, such as Italian Easter Bread and Flaky Biscuits with Herb Butter, to more adventurous options, like Lime Muffins with Coconut Streusel and Peppered Bacon and Cheese Scones, there are sweet and savory recipes fit for any meal.

FRESH FROM THE OVEN
(PICTURED AT RIGHT)

Mom's Almond-Filled Coffee Rings (p. 150)

easter
BREAD BASKET

mom's almond-filled coffee rings

(PICTURED ON PAGE 149)

The recipe for my mom's coffee cake goes back more than 50 years.
Perfect for special occasions, her nut-filled ring is full of visual appeal and wonderful flavor.

Arlene Murphy | PHILADELPHIA, PA

1 package (1/4 ounce) active dry yeast

2/3 cup warm 2% milk (110° to 115°)

3 eggs

1/2 cup sugar

1/2 cup butter, melted

3/4 teaspoon salt

3-1/2 to 4 cups all-purpose flour

FILLING:

1-1/2 cups finely chopped almonds

1-1/4 cups packed brown sugar

3/4 teaspoon ground cinnamon

1/4 cup butter, softened

ICING:

2-1/2 cups confectioners' sugar

3 tablespoons 2% milk

1 teaspoon vanilla extract

In a large bowl, dissolve yeast in warm milk. Add the eggs, sugar, butter, salt and 1 cup flour. Beat until smooth. Stir in enough remaining flour to form a soft dough (dough will be sticky).

Turn onto a floured surface; knead until smooth and elastic, about 6-8 minutes. Place in a greased bowl, turning once to grease the top. Cover and let rise in a warm place until doubled, about 1 hour. Combine the chopped almonds, brown sugar and cinnamon; set aside.

Punch dough down; turn onto a lightly floured surface. Divide in half. Roll each half into a 12-in. x 9-in. rectangle. Spread butter over rectangles to within 1 in. of edges; sprinkle with almond mixture. Roll up jelly-roll style, starting with a long side; pinch seams to seal.

Place each portion seam side down on a greased baking sheet; pinch ends together to form a ring. With scissors, cut from outside edge to two-thirds of the way toward center of ring at 1-1/2-in. intervals. Separate strips slightly; twist to allow filling to show. Cover and let rise until doubled, about 1 hour.

Bake at 375° for 12-15 minutes or until golden brown. Combine the confectioners' sugar, milk and vanilla; drizzle over rings. **YIELD:** 2 rings (10 slices each).

> ### FREEZER PLEASERS
>
> Save time by baking and freezing your Easter breads up to a month before the holiday. After baking, let the loaves cool completely before wrapping them tightly in freezer-safe plastic bags, heavy-duty aluminum foil or freezer paper. When ready to use, remove loaves from freezer, unwrap slightly and thaw at room temperature for 2 to 3 hours.

lime muffins with coconut streusel

(PICTURED AT RIGHT)

Looking for a way to make your brunch dazzle? A dozen of these tempting gems should do the trick. The coconut-macadamia nut struesel is the perfect complement to the fresh lime taste.

Teresa Grissom | ZIONSVILLE, IN

2 cups all-purpose flour

3/4 cup sugar

1 teaspoon baking powder

3/4 teaspoon baking soda

1/2 teaspoon salt

3/4 cup buttermilk

3/4 cup (6 ounces) key lime yogurt

1 egg

1/4 cup butter, melted

2 teaspoons key lime juice

1 teaspoon grated lime peel

1 teaspoon vanilla extract

TOPPING:

3 tablespoons sugar

2 tablespoons all-purpose flour

2 tablespoons flaked coconut

2 tablespoons finely chopped macadamia nuts

2 tablespoons butter, melted

In a large bowl, combine the first five ingredients. In another bowl, combine the buttermilk, yogurt, egg, butter, lime juice, lime peel and vanilla. Stir into dry ingredients just until moistened. Fill greased muffin cups three-fourths full.

In a small bowl, combine topping ingredients; sprinkle over muffins. Bake at 375° for 18-22 minutes or until a toothpick inserted in muffin comes out clean. Cool for 5 minutes before removing from pan to a wire rack. Serve warm. YIELD: 1 dozen.

asiago bagels

These thick and chewy bagels feature a mild cheese flavor sure to be a popular part of any morning meal. They're delicious as is or toasted and topped with cream cheese or butter.

Tami Kuehl | LOUP CITY, NE

1 cup water (70° to 80°)

2 eggs

1/4 cup plus 1 tablespoon olive oil

2 tablespoons honey

3/4 cup shredded Asiago cheese, divided

1/3 cup nonfat dry milk powder

1-1/2 teaspoons salt

1 teaspoon dried basil

2 cups whole wheat flour

1-1/2 cups plus 2 tablespoons all-purpose flour

4 teaspoons active dry yeast

1 egg white

1 tablespoon water

In bread machine pan, place the water, eggs, oil, honey, 1/2 cup cheese, milk powder, salt, basil, flours and yeast in order suggested by manufacturer. Select dough setting (check dough after 5 minutes of mixing; add 1 to 2 tablespoons of water or flour if needed).

When cycle is completed, turn dough onto a lightly floured surface. Shape into 12 balls. Push thumb through centers to form a 1-1/2-in. hole. Stretch and shape dough to form an even ring. Cover and let rest for 10 minutes; flatten bagels slightly.

Fill a Dutch oven two-thirds full with water; bring to a boil. Drop bagels, two at a time, into boiling water. Cook for 45 seconds; turn and cook 45 seconds longer. Remove with a slotted spoon; drain well on paper towels.

In a small bowl, combine egg white and water; brush over bagels. Sprinkle with remaining cheese. Place 2 in. apart on greased baking sheets. Bake at 400° for 15-20 minutes or until golden brown. Remove to wire racks to cool. **YIELD:** 1 dozen.

lemon thyme bread

I created this fabulous spring quick bread to satisfy my love of all things lemon and to use up some fresh herbs from my garden. I was quite pleased with the results and think you will be, too.

Deanna Smith | DES MOINES, IA

1-3/4 cups all-purpose flour

3/4 cup sugar

1/2 teaspoon baking soda

1/4 teaspoon salt

1 egg

1 cup buttermilk

1/4 cup canola oil

2 tablespoons minced fresh thyme or 2 teaspoons dried thyme

1 tablespoon lemon juice

2 teaspoons grated lemon peel

1/4 cup pine nuts, optional

DRIZZLE:

1/2 cup confectioners' sugar

1 tablespoon lemon juice

In a large bowl, combine the flour, sugar, baking soda and salt. In a small bowl, whisk the egg, buttermilk, oil, thyme, lemon juice and lemon peel. Stir into dry ingredients just until moistened.

Transfer to a greased 8-in. x 4-in. loaf pan. Sprinkle with pine nuts if desired. Bake at 350° for 35-40 minutes or until a toothpick inserted near the center comes out clean. Cool for 10 minutes before removing from pan to a wire rack.

In a small bowl, whisk confectioners' sugar and lemon juice; drizzle over warm bread. **YIELD:** 1 loaf (12 slices).

italian easter bread

(PICTURED AT RIGHT)

It is an Italian tradition to make this sweet, golden braid at Easter. A family heirloom, this recipe came from my mother-in-law, who received it from her mother. If you're not a fan of raisins, the bread is just as wonderful without them.

Kathi West | CANTON, MI

2 packages (1/4 ounce each) active dry yeast

3 tablespoons warm water (110° to 115°)

1-1/3 cups warm milk (110° to 115°)

2/3 cup sugar

2/3 cup butter, softened

1-1/4 teaspoons salt

2 eggs

3 teaspoons anise extract

6 to 6-1/2 cups all-purpose flour

2/3 cup raisins

1 egg white, beaten

1 tablespoon water

In a large bowl, dissolve yeast in warm water. Add the milk, sugar, butter and salt; mix well. Add eggs, extract and 2 cups flour; beat until smooth. Stir in enough remaining flour to form a soft dough.

Turn onto a floured surface; knead until smooth and elastic, about 8-10 minutes. Place in a greased bowl, turning once to grease the top. Cover and let rise in a warm place until doubled, about 1 hour.

Punch dough down. Turn onto a lightly floured surface; sprinkle with raisins and knead in. Divide in half. Divide each portion into thirds. Shape each into a 14-in. rope. Place three ropes on a greased baking sheet and braid; pinch ends to seal and tuck under. Repeat with remaining dough. Cover and let rise until doubled, about 45 minutes.

Whisk egg white and water; brush over braids. Bake at 325° for 35-40 minutes or until golden brown. Remove from pans to wire racks to cool. **YIELD:** 2 loaves.

peppered bacon and cheese scones

Mmm! That's what you'll hear as you serve a platter of these buttery, savory scones.
The bacon and cheese flavor combination is a welcome change of pace from the usual sweet variety.

Janice Elder | CHARLOTTE, NC

3 cups all-purpose flour

3 teaspoons baking powder

2 teaspoons coarsely ground pepper

1 teaspoon salt

1/4 teaspoon cayenne pepper

1/2 cup cold butter

1-1/2 cups (6 ounces) shredded Gouda cheese

4 bacon strips, cooked and crumbled

1 shallot, finely chopped

1 cup buttermilk

1 egg

In a large bowl, combine the first five ingredients. Cut in butter until mixture resembles coarse crumbs. Stir in the cheese, bacon and shallot. Whisk buttermilk and egg; set aside 1 tablespoon. Stir remainder into crumb mixture just until moistened. Turn onto a floured surface; knead 10 times.

Pat into an 8-in. circle. Cut into eight wedges. Separate wedges and place on a greased baking sheet. Brush with reserved milk mixture. Bake at 400° for 20-25 minutes or until golden brown. Serve warm. YIELD: 8 scones.

sunshine state orange bread

This pretty glazed loaf is bursting with fresh citrus tones. Walnuts add a subtle nuttiness and
yummy texture to the moist slices. It's one recipe you can serve year after year without tiring of it.

Priscilla Gilbert | INDIAN HARBOUR BEACH, FL

2 cups all-purpose flour

1 cup sugar

2 tablespoons grated orange peel

1 teaspoon baking powder

1 teaspoon baking soda

1/2 cup water

1/3 cup orange juice

1 egg, lightly beaten

2 tablespoons butter, melted

2 teaspoons vanilla extract

1/2 cup chopped walnuts

ICING:

1 cup confectioners' sugar

1 teaspoon butter, melted

1/2 teaspoon grated orange peel

2 tablespoons orange juice

In a large bowl, combine the flour, sugar, orange peel, baking powder and baking soda. In a small bowl, whisk water, orange juice, egg, butter and vanilla. Stir into dry ingredients just until moistened. Fold in walnuts.

Transfer to greased 9-in. x 5-in. loaf pan. Bake at 350° for 35-40 minutes or until a toothpick inserted near the center comes out clean. Cool for 10 minutes before removing from pan to a wire rack to cool completely.

In a small bowl, combine icing ingredients. Drizzle over bread. YIELD: 1 loaf (16 slices).

USING FRESH CITRUS PEEL

Grating fresh orange peel for recipes such as Sunshine State Orange Bread is a lot easier when you place the orange in the freezer the night before. For slightly thicker and longer shreds, use the zester; for long, continuous strips, use a stripper.

cardamom twist

(PICTURED AT RIGHT)

Every bite of these soft and tender loaves offers the perfect amount of cardamom flavor. Slices are especially good with a cream cheese spread or fresh honey butter.

Carla Miller | PASCO, WA

1/2 cup sliced fresh carrots

2 packages (1/4 ounce each) active dry yeast

1-3/4 cups warm water (110° to 115°)

4-1/2 teaspoons cardamom pods (about 40)

3/4 cup sugar

1/3 cup canola oil

2 teaspoons salt

4-3/4 to 5-1/4 cups all-purpose flour

1 egg white

1 tablespoon water

2 teaspoons coarse sugar

Place 1 in. of water in a small saucepan; add carrots. Bring to a boil. Reduce heat; cover and simmer for 6-8 minutes or until tender. Drain, reserving 1/4 cup water. Transfer carrots and reserved water to a small food processor; cover and process until smooth.

In a large bowl, dissolve yeast in warm water. Remove seeds from cardamom pods; coarsely crush seeds. Add the seeds, sugar, oil, salt, pureed carrots and 2-1/2 cups flour to yeast mixture. Beat until smooth. Stir in enough remaining flour to form a firm dough (dough will be sticky).

Turn onto a floured surface; knead until smooth and elastic, about 6-8 minutes.

Place in a greased bowl, turning once to grease the top. Cover and let rise in a warm place until doubled, about 1 hour.

Punch dough down; turn onto a lightly floured surface. Divide into thirds; shape each into a 25-inch rope. Place ropes on a greased baking sheet and braid; pinch ends together, forming a round loaf. Cover and let rise until doubled, about 30 minutes.

Beat egg white and water; brush over loaf. Sprinkle with coarse sugar. Bake at 350° for 25-35 minutes or until golden brown. Remove to a wire rack. YIELD: 1 loaf (18 slices).

flaky biscuits with herb butter

Nothing says spring like fresh herbs. These melt-in-your-mouth biscuits showcase tarragon and chives and can be on the table in 30 minutes, which makes them an ideal choice for last-minute entertaining.

Theresa Stanek | EVANS CITY, PA

2 cups all-purpose flour

3 teaspoons baking powder

1 tablespoon sugar

1-1/2 teaspoons minced fresh chives

1-1/2 teaspoons minced fresh tarragon

1 teaspoon salt

1/2 teaspoon garlic powder

1/2 cup shortening

3/4 cup 2% milk

HERB BUTTER:

1/2 cup butter, softened

1-1/2 teaspoons minced fresh chives

1-1/2 teaspoons minced fresh tarragon

1/2 teaspoon garlic powder

In a small bowl, combine the first seven ingredients. Cut in shortening until mixture resembles coarse crumbs. Stir in milk just until moistened. Turn onto a lightly floured surface; knead 8-10 times.

Pat or roll out to 1/2-in. thickness; cut with a floured 2-1/2-in. biscuit cutter. Place 2 in. apart on an ungreased baking sheet.

Bake at 425° for 8-12 minutes or until golden brown.

Meanwhile, in a small bowl, beat the butter ingredients until blended; serve with warm biscuits. YIELD: 1 dozen.

coconut bread

A tropical aroma fills the kitchen whenever I bake my irresistible quick bread. The coconut topping adds a touch of visual flair.

Cindy Steffen | CEDARBURG, WI

2-1/2 cups all-purpose flour

3/4 cup sugar

2 teaspoons baking powder

1/2 teaspoon salt

1/2 teaspoon ground cinnamon

1/4 teaspoon baking soda

2-1/3 cups flaked coconut, divided

1 egg

1-1/4 cups buttermilk

6 tablespoons butter, melted

1 teaspoon coconut extract

1 teaspoon vanilla extract

In a large bowl, combine the flour, sugar, baking powder, salt, cinnamon and baking soda. Add 2 cups coconut and mix well. Combine the egg, buttermilk, butter and extracts; stir into dry ingredients just until moistened.

Pour into a greased 9-in. x 5-in. loaf pan. Sprinkle with remaining coconut; press lightly into batter. Bake at 350° for 60-65 minutes or until a toothpick inserted near the center comes out clean. Cool for 10 minutes before removing from pan to a wire rack. YIELD: 1 loaf.

chocolate panini

(PICTURED AT RIGHT)

Pretty chocolate swirls through the interior of my Italian-style rolls make them a must-try. These tempting treats really stand out when served with brunch or as dessert.

Sara Bonetti | OAKLAND, CA

2-1/4 cups bread flour

5 teaspoons active dry yeast

1 teaspoon sugar

1/4 teaspoon salt

3/4 cup water

1/3 cup 2% milk

1/4 cup butter, cubed

1 egg

2/3 cup semisweet chocolate chunks

EGG WASH:

1 egg

1 tablespoon water

2 teaspoons sugar

In a large bowl, combine 1-1/2 cups flour, yeast, sugar and salt. In a small saucepan, heat the water, milk and butter to 120°-130°. Add to dry ingredients; beat just until moistened. Add egg; beat until smooth. Stir in enough remaining flour to form a soft dough.

Turn onto a floured surface; knead in chocolate chunks until smooth and elastic, about 6-8 minutes. Place in a greased bowl, turning once to grease the top. Cover and let rise in a warm place until doubled, about 45 minutes.

Turn onto a lightly floured surface; divide into 16 pieces. Shape each into a roll. Place 2 in. apart on a greased baking sheets. Cover and let rise until doubled, about 30 minutes. Beat egg and water; brush over rolls. Sprinkle with sugar.

Bake at 375° for 10-12 minutes or until golden brown. Remove to wire racks to cool completely. **YIELD:** 16 rolls.

*A*h, spring! After a season of cold, dreary weather, it's wonderful to open up the windows and let in the warm, blowing breeze.

The season also signals the time to take a break from heavy, rich foods and replace them with some fresher, lighter fare.

A great way to introduce the spring's finest produce is through a palate-pleasing selection of sides.

Maple-Ginger Glazed Carrots and Dijon Roasted Asparagus are classic choices that bring color and flavor to your table.

For an earthier item, you can't go wrong with Shiitake & Goat Cheese Rustic Tart.

GARDEN-FRESH GOODNESS
(PICTURED AT RIGHT)

Maple-Ginger Glazed Carrots (p. 162)
Dijon Roasted Asparagus (p. 160)
Shiitake & Goat Cheese Rustic Tart (p. 160)

spectacular
SPRING SIDES

shiitake & goat cheese rustic tart

(PICTURED ON PAGE 158)

I almost always prefer sweet over savory but was inspired to try this tart showcasing shiitake mushrooms and goat cheese. Refrigerated pie pastry allows for easy assembly.

Karen Watts | CORTLANDT MANOR, NY

1/2 pound sliced fresh shiitake mushrooms

2 shallots, thinly sliced

1 tablespoon butter

1 tablespoon olive oil

1 teaspoon minced fresh thyme
or 1/4 teaspoon dried thyme

1/8 teaspoon salt

1/8 teaspoon pepper

1 sheet refrigerated pie pastry

4 ounces fresh goat cheese, crumbled

In a large skillet, saute mushrooms and shallots in butter and oil until tender. Remove from heat; add thyme, salt and pepper.

On a lightly floured surface, roll pastry into a 14-in. circle. Transfer to a parchment paper-lined baking sheet. Spoon the mushroom mixture over the pastry to within 2 in. of edges; sprinkle with cheese.

Fold up edges of pastry over filling, leaving center uncovered. Bake at 375° for 30-35 minutes or until crust is golden brown. Serve warm. **YIELD:** 6 servings.

dijon roasted asparagus

(PICTURED ON PAGE 158)

Asparagus is a natural side dish to serve at Easter. In this mouthwatering recipe, Dijon mustard, cayenne pepper and Asiago cheese provide big, bold flavor.

Jamie Brown-Miller | NAPA, CA

1/4 cup Dijon mustard

1/4 cup olive oil

4 garlic cloves, minced

1/4 teaspoon cayenne pepper

1 slice brioche bread (1/2 inch thick), toasted

1 pound fresh asparagus, trimmed

1/2 cup shredded Asiago cheese

In a small bowl, combine the mustard, oil, garlic and cayenne. Place bread in a food processor; cover and process until fine crumbs form. In a small bowl, combine the bread crumbs and 1 tablespoon of the mustard mixture.

Place asparagus in an ungreased 13-in. x 9-in. baking dish; drizzle with remaining mustard mixture. Sprinkle with bread crumb mixture and cheese. Bake, uncovered, at 425° for 14-18 minutes or until golden brown. **YIELD:** 4 servings.

ASPARAGUS TIPS

The peak months for buying asparagus are April and May. Look for firm, straight, uniform-size spears. The tips should be closed with crisp stalks.

It's best to use asparagus within a few days of purchase. For slightly longer storage, place bundled stalks upright in a bowl filled with 1 inch of water. Or wrap the cut ends in moist paper towels. Cover the towels with plastic wrap. Refrigerate.

To clean, soak asparagus in cold water. Cut or snap off the tough white portion.

tahitian fruit salad

(PICTURED AT RIGHT)

If you're tired of the same old fruit salad, try this tropical version featuring papaya, mango and a creamy topping!

Doty Emory | JASPER, GA

1 fresh pineapple, peeled and cubed

1 medium mango, peeled and cubed

1 medium papaya, peeled, seeded and cubed

3 large navel oranges, peeled and sectioned

2 cups halved fresh strawberries

4 medium kiwifruit, peeled and sliced

2 medium ripe bananas, peeled and sliced

1 cup green grapes, halved

1/2 cup flaked coconut

1/4 cup lemon juice

3 teaspoons vanilla extract

1 teaspoon honey

TOPPING:

1 package (8 ounces) cream cheese, softened

1 jar (7 ounces) marshmallow creme

1 teaspoon vanilla extract

1/2 cup chopped pistachios

In a large bowl, combine the first nine ingredients. In a small bowl, whisk the lemon juice, vanilla and honey. Pour over fruit; toss to coat. Cover and refrigerate for at least 30 minutes.

Just before serving, in a small bowl, combine the cream cheese, marshmallow creme and vanilla; stir in pistachios. Serve with fruit salad. **YIELD:** 12 servings.

maple-ginger glazed carrots

(PICTURED ON PAGE 159)

I first made this dish for my family and friends one Thanksgiving. Now, I prepare it throughout the year. Not only are the carrots lovely on a spring table, they taste terrific, too!

Jeannette Sabo | LEXINGTON PARK, MD

4 pounds medium carrots, cut into 1/4-inch slices

1/4 cup water

3 tablespoons butter, divided

1 tablespoon minced fresh gingerroot

1/3 cup maple syrup

1 tablespoon cider vinegar

1/2 teaspoon salt

1/4 teaspoon pepper

Minced fresh parsley, optional

In a Dutch oven, combine the carrots, water, 2 tablespoons butter and ginger. Cover and cook for 10 minutes. Cook, uncovered, 6-8 minutes longer or until carrots are crisp-tender.

Stir in the syrup, vinegar, salt and pepper. Cook for 5-6 minutes, stirring frequently, or until sauce is thickened. Stir in remaining butter. Garnish with parsley if desired. YIELD: 16 servings.

three-pea salad with creamy tarragon dressing

Brightly colored peas make a beautiful addition to any warm-weather menu. A tarragon dressing keeps this salad on the lighter side.

Mary Wilhelm | SPARTA, WI

2 tablespoons white wine vinegar

2 tablespoons reduced-fat sour cream

1 tablespoon olive oil

2 teaspoons minced fresh tarragon or 1/2 teaspoon dried tarragon

1 teaspoon honey

2 cups fresh sugar snap peas

3/4 cup frozen peas

3/4 cup frozen shelled edamame

4 cups spring mix salad greens

1/2 cup sliced radishes

For dressing, in a small bowl, combine the vinegar, sour cream, oil, tarragon and honey; set aside.

In a large saucepan, bring 4 cups water to a boil. Add sugar snap peas, frozen peas and edamame; cover and boil for 4-5 minutes or until tender. Drain and rinse under cold water.

Divide salad greens among four plates. Top with pea mixture and radishes; drizzle with dressing. YIELD: 4 servings.

ravishing radish salad

(PICTURED AT RIGHT)

Here is a recipe that showcases radishes in all their glory. The fresh, crunchy salad really complements grilled entrees.

Maggie Ruddy | ALTOONA, IA

24 radishes, quartered

1 teaspoon salt

1 teaspoon pepper

6 green onions, chopped

1/2 cup thinly sliced fennel bulb

6 fresh basil leaves, thinly sliced

1/4 cup snipped fresh dill

1/4 cup olive oil

2 tablespoons champagne wine vinegar

2 tablespoons honey

2 garlic cloves, minced

1/2 cup chopped walnuts, toasted

Place radishes in a large bowl. Sprinkle with salt and pepper; toss to coat. Add the onions, fennel, basil and dill. In a small bowl, whisk the oil, vinegar, honey and garlic. Pour over salad and toss to coat.

Cover and refrigerate for at least 1 hour. Sprinkle with walnuts just before serving.
YIELD: 6 servings.

THE DISH ON RADISHES

Look for radishes that are crisp, firm and free of blemishes. Avoid any with greens that are not brightly colored or that do not look particularly fresh. Remove the greens before washing. Spring radishes can be stored in a plastic bag in the refrigerator for a week.

szechuan sugar snap peas

Simple seasonings transform crisp, sweet sugar snap peas into an unbeatable side dish everyone will favor. Chopped walnuts can be used in place of the cashews.

Jeanne Holt | MENDOTA HEIGHTS, MN

6 cups fresh sugar snap peas

2 teaspoons peanut oil

1 teaspoon sesame oil

3 tablespoons thinly sliced green onions

1 teaspoon grated orange peel

1/2 teaspoon minced garlic

1/2 teaspoon minced fresh gingerroot

1/8 teaspoon crushed red pepper flakes

1 tablespoon minced fresh cilantro

1/4 teaspoon salt

1/8 teaspoon pepper

1/3 cup salted cashew halves

In a Dutch oven, saute peas in peanut oil and sesame oil until crisp-tender. Add the onions, orange peel, garlic, ginger and pepper flakes; saute 1 minute longer.

Remove from the heat; stir in the cilantro, salt and pepper. Sprinkle with cashews just before serving. **YIELD:** 8 servings.

lemon herb quinoa

My family is turning to quinoa more and more these days. It's a super grain that's packed with protein and vitamins. Plus it can be paired with any kind of main course.

Jenn Tidwell | FAIR OAKS, CA

2 cups water

1 cup quinoa, rinsed

1/2 teaspoon salt, divided

1 tablespoon minced fresh basil

1 tablespoon minced fresh cilantro

1-1/2 teaspoons minced fresh mint

1 teaspoon grated lemon peel

In a small saucepan, bring water to a boil. Add quinoa and 1/4 teaspoon salt. Reduce heat; cover and simmer for 12-15 minutes or until liquid is absorbed.

Remove from the heat. Add the basil, cilantro, mint, lemon peel and remaining salt; fluff with a fork. **YIELD:** 4 servings.

EDITOR'S NOTE: Look for quinoa in the cereal, rice or organic food aisle.

TRIMMING CILANTRO

To easily trim cilantro from its stems, hold the bunch, and then angle the blade of a chef's knife almost parallel with the stems. With short, downward strokes, shave off the leaves where they meet the stems. Mince or chop the leaves.

arugula salad with berry dressing

(PICTURED AT RIGHT)

My family enjoys this refreshing salad during the spring and summer months. Sweet strawberries balance the slightly tart balsamic dressing.

Jennifer Kunz | TROY, MI

1 cup halved fresh strawberries, divided

2 tablespoons balsamic vinegar

1 tablespoon canola oil

1 teaspoon honey

Dash salt

1 log (4 ounces) fresh goat cheese

2 tablespoons finely chopped pistachios

4 cups fresh arugula or baby spinach

3/4 cup fresh blackberries

3/4 cup fresh blueberries

1/4 cup julienned peeled jicama

For dressing, place 1/4 cup strawberries, vinegar, oil, honey and salt in a blender; cover and process until smooth.

Roll goat cheese in pistachios; cut into eight slices. Divide the arugula among four salad plates; top each with blackberries, blueberries, jicama, remaining strawberries and two slices of goat cheese. Drizzle with dressing. YIELD: 4 servings.

tarragon peas with lemon-thyme butter

This recipe is an example of how the right combination of herbs can turn an ordinary dish into something extraordinary. Use any leftover butter on grilled fish, chicken and steak.

Katherine White | CLEMMONS, NC

1/2 cup butter, softened

1-1/2 teaspoons grated lemon peel

1-1/2 teaspoons minced fresh thyme

1/2 teaspoon salt

3 cups fresh peas

3 teaspoons minced fresh tarragon

In a small bowl, combine the butter, lemon peel, thyme and salt. Shape into a 1-in.-thick log; wrap in plastic wrap. Refrigerate for 30 minutes or until firm.

In a large saucepan, bring 1/2 in. of water to a boil. Add peas; cover and cook for 5-8 minutes or until tender. Drain. Stir in tarragon and 2 tablespoons lemon-thyme butter.

Rewrap remaining butter; refrigerate for 1 week or freeze for up to 3 months. YIELD: 4 servings.

creamy penne pasta with walnuts

My husband says I'm spoiling him when I prepare this recipe. Crunchy walnuts are a wonderful complement to the creamy sauce. You can serve this as an entree or side.

Cheryl Strahm | ST. LOUIS, MO

3 cups uncooked penne pasta

1 small onion, chopped

1/3 cup olive oil

3/4 cup finely chopped walnuts

2 garlic cloves, minced

1/2 teaspoon salt

1/4 teaspoon crushed red pepper flakes

1/4 teaspoon pepper

1 tablespoon brandy

1 cup heavy whipping cream

1 tablespoon minced fresh parsley

Grated Parmesan cheese, optional

Cook pasta according to package directions. Meanwhile, in a large skillet, saute onion in oil until tender. Add the walnuts, garlic, salt, pepper flakes and pepper; saute 1 minute longer. Remove from the heat.

Stir in brandy; cook over medium heat until liquid is evaporated. Stir in cream; bring to a gentle boil. Reduce heat; cook for 4-6 minutes or until slightly thickened, stirring occasionally.

Drain pasta; toss pasta and parsley with cream sauce. Garnish with cheese if desired. **YIELD:** 7 servings.

rich onion gratin

A staple at many of our special dinners, this comforting casserole is a tasty change of pace from potatoes. The aroma while baking is irresistible!

Carla den Dulk | MODESTO, CA

2 large onions, cut into 8 wedges

3-1/2 cups frozen pearl onions

3 cups sliced leeks (white portion only)

2 garlic cloves, minced

1/4 cup butter, melted

1-1/2 cups heavy whipping cream

1 tablespoon all-purpose flour

1/4 teaspoon salt

1/4 teaspoon pepper

1/2 cup dry bread crumbs

2 tablespoons minced fresh parsley

1 teaspoon paprika

Place the onions, leeks and garlic in an ungreased 13-in. x 9-in. baking dish; drizzle with butter.

Combine the cream, flour, salt and pepper until smooth; pour over onion mixture and stir to coat. Sprinkle with bread crumbs, parsley and paprika.

Bake, uncovered, at 325° for 45-50 minutes or until onions are tender. Let stand for 10 minutes before serving. **YIELD:** 8 servings.

oven-roasted spring vegetable medley

(PICTURED AT RIGHT)

With potatoes, asparagus, squash and radishes, this dish has something for everyone. What a terrific way to present a variety of spring veggies.

Trisha Kruse | EAGLE, ID

9 small red potatoes, quartered

2 tablespoons olive oil

1/2 teaspoon salt

1/4 teaspoon pepper

1 pound fresh asparagus, trimmed and cut into 1-inch pieces

2 small yellow summer squash, quartered and cut into 1/2-inch slices

2 small zucchini, quartered and cut into 1/2-inch slices

6 radishes, quartered

1/3 cup balsamic vinegar

3 tablespoons brown sugar

In a large bowl, toss the potatoes with oil, salt and pepper. Transfer to a shallow roasting pan. Bake at 425° for 15 minutes.

In the same bowl, combine the remaining ingredients; add to pan. Bake 20-25 minutes longer or until vegetables are tender. YIELD: 10 servings.

SPECIAL
celebrations

This year, why not look for an out-of-the-ordinary reason to entertain? Invite a few friends over for coffee and cupcakes, create a cherry blossom festival in your own backyard or share your harvest bounty with family and friends. Here, you'll also discover how to fire up your next graduation party, spread the luck of the Irish, take a real bite out of Halloween and so much more!

It's the big game, and you're not just hungry for a win but for some serious game-time grub. This smorgasbord of cheer-worthy, crowd-pleasing fare has you and your fellow fans covered.

Kick off eager appetites with rich and zesty Bacon-Jalapeno Mushrooms with Ranch Sauce... piled-high Smoky Chicken Nachos... crunchy Rainbow Potato Chips with Creamy Onion Dip.

Come halftime, huddle around Loaded Philly Cheese Steaks or a Focaccia Party Sandwich.

And when it's time to celebrate your team's win, savor the sweet taste of victory with Double Chocolate Chipotle Cookies.

GAME DAY BITES
(PICTURED AT RIGHT)

Bacon-Jalapeno Mushrooms
with Ranch Sauce (p. 176)
Focaccia Party Sandwich (p. 172)
Double Chocolate Chipotle Cookies (p. 174)
Loaded Philly Cheese Steaks (p. 174)
Smoky Chicken Nachos (p. 172)
Rainbow Potato Chips
with Creamy Onion Dip (p. 178)

game day
GATHERING

smoky chicken nachos

(PICTURED ON PAGE 171)

What's game day without can't-stop-munching nachos? Featuring layers of crunchy tortilla chips, black beans and a creamy, smoky chicken mixture, this appetizer will disappear before the second quarter!

Whitney Smith | WINTER HAVEN, FL

1 pound ground chicken

2/3 cup water

1 envelope taco seasoning

1/4 cup cream cheese, softened

3 tablespoons minced fresh chives

2 tablespoons plus 1-1/2 teaspoons 2% milk

2 tablespoons dry bread crumbs

1 teaspoon prepared mustard

1/2 teaspoon paprika

3/4 teaspoon Liquid Smoke, optional

6 cups tortilla chips

1 can (15 ounces) black beans, rinsed and drained

1 cup (4 ounces) shredded cheddar-Monterey Jack cheese

Optional toppings: chopped tomatoes and sliced ripe olives

In a large skillet over medium heat, cook chicken until no longer pink; drain. Add water and taco seasoning; bring to a boil. Reduce heat and simmer for 5 minutes. Combine the cream cheese, chives, milk, bread crumbs, mustard, paprika and Liquid Smoke if desired; stir into chicken mixture until blended.

In an ungreased 13-in. x 9-in. baking dish, layer half of the chips, chicken mixture, beans and cheese. Repeat layers.

Bake at 350° for 15-20 minutes or until cheese is melted. Serve with tomatoes and olives if desired. **YIELD:** 12 servings.

focaccia party sandwich

(PICTURED ON PAGE 170)

The men in your family will go crazy for this hearty loaf. When the weather cooperates, I wrap the sandwich in foil and cook it on the grill.

Jeanette Jones | MUNCIE, IN

1 medium onion, halved and sliced

1 tablespoon olive oil

1 teaspoon minced fresh thyme or 1/4 teaspoon dried thyme

1 loaf (1 pound) focaccia bread

1/3 cup mayonnaise

2 tablespoons minced fresh basil or 2 teaspoons dried basil

8 slices deli pastrami

6 slices smoked deli ham

6 thin slices hard salami

1 small tomato, thinly sliced

6 slices provolone cheese

In a large skillet, saute the onion in oil until tender. Stir in the thyme; set aside.

Cut focaccia in half horizontally. Combine mayonnaise and basil; spread over bread bottom. Layer with onion mixture, pastrami, ham, salami, tomato and cheese; replace bread top. Place sandwich on a baking sheet.

Bake at 350° for 15-20 minutes or until heated through and cheese is melted. Cut into wedges. **YIELD:** 8 servings.

puttanesca meatball sliders

(PICTURED AT RIGHT)

Their just-right size and spice set these tender meatballs apart from others you may have tried. Placed on soft dinner rolls and topped with a zesty sauce, these unique "sliders" quickly win over a crowd.

Amy Coeler | LEMOORE, CA

1 can (28 ounces) whole tomatoes

1 medium onion, finely chopped

3 tablespoons olive oil

2 garlic cloves, minced

1 teaspoon crushed red pepper flakes

1/2 teaspoon fennel seed, crushed

1 tablespoon chopped capers

1/8 teaspoon salt

1/4 teaspoon pepper

MEATBALLS:

1 cup shredded Parmesan cheese, divided

1/2 cup panko (Japanese) bread crumbs

1/4 cup 2% milk

1 egg, beaten

2 tablespoons minced fresh parsley

1 garlic clove, minced

1/2 teaspoon pepper

1/4 teaspoon salt

1/2 pound lean ground beef (90% lean)

1/2 pound ground pork

1 tablespoon canola oil

15 dinner rolls

Place tomatoes in a food processor; cover and process until pureed. Set aside. In a

large skillet, saute onion in oil until tender. Add the garlic, pepper flakes and fennel; cook 2 minutes longer. Stir in the tomatoes, capers, salt and pepper. Bring to a boil. Reduce heat; simmer for 15-20 minutes or until thickened, stirring occasionally.

Meanwhile, in a large bowl, combine 1/2 cup cheese, bread crumbs, milk, egg, parsley, garlic, pepper and salt. Crumble meat over mixture and mix well. Shape into fifteen 1-1/2-in. balls. In a large skillet, brown meatballs in oil; drain. Transfer meatballs to sauce; simmer, uncovered, for 15-20 minutes or until a meat thermometer reads 160°.

Place a meatball on each roll. Top with sauce and remaining cheese. **YIELD:** 15 sliders.

loaded philly cheese steaks

(PICTURED ON PAGE 171)

*For a scrumptious twist on a Philly favorite, take a bite of this
hearty bomber. With cheese sauce, tender steak and sauteed veggies, it has mass appeal.*

Diane Higgins | TAMPA, FL

2 tablespoons butter

2 tablespoons all-purpose flour

1 cup 2% milk

2 cups (8 ounces) shredded cheddar cheese

1 cup (4 ounces) shredded pepper Jack cheese

1/4 teaspoon pepper

1/8 teaspoon salt

3 boneless beef top loin steaks (10 ounces each)

3 tablespoons canola oil, divided

3 medium onions, sliced

3 small green peppers, sliced

6 hoagie buns

In a large saucepan, melt butter. Stir in flour until smooth; gradually add milk. Bring to a boil; cook and stir for 2 minutes or until thickened. Stir in the cheeses, pepper and salt just until melted. Remove from the heat; keep warm.

In a large skillet over medium heat, cook steaks in 1 tablespoon oil for 4-6 minutes on each side or until meat reaches desired doneness (for medium-rare, a meat thermometer should read 145°; medium, 160°; well-done, 170°). Remove and keep warm.

In the same skillet, saute onions and peppers in remaining oil until tender. Slice steak; place in hoagie buns. Add onions and peppers; top with cheese sauce. **YIELD:** 6 servings.

double chocolate chipotle cookies

(PICTURED ON PAGE 170)

Chipotle and cayenne peppers give these chewy, fudgy delights a yummy twist.

Lisa Meredith | EAGAN, MN

2/3 cup butter, softened

1/2 cup sugar

1/2 cup packed brown sugar

1 egg

1 teaspoon vanilla extract

1/2 teaspoon minced chipotle pepper in adobo sauce

1 cup plus 2 tablespoons all-purpose flour

1/3 cup baking cocoa

1 teaspoon ground cinnamon

1/2 teaspoon salt

1/2 teaspoon baking soda

1/4 teaspoon cayenne pepper

3 milk chocolate candy bars (1.55 ounces each), chopped

Confectioners' sugar, optional

In a large bowl, cream butter and sugars until light and fluffy. Beat in the egg, vanilla and chipotle pepper. Combine the flour, cocoa, cinnamon, salt, baking soda and cayenne; gradually add to creamed mixture and mix well. Stir in chopped candy. Chill for 1 hour or until easy to handle.

Roll into 1-1/2-in. balls; place 4 in. apart on ungreased baking sheets. Bake at 350° for 10-12 minutes or until set. Cool for 4 minutes before removing from pans to wire racks. Dust with confectioners' sugar if desired. **YIELD:** 1-1/2 dozen.

potato cheese soup

(PICTURED AT RIGHT)

This satisfying potato soup has a velvety texture that's not too thick or too thin. The subtle flavors of beer and cheese balance each other nicely, creating a soup that's sure to warm you head to toe.

Patti Lavell | ISLAMORADA, FL

2 pounds potatoes (about 6 medium), peeled and cubed

1 small onion, chopped

2 cups water

1-1/2 cups 2% milk

1 cup beer or chicken broth

2 tablespoons Worcestershire sauce

2 chicken bouillon cubes

3/4 teaspoon salt

1/2 teaspoon ground mustard

1/2 teaspoon white pepper

2 cups (8 ounces) shredded cheddar cheese

Salad croutons and/or crumbled cooked bacon, optional

Place the potatoes, onion and water in a large saucepan. Bring to a boil. Reduce heat; cover and cook for 15-20 minutes or until tender. Remove from the heat; cool slightly (do not drain). In a blender, cover and process mixture in batches until smooth. Return all to the pan and heat through.

Stir in milk, beer, Worcestershire, bouillon, salt, mustard and white pepper; heat through. Stir in cheese just until melted. Top with croutons and/or bacon if desired. YIELD: 8 servings (2 quarts).

bacon-jalapeno mushrooms with ranch sauce

(PICTURED ON PAGE 170)

Tender mushrooms are stuffed with a zesty bacon and jalapeno cream cheese mixture then baked to golden perfection. When served alongside the flavorful lime-ranch dipping sauce, it's a great game day snack.

Kelly Byler | GOSHEN, IN

8 bacon strips, chopped

24 medium fresh mushrooms

1 package (8 ounces) cream cheese, softened

2 jalapeno peppers, seeded and minced

1/4 cup shredded cheddar cheese

2 tablespoons finely chopped onion

SAUCE:

2 cups (16 ounces) sour cream

1 envelope ranch dip mix

1 tablespoon lime juice

1 teaspoon grated lime peel

In a small skillet, cook bacon over medium heat until crisp. Remove to paper towels with a slotted spoon; drain.

Remove stems from mushrooms and set caps aside; discard stems or save for another use. In a small bowl, combine the cream cheese, peppers, cheddar cheese, onion and bacon. Stuff into the mushroom caps.

Place in a greased 15-in. x 10-in. x 1-in. baking pan. Bake, uncovered, at 400° for 12-15 minutes or until tender.

Broil 3-4 in. from the heat for 1-2 minutes or until tops are golden brown. Meanwhile, in a small bowl, combine the sauce ingredients. Dollop 1 teaspoon sauce over each mushroom. Serve remaining sauce with fresh vegetables or save for another use. **YIELD:** 2 dozen mushrooms plus 1-1/2 cups leftover sauce.

EDITOR'S NOTE: We recommend wearing disposable gloves when cutting hot peppers. Avoid touching your face.

eat-twice chili pizza

This homemade pie's mild kick and hearty toppings make it a winner with everyone.

Zhee Zhee Aguirre | SAN DIEGO, CA

1 pound lean ground beef (90% lean)

1 small onion, chopped

1 small green pepper, chopped

1 garlic clove, minced

1 can (16 ounces) mild chili beans, undrained

1 tablespoon A1 steak sauce

1 teaspoon ground cumin

1 teaspoon chili powder

1/2 teaspoon hot pepper sauce

1 prebaked 12-inch pizza crust

1/2 cup marinara or spaghetti sauce

1 cup (4 ounces) shredded Monterey Jack cheese

1 cup (4 ounces) shredded cheddar cheese

4 green onions, chopped

Sour cream and shredded lettuce, optional

In a large skillet, cook the beef, onion, green pepper and garlic over medium heat until meat is no longer pink; drain. Stir in the beans, steak sauce, cumin, chili powder and pepper sauce. Bring to a boil. Reduce heat; simmer, uncovered, for 5 minutes.

Place crust on an ungreased baking sheet; spread with marinara sauce. Top with half of the chili; sprinkle with cheeses and onions. (Save remaining chili for another use.)

Bake at 400° for 15-20 minutes or until cheese is melted. Serve with sour cream and lettuce if desired. **YIELD:** 1 pizza (8 slices) plus 2 cups leftover chili.

blondie sundaes

(PICTURED AT RIGHT)

Just when we thought rich and chewy blondies couldn't get any better, our home economists dreamed up this luscious sundae version. Topped with creamy vanilla ice cream and sweet butterscotch sauce, this dessert takes decadence to the next level.

1 egg

1 cup packed brown sugar

1/2 cup butter, melted

1 teaspoon vanilla extract

1-1/4 cups all-purpose flour

1/8 teaspoon salt

1 cup butterscotch chips

BUTTERSCOTCH SAUCE:

1/2 cup butter, cubed

1 cup packed brown sugar

1 cup heavy whipping cream

1/2 teaspoon salt

1-1/2 teaspoons vanilla extract

4-1/2 cups vanilla ice cream

In a large bowl, beat the egg, brown sugar, butter and vanilla. Combine the flour and salt; gradually beat into the egg mixture. Fold in the chips.

Transfer to a greased 8-in. square baking dish. Bake at 350° for 20-25 minutes or until a toothpick inserted near the center comes out with moist crumbs (do not overbake). Cool on a wire rack.

For sauce, in a large saucepan, melt butter. Stir in the brown sugar, cream and salt. Bring to a boil; cook and stir for 5 minutes or until slightly thickened. Remove from the heat. Stir in vanilla. Cut brownies into squares; serve with ice cream and sauce. **YIELD:** 9 servings (1-1/2 cups sauce).

SOFTENING BROWN SUGAR

Even when stored in an airtight container, brown sugar can become hard over time.

To soften brown sugar, place a slice of bread or an apple wedge with the brown sugar in a covered container for a few days. If you're in a hurry, microwave on high for 20-30 seconds. Repeat if necessary, but watch carefully, because the sugar will begin to melt.

rainbow potato chips with creamy onion dip

(PICTURED ON PAGE 171)

Forget store-bought potato chips! You won't want them after you munch on these crispy, perfectly seasoned baked chips served with a creamy onion dip.

Jenn Tidwell | FAIR OAKS, CA

1-1/4 pounds assorted potatoes
(such as gold, red and purple)

3 tablespoons canola oil

1/2 teaspoon salt

DIP:

1 small onion, finely chopped

2 teaspoons olive oil

1-1/4 cups fat-free plain Greek yogurt

1/4 cup mayonnaise

2 green onions, sliced

3/4 teaspoon garlic powder

1/2 teaspoon salt

1/2 teaspoon onion powder

1/4 teaspoon pepper

Scrub potatoes; with a mandoline or vegetable peeler, cut into 1/32-in.-thick slices. Place in a large bowl; cover with cold water. Soak for 30 minutes.

Drain; pat dry with paper towels. Place potatoes in a large bowl; drizzle with oil and toss to coat.

Arrange in a single layer in ungreased 15-in. x 10-in. x 1-in. baking pans. Bake at 400° for 18-22 minutes or until golden brown, turning once. Sprinkle with salt.

Meanwhile, in a small skillet, saute onion in oil until tender; cool to room temperature. In a small bowl, combine the yogurt, mayonnaise, green onions, seasonings and cooked onion. Serve with chips. **YIELD:** 5 cups chips (1-1/2 cups dip).

EDITOR'S NOTE: If Greek yogurt is not available in your area, line a strainer with a coffee filter and place over a bowl. Place 2-1/2 cups fat-free yogurt in prepared strainer; refrigerate overnight. Discard liquid from bowl; proceed as directed.

buffalo wing munch mix

This spicy mix is my take on hot wings. Every handful of the crunchy snack has just the right amount of heat, combined with a hint of cool ranch flavor.

Keri Thompson | PLEASANT HILL, IA

4 cups Corn Chex

4 cups Wheat Chex

2 cups cheddar-flavored snack crackers

2 cups potato sticks

6 tablespoons butter, melted

2 tablespoons hot pepper sauce

1 tablespoon Worcestershire sauce

1 envelope ranch salad dressing mix

1/8 teaspoon cayenne pepper

In a large bowl, combine the cereals, crackers and potato sticks. Combine the butter, pepper sauce and Worcestershire sauce. Drizzle over cereal mixture and toss to coat. Sprinkle with salad dressing mix and cayenne; toss to coat.

Microwave half of mixture on high for 2 minutes, stirring once. Spread onto waxed paper to cool. Repeat. Store in an airtight container. **YIELD:** 3 quarts.

EDITOR'S NOTE: This recipe tested in a 1,100-watt microwave.

cheering station setup

(PICTURED AT RIGHT)

Looking for a way to score a few extra points with the friends and relatives attending your pigskin party?

Just purchase an assortment of football fan favors and encourage guests to cheer on the home team!

Fun-filled items include clappers, beads, pom-poms, foam fingers, megaphones and mini footballs. (Look for these items online or at your local party supplier.)

For an easy, homemade idea, enlist the kids to help make interactive Penalty Flag Favors. Folks can safely throw them at the TV when they disagree with a ref's call. (See instructions below.)

Do you know die-hard fans who proudly sport their team spirit on their sleeves...as well as their faces? Don't forget to set out a few tubes of face paint!

Place the items in a bucket on a table near the television so everyone can quickly grab an item when it's time to cheer.

PENALTY FLAG FAVORS

Foolish fumbles...quarterback sacks...missed calls from the refs. Bad events are just part of the game of football. Take out your frustration by throwing your own penalty flags at the television!

Start with squares of inexpensive yellow fabric. Place a mini Styrofoam ball in the center of each. Wrap the fabric around each ball and secure with small rubber bands.

It's little wonder the cupcake craze has spread from coast to coast! These cute, individual-sized offerings allow folks to indulge in tasty treats without feeling too guilty. Plus, when decorated, they look like edible pieces of art!

Beyond classic vanilla and chocolate, cupcakes now feature a large variety of flavor combinations.

Tempt your taste buds with Coconut Tres Leches, Orange Creamsicle, Gin & Tonic and Salted Caramel Cupcakes (pictured at right).

And for the more adventurous baker, this chapter also offers a few uniquely delicious options, such as Dark Chocolate Bacon, Pad Thai and Jalapeno Popper Corn Cupcakes.

LITTLE GEMS
(PICTURED AT RIGHT)

Coconut Tres Leches Cupcakes (p. 182)
Orange Creamsicle Cupcakes (p. 186)
Gin & Tonic Cupcakes (p. 184)
Salted Caramel Cupcakes (p. 182)

crazy for
CUPCAKES

coconut tres leches cupcakes

(PICTURED ON PAGE 180)

Three types of milk wonderfully moisten cupcakes created by our Test Kitchen staff.

1/2 cup butter, softened

1-1/2 cups sugar

4 egg whites

1-1/2 teaspoons vanilla extract

2 cups all-purpose flour

1 teaspoon baking powder

1/2 teaspoon baking soda

1/4 teaspoon salt

1-1/3 cups buttermilk

1 can (14 ounces) sweetened condensed milk

2/3 cup evaporated milk

1/2 cup coconut milk

1 cup heavy whipping cream

3 tablespoons confectioners' sugar

Toasted flaked coconut

In a large bowl, cream butter and sugar until light and fluffy. Add egg whites, one at a time, beating well after each addition. Beat in vanilla. Combine next four ingredients; add to creamed mixture alternately with buttermilk, beating well after each addition.

Fill paper-lined muffin cups three-fourths full. Bake at 350° for 18-22 minutes or until a toothpick inserted near the center comes out clean. Place pan on a wire rack; cool for 10 minutes. Remove paper liners from cupcakes; return to pan.

Poke holes in cupcakes with a skewer, about 1/2 in. apart. Combine the sweetened condensed milk, evaporated milk and coconut milk; slowly pour over cupcakes, allowing mixture to absorb into cake. Cover and refrigerate for 2 hours.

In a large bowl, beat cream until it begins to thicken. Add confectioners' sugar; beat until soft peaks form. Frost cupcakes. Sprinkle with coconut. Store in the refrigerator. **YIELD:** 1 dozen.

salted caramel cupcakes

(PICTURED ON PAGE 180)

To help balance the sweetness of the brown sugar cupcake, our staff created a unique salty frosting.

1/2 cup butter, softened

1 cup packed dark brown sugar

1/2 cup sugar

2 eggs

1 teaspoon vanilla extract

1-1/4 cups all-purpose flour

3/4 teaspoon baking powder

1/4 teaspoon salt

1/2 cup 2% milk

FROSTING:

1/3 cup sugar

4 teaspoons water

1/8 teaspoon salt

1-1/3 cups heavy whipping cream

In a large bowl, cream butter and sugars until light and fluffy. Add eggs, one at a time, beating well after each addition. Beat in vanilla. Combine the flour, baking powder and salt; add to the creamed mixture alternately with milk, beating well after each addition.

Fill paper-lined muffin cups three-fourths full. Bake at 350° for 18-22 minutes or until a toothpick inserted near the center comes out clean. Cool for 10 minutes before removing from pan to a wire rack to cool completely.

In a large heavy saucepan, combine the sugar, water and salt. Cook over medium-low heat until sugar begins to melt. Gently pull sugar to the center of the pan until sugar melts evenly. Cook, without stirring, until mixture turns an amber color.

Remove from the heat; gradually stir in cream until smooth. Transfer to a small bowl; cover and refrigerate for 4 hours. Beat until stiff peaks form. Frost cupcakes. **YIELD:** 10 cupcakes.

bananas foster surprise cupcakes

(PICTURED AT RIGHT)

This recipe was inspired by the classic dessert, which I had for the first time at a restaurant many years ago. The flavor is simply magical!

Julie Ohnstad | MARIETTA, GA

3/4 cup butter, softened

2 cups sugar

2 tablespoons dark brown sugar

3 eggs

1-3/4 cups mashed ripe bananas (about 4-5 medium)

1-1/2 cups buttermilk

2 teaspoons lemon juice

2 teaspoons vanilla extract

3 cups all-purpose flour

1-1/2 teaspoons baking soda

1 teaspoon ground cinnamon

1/4 teaspoon salt

FILLING:

1 jar (12 ounces) hot caramel ice cream topping

1/2 teaspoon ground cinnamon

1/4 teaspoon rum extract

FROSTING:

2-1/4 cups packed brown sugar

1 cup heavy whipping cream

1/2 teaspoon baking soda

1/2 cup butter, cubed

1/4 teaspoon rum extract

Sliced bananas, whipped cream and turbinado (washed raw) sugar

In a large bowl, cream the butter, sugar and brown sugar until light and fluffy. Add eggs, one at a time, beating well after each addition. Beat in the bananas, buttermilk,

lemon juice and vanilla. Combine the flour, baking soda, cinnamon and salt; add to creamed mixture just until moistened.

Fill greased or paper-lined muffin cups three-fourths full. Bake at 375° for 18-22 minutes or until a toothpick inserted in cupcake comes out clean. Cool for 10 minutes before removing from pans to wire racks to cool completely.

In a small bowl, combine the filling ingredients. Cut a small hole in the corner of a pastry or plastic bag; insert a very small tip. Fill with caramel filling. Push the tip through the top to fill each cupcake.

For frosting, in a large saucepan, combine brown sugar and cream. Bring to a boil over medium-low heat. Stir in baking soda; cook and stir until smooth. Stir in butter and extract. Remove from the heat; cool slightly. Transfer to a small bowl; refrigerate for at least 30 minutes or until chilled.

Beat frosting on high until thickened, about 15-20 minutes. Top cupcakes with frosting, banana slices and whipped cream; sprinkle with turbinado sugar. YIELD: 2 dozen.

gin & tonic cupcakes

(PICTURED ON PAGE 181)

A creamy frosting infused with gin is the crowning touch on these luscious lime cakes from our staff.

3 eggs, separated

3/4 cup all-purpose flour

3/4 cup sugar

1-1/2 teaspoons baking powder

1/4 teaspoon salt

1/4 cup tonic water

1/4 cup canola oil

2 tablespoons lime juice

2 teaspoons grated lime peel

1/2 teaspoon vanilla extract

1/4 teaspoon cream of tartar

FROSTING:

2 cartons (8 ounces each) Mascarpone cheese

2/3 cup heavy whipping cream

1/2 cup confectioners' sugar

1/3 cup gin

6 to 8 drops green food coloring

Lime slices

Place egg whites in a large bowl; let stand at room temperature for 30 minutes. In a large bowl, combine flour, sugar, baking powder and salt. In another bowl, whisk the egg yolks, water, oil, lime juice, peel and vanilla. Add to dry ingredients; beat until well blended.

Add cream of tartar to egg whites; beat with clean beaters until stiff peaks form. Fold into batter. Fill paper-lined muffin cups three-fourths full. Bake at 325° for 18-22 minutes or until a toothpick inserted near the center comes out clean. Cool for 10 minutes before removing wire racks to cool completely.

In a large bowl, beat the cheese, cream, confectioners' sugar, gin and food coloring until stiff peaks form. Pipe over cupcakes. Garnish with lime slices. Refrigerate leftovers. **YIELD:** 16 cupcakes.

pad thai cupcakes

A sweet peanut butter frosting complements the slight heat from the cayenne and pepper flakes in this Test Kitchen creation.

3/4 cup creamy peanut butter

1/2 cup butter, softened

1-1/2 cups sugar

4 eggs

2 teaspoons vanilla extract

2 cups all-purpose flour

1 teaspoon baking powder

1/2 teaspoon salt

1/4 teaspoon baking soda

1/4 teaspoon cayenne pepper

3/4 cup sour cream

FROSTING:

1 cup creamy peanut butter

6 ounces cream cheese, softened

1/2 cup heavy whipping cream

1/3 cup confectioners' sugar

1/4 teaspoon salt

Chopped salted peanuts, minced fresh cilantro and crushed red pepper flakes

In a large bowl, cream the peanut butter, butter and sugar until light and fluffy. Beat in eggs and vanilla. Combine the flour, baking powder, salt, baking soda and cayenne; add to the creamed mixture alternately with sour cream, beating well after each addition.

Fill paper-lined muffin cups two-thirds full. Bake at 350° for 22-26 minutes or until a toothpick inserted near the center comes out clean. Cool for 10 minutes before removing to wire racks to cool.

In a small bowl, cream peanut butter and cream cheese until light and fluffy. Gradually beat in the cream, confectioners' sugar and salt. Frost cupcakes. Sprinkle with peanuts, cilantro and pepper flakes. **YIELD:** 1-1/2 dozen.

dark chocolate bacon cupcakes

(PICTURED AT RIGHT)

These adventurous cupcakes were a challenge by friends that turned into a great success. Use extra-smoky bacon to really get the salty, rich flavor.

Sandy Ploy | WEST ALLIS, WI

2 cups sugar

1 cup buttermilk

2 eggs

1/2 cup canola oil

1/2 cup strong brewed coffee

2 cups all-purpose flour

3/4 cup plus 1 tablespoon baking cocoa, divided

1-1/4 teaspoons baking powder

1/2 teaspoon sea salt

1/4 teaspoon baking soda

3/4 pound bacon strips, cooked and crumbled, divided

1 can (16 ounces) chocolate frosting

In a large bowl, beat the sugar, buttermilk, eggs, oil and coffee until well blended. In a small bowl, combine the flour, 3/4 cup cocoa, baking powder, salt and baking soda; gradually beat into sugar mixture until blended. Stir in two-thirds of the bacon.

Fill paper-lined muffin cups two-thirds full. Bake at 375° for 18-22 minutes or until a toothpick inserted near the center comes out clean. Cool for 10 minutes before removing from the pans to wire racks to cool completely.

Frost cupcakes. Sprinkle with remaining bacon; dust with the remaining cocoa. Refrigerate leftovers. **YIELD:** 22 cupcakes.

FAST CUPCAKE FIXES

To make cupcakes of the same size, use a solid plastic ice cream scoop to measure out the batter and fill the muffin cups.

To quickly frost cooled cupcakes, place the frosting in a bowl. (The frosting should be a soft, spreadable consistency. If it is too stiff, add milk, a teaspoon at a time, until it reaches desired consistency.) Dip the tops of the cupcakes into the frosting, twist slightly and lift.

orange creamsicle cupcakes

(PICTURED ON PAGE 180)

Our Test Kitchen staff members bring the flavor of a favorite frozen treat to palate-pleasing cupcakes. A scoop of vanilla ice cream adds even more indulgence!

3 eggs

1-1/2 cups sugar

1 cup canola oil

1/2 cup buttermilk

1/3 cup orange juice

2 teaspoons grated orange peel

1 teaspoon orange extract

1 teaspoon vanilla extract

3 cups all-purpose flour

2 teaspoons baking powder

1 teaspoon baking soda

3/4 teaspoon salt

FROSTING:

3/4 cup butter, softened

1 cup confectioners' sugar

1/4 teaspoon vanilla extract

1/4 teaspoon orange extract

1 jar (7 ounces) marshmallow creme

2 cups vanilla ice cream

Orange peel strips

In a large bowl, beat the first eight ingredients until well blended. Combine the flour, baking powder, baking soda and salt; gradually beat into egg mixture until blended.

Fill paper-lined muffin cups three-fourths full. Bake at 350° for 18-22 minutes or until a toothpick inserted near the center comes out clean. Cool for 10 minutes before removing from pans to wire racks to cool completely.

In a large bowl, beat butter until fluffy; beat in confectioners' sugar and extracts until smooth. Add marshmallow creme; beat until light and fluffy. Using a melon scoop, remove a small amount of cake from tops of cupcakes. Top each with a small scoop of ice cream. Decorate with frosting and orange peel strips. Serve immediately. YIELD: 20 cupcakes.

chocolate and red wine cupcakes

A rich chocolate frosting tops our home economists' tender cupcakes that have a subtle red wine flavor.

1-1/2 cups dry red wine

2 eggs

3 tablespoons canola oil

1 teaspoon vanilla extract

1-1/2 cups all-purpose flour

1-1/2 cups sugar

3/4 cup baking cocoa

1-1/2 teaspoons baking soda

3/4 teaspoon salt

3/4 teaspoon baking powder

16 ounces bittersweet chocolate, chopped

2 cups heavy whipping cream

In a large bowl, beat the wine, eggs, oil and vanilla until well blended. Combine the flour, sugar, cocoa, baking soda, salt and baking powder; gradually beat into wine mixture until blended.

Fill paper-lined muffin cups half full. Bake at 350° for 18-20 minutes or until a toothpick comes out clean. Cool for 10 minutes before removing from pans to wire racks to cool completely.

Place chocolate in a small bowl. In a small saucepan, bring cream just to a boil. Pour over chocolate; whisk until smooth. Refrigerate until chilled. Beat until soft peaks form, about 15 seconds. Pipe over cupcakes. YIELD: 2 dozen.

jalapeno popper corn cupcakes

(PICTURED AT RIGHT)

Cream cheese frosting may seem like an unlikely partner for a jalapeno and cornmeal cupcake, but our Test Kitchen staff guarantees the treats are terrific!

1-1/4 cups all-purpose flour

1 cup sugar

1/2 cup cornmeal

2 teaspoons baking powder

1/4 teaspoon salt

2 eggs

1/2 cup 2% milk

1/2 cup olive oil

1/2 teaspoon vanilla extract

3/4 cup frozen corn, thawed

2 tablespoons finely chopped seeded jalapeno pepper

FROSTING:

1/4 cup panko (Japanese) bread crumbs

4 ounces cream cheese, softened

1/4 cup butter, softened

1-3/4 cups confectioners' sugar

1 teaspoon vanilla extract

Sliced jalapeno peppers

In a large bowl, combine the flour, sugar, cornmeal, baking powder and salt. In another bowl, combine the eggs, milk, oil and vanilla. Stir into the dry ingredients just until moistened. Fold in the corn and jalapeno.

Fill greased or paper-lined muffin cups three-fourths full. Bake at 350° for 24-28 minutes or until a toothpick inserted in cupcake comes out clean. Cool for 5 minutes before removing from pan to a wire rack to cool completely.

Place bread crumbs on an ungreased baking sheet. Bake at 400° for 2-3 minutes or until toasted. Cool. In a large bowl, beat cream cheese and butter until fluffy. Add confectioners' sugar and vanilla; beat until smooth. Frost cupcakes. Garnish with toasted bread crumbs and jalapeno slices. **YIELD:** 1 dozen.

EDITOR'S NOTE: We recommend wearing disposable gloves when cutting hot peppers. Avoid touching your face.

You won't need the luck of the Irish to throw a successful St. Patrick's Day celebration...just an appetite for merriment and a menu filled with Irish-inspired fare.

Blending a classic taste of the old country with a modern-day twist, West Virginia Shepherd's Pie features tender ground lamb and fresh peas under a pillow of mashed potatoes and parsnips.

Instead of traditional Irish soda bread, pass around a basket filled with slices of Boston Brown Bread.

To end the festivities in fashion, try this chapter's Creamy Mocha Cocktail or Irish Whiskey Float and a generous slice of Malted Chocolate & Stout Layer Cake.

ST. PADDY'S DAY PICKS
(PICTURED AT RIGHT)

West Virginia Shepherd's Pie (p. 190)
Boston Brown Bread (p. 192)

st.patrick's day
PARTY

west virginia shepherd's pie

(PICTURED ON PAGE 188)

*The combination of mashed parsnips and potatoes atop a flavorful
mixture of cooked ground lamb and fresh herbs makes this dish a standout.*

Tina Price | DEEP WATER, WV

4 medium potatoes, peeled and cubed

2 medium parsnips, peeled and cubed

3/4 cup evaporated milk

2 tablespoons butter

1 teaspoon salt

1 teaspoon pepper, divided

2 eggs

1 teaspoon dried mint

1 teaspoon dried rosemary, crushed

1 teaspoon Worcestershire sauce

1/4 teaspoon ground allspice

1 pound ground lamb

1/2 cup chopped onion

1/4 cup chopped celery

1 tablespoon olive oil

1/2 cup fresh peas

Place potatoes and parsnips in a large saucepan and cover with water. Bring to a boil. Reduce the heat; cover and cook for 15-20 minutes or until tender. Drain; mash potato mixture. Add milk, butter, salt and 1/2 teaspoon pepper; mash until combined.

In a large bowl, combine the eggs, mint, rosemary, Worcestershire sauce, allspice and remaining pepper. Crumble lamb over mixture and mix well.

In a large skillet, cook onion and celery in oil over medium heat until tender. Add lamb mixture; cook and stir until lamb is no longer pink; drain.

Place lamb mixture in a greased 11-in. x 7-in. baking dish; sprinkle with peas. Spread potato mixture over peas. Bake, uncovered, at 375° for 30-35 minutes or until golden brown. **YIELD:** 6 servings.

MAKE-AHEAD SHEPHERD'S PIE

To save time when dinner rolls around, prepare the mashed potato and lamb mixtures for this shepherd's pie the day before. Refrigerate, tightly covered, in separate containers.

The next day, reheat in the microwave until warm. Assemble and bake the pie as directed.

irish whiskey float

*Our home economists offer a yummy adult spin on a
favorite childhood ice cream treat. Every sip is cool, creamy and fun!*

1 scoop vanilla ice cream

1 cup cola

1 ounce whiskey

Place ice cream in a tall glass; top with cola and whiskey. Serve immediately. **YIELD:** 1 serving.

my underground vegetable salad

(PICTURED AT RIGHT)

*Here's a deliciously different way
to serve root vegetables that's sure
to delight and impress. The homemade
vinaigrette really enhances the
vegetables' color and earthy flavor.*

Peter Halferty | CORPUS CHRISTI, TX

1 pound medium fresh mushrooms, quartered

8 small carrots, peeled and halved lengthwise

2 cups cubed peeled sweet potatoes

2 cups cubed peeled celery root

2 cups cubed peeled rutabaga

2 tablespoons canola oil

1/4 teaspoon salt

2 cups cherry tomatoes, halved

8 cups torn curly endive

VINAIGRETTE:

1/2 cup olive oil

3 tablespoons apple cider or juice

2 tablespoons lemon juice

2 tablespoons cider vinegar

1 teaspoon grated lemon peel

1 teaspoon yellow mustard

1/2 teaspoon fennel seed, crushed

1/2 teaspoon mustard seed, crushed

1/4 teaspoon salt

1/4 teaspoon pepper

In a large bowl, combine the first seven ingredients. Transfer to a greased shallow roasting pan.

Bake, uncovered, at 400° for 30 minutes, stirring occasionally. Add the tomatoes; bake 10-15 minutes longer or until vegetables are tender.

Place endive in a large bowl. In a small bowl, whisk the vinaigrette ingredients. Pour over endive and toss to coat. Divide endive among eight serving plates; top with vegetables. YIELD: 8 servings.

boston brown bread

(PICTURED ON PAGE 189)

*This bread is one of my favorites, and I'm sure it will become one of yours as well.
The loaf's dense, chewy texture and slight sweetness from the molasses make it irresistible.*

NannyKay | TASTE OF HOME ONLINE COMMUNITY

1 cup all-purpose flour

1 cup whole wheat flour

1/2 cup steel-cut oats

1/2 cup cornmeal

1/2 cup rye flour

1 teaspoon salt

1 teaspoon baking soda

1 teaspoon baking powder

1 egg

2 cups buttermilk

1/4 cup molasses

In a large bowl, combine the first eight ingredients. In another bowl, whisk the egg, buttermilk and molasses. Stir into the dry ingredients just until moistened. Transfer to a greased 9-in. x 5-in. loaf pan.

Bake at 325° for 45-50 minutes or until a toothpick inserted near the center comes out clean. Cool for 10 minutes before removing from pan to a wire rack. **YIELD:** 1 loaf (16 slices).

EDITOR'S NOTE: Steel-cut oats are also known as Scotch oats or Irish oatmeal.

corned beef & cabbage for the wine lover

*With its exquisite flavor and lovely appearance, you'd never guess how easy it is to prepare this
St. Patrick's Day favorite. Thanks to the slow-cooker, it comes together effortlessly.*

Susan Cepeda | MIAMI LAKES, FL

8 fingerling potatoes, halved

2 cups fresh baby carrots

2 medium onions, cut into wedges

4 garlic cloves, minced

1-1/2 cups white wine or beef broth

1 corned beef brisket with spice packet
(3 to 3-1/2 pounds)

1/2 cup stone-ground mustard

1 small head cabbage, cut into wedges

1 can (14 ounces) sauerkraut,
rinsed and well drained

In a 6- or 7-qt. slow cooker, combine the potatoes, carrots, onions and garlic. Pour wine over vegetables. Cut brisket in half. Spread with mustard; place over vegetables (discard spice packet from corned beef or save for another use).

Cover and cook on low for 8-10 hours or until meat and vegetables are tender, adding cabbage and sauerkraut during the last hour of cooking.

To serve, thinly slice beef across the grain; serve with vegetables. **YIELD:** 6 servings.

chive horseradish sauce

(PICTURED AT RIGHT)

Smoked salmon gets a delicious treatment when paired with a creamy horseradish sauce. People always compliment me on it having just the right amount of "bite."

Connie Fickes | YORK, PA

1-1/2 cups sour cream

3 tablespoons prepared horseradish

2 tablespoons minced chives

2 teaspoons lemon juice

1/4 teaspoon salt

Smoked salmon or lox

Pumpernickel bread slices

In a small bowl, combine the sour cream, horseradish, chives, lemon juice and salt. Refrigerate until serving. Serve with salmon and pumpernickel bread. **YIELD:** 1-1/2 cups.

colcannon with onions and leek

Colcannon is a traditional Irish dish that combines mashed potatoes and cabbage. The addition of green onions and leeks punches up the flavors. It's a delicious side that pairs well with any meat.

Angela Spengler | CLOVIS, NM

3 medium potatoes, peeled and cubed

2 cups chopped cabbage

2 tablespoons 2% milk

1/2 teaspoon salt

1/2 teaspoon pepper

2 green onions, chopped

2 tablespoons chopped leek (white portion only)

1/4 cup butter, cubed

2 tablespoons minced fresh parsley

Place the potatoes in a large saucepan and cover with water. Bring to a boil. Reduce the heat; cover and cook for 10-15 minutes or until tender.

Meanwhile, place cabbage in a small saucepan and cover with water. Bring to a boil. Reduce the heat; cover and simmer for 6-8 minutes or until tender.

Drain potatoes; mash with milk, salt and pepper. Set aside. In a large skillet, saute onions and leek in butter until tender. Drain cabbage; add to skillet with potato mixture. Heat through; sprinkle with parsley. **YIELD:** 4 servings.

malted chocolate & stout layer cake

(PICTURED AT FAR RIGHT)

If you want a dessert that will "take the cake" at your St. Patrick's Day celebration, look no further! This rich chocolate cake is incredibly moist and has a nice malt flavor that's perfectly complemented by its creamy frosting.

Jennifer Wayland | MORRIS PLAINS, NJ

2 cups stout beer

1-3/4 cups butter, cubed

3 ounces bittersweet chocolate, chopped

1 cup malted milk powder

1 cup baking cocoa

1-1/2 cups (12 ounces) sour cream

4 eggs

3-1/2 cups sugar

3 cups cake flour

1 tablespoon baking soda

1 teaspoon salt

FROSTING:

2 cups sugar

1 cup Irish cream liqueur

12 egg yolks, beaten

3 teaspoons vanilla extract

3 cups butter, softened

1 cup malted milk powder

Grease and flour three 9-in. round baking pans; set aside.

In a large saucepan, combine the beer, butter and chocolate. Cook and stir over medium-low heat until butter and chocolate are melted. Remove from the heat; whisk in milk powder and cocoa. Transfer to a large bowl. Let stand for 15 minutes.

Add sour cream and eggs to chocolate mixture; beat until well blended. Combine the sugar, flour, baking soda and salt; gradually beat into chocolate mixture until blended. Pour batter into prepared pans.

Bake at 350° for 32-36 minutes or until a toothpick inserted near the center comes out clean. Cool for 10 minutes before removing from pans to wire racks to cool completely.

In a large heavy saucepan, bring sugar and liqueur to a gentle boil over medium heat; cook until sugar is dissolved. Remove from the heat. Add a small amount of hot mixture to egg yolks; return all to the pan, stirring constantly. Cook 2 minutes longer or until mixture thickens, stirring constantly. Remove from the heat; stir in vanilla. Cool to room temperature.

In a large bowl with a whisk attachment, cream butter until fluffy, about 5 minutes. Gradually beat in sugar mixture. Add milk powder; beat until fluffy, about 5 minutes. If necessary, refrigerate until frosting reaches spreading consistency.

Place bottom cake layer on a serving plate; spread with 1 cup frosting. Repeat layers. Top with remaining cake layer. Spread remaining frosting over top and sides of cake. Refrigerate for at least 1 hour before serving. **YIELD:** 16 servings.

creamy mocha cocktail

(PICTURED AT RIGHT)

This upscale cocktail is sure to bring any menu a stroke of good luck. A truly decadent indulgence, the mocha- and Irish-cream infused beverage makes a lovely dessert drink.

Mariam Ishaq | BUFFALO, NY

1 cup ice cubes

2/3 cup half-and-half cream

5 ounces Irish cream liqueur

5 ounces Amaretto

1 ounce coffee liqueur

2 tablespoons chocolate syrup

In a blender, combine the first five ingredients; cover and process until smooth. Drizzle sides of chilled glasses with syrup. Pour cream liqueur mixture into glasses. Serve immediately. YIELD: 3 servings.

beer fondue

This cheesy, rich mixture keeps well in a fondue pot and is likely to be the star of the buffet.

Sonya Labbe | LOS ANGELES, CA

1-1/2 cups fresh cauliflowerets

2 cups fresh broccoli florets

2 cups (8 ounces) shredded cheddar cheese

1 cup (4 ounces) shredded Swiss cheese

1 cup (4 ounces) shredded Gruyere or additional Swiss cheese

1 tablespoon all-purpose flour

1 cup Irish or nonalcoholic beer

2 teaspoons lemon juice

2 tablespoons Dijon mustard

1 French bread baguette (10-1/2 ounces), cubed

In a large saucepan, bring 4 cups water to a boil. Add broccoli and cauliflower; cover and cook for 3 minutes. Drain and immediately place vegetables in ice water. Drain and pat dry; set aside.

In a large bowl, combine the cheeses and flour. In a large saucepan, heat beer and lemon juice over medium heat until bubbles form around sides of pan.

Reduce heat to medium-low; add a handful of cheese mixture. Stir constantly, using a figure-eight motion, until cheese is almost completely melted. Continue adding cheese, one handful at a time, allowing cheese to almost completely melt between additions. Add mustard; cook and stir until mixture is thickened and smooth.

Transfer to a fondue pot and keep warm. Serve with bread cubes and reserved vegetables. YIELD: 2-1/2 cups.

irish onion soup

The inspiration behind this recipe came from my father, who owned a restaurant and created the original. This version stars contemporary ingredients but still serves the same popular robust flavor.

Theresa Miller | SAULT ST. MARIE, MI

3 medium red potatoes, cut into 1/2-inch cubes

1 tablespoon olive oil

1 teaspoon salt, divided

3 large sweet onions, halved and thinly sliced

2 tablespoons butter

1/2 pound sliced baby portobello mushrooms

1/2 cup sunflower kernels

1 teaspoon minced fresh rosemary
or 1/4 teaspoon dried rosemary, crushed

1/2 teaspoon pepper

5 cups chicken broth

3/4 cup stout beer or additional chicken broth

2 tablespoons brown sugar

10 slices French bread baguette
(1/4 inch thick)

10 slices white cheddar cheese

1 log (11 ounces) fresh goat cheese, sliced

Place potatoes on a baking sheet. Drizzle with oil and sprinkle with 1/2 teaspoon salt. Bake at 425° for 20-25 minutes or until tender.

Meanwhile, in a Dutch oven, saute onions in butter until tender. Reduce heat to medium-low; cook for 30 minutes or until deep golden brown, stirring occasionally. Add the mushrooms, sunflower kernels, rosemary, pepper and remaining salt. Cook 8-10 minutes longer or until mushrooms are tender. Stir in the broth, beer, brown sugar and potatoes; heat through.

Place the bread slices on a baking sheet; top with cheeses. Broil 3-4 inches from heat for 3-5 minutes or until cheese is melted. Ladle the soup into bowls; top each with a cheese toast. Serve immediately. **YIELD:** 10 servings (2-1/2 quarts).

CLOVER CUTLERY

Forgo paper napkins and plastic utensils at your St. Patrick's Day celebration...give your everyday cloth napkins a fast, refreshing facelift!

First, simply fold the napkins as desired. Set silverware on top, and then tie together with a piece of twine or ribbon.

Although four-leaf clovers may be as hard to find as leprechauns, English ivy is readily available. (Plus, its three-pointed shape resembles a shamrock.) So tuck in a pretty green leaf.

Instead of stacking the bundles in a basket, lay them on the table for a more sophisticated look.

bells of ireland beauty

(PICTURED AT RIGHT)

Bring a wee bit of the Emerald Isle—and a little luck of the Irish—to your St. Patrick's Day table by fashioning an eye-catching display with Bells of Ireland.

Bells of Ireland is an annual plant, which actually hails from the Mediterranean. It gets its name from the bright green "bells" or outer leaves (called calyxes) surrounding the small white flowers tucked inside.

Because bells symbolize good luck, the attractive flower is often used in St. Patrick's Day arrangements.

The stems have tiny thorns, so wear protective gloves when handling them and placing in water-filled vases. Do not submerge any bells in the water.

While Bells of Ireland is a long-lasting cut flower, some steps can ensure a longer life.

First, use a floral preservative in the water. You can purchase plant food or make your own by adding 2 teaspoons bleach, 1 teaspoon lemon juice and 1 teaspoon white sugar to a quart of cold water.

Next, replace the water in the vase every 3 days with more floral preservative. Under cold running water, trim ½ inch from the base of each stem with a sharp knife.

Enjoy the striking, tall stalks well into winter by drying them when they are at their peak. Tie the stems together and hang upside-down in a cool, dark, well-ventilated location. The colorful green bells become pretty pale beige.

For centuries, people in Japan have been holding hanami (flower viewing) under the breathtaking, blooming sakura (cherry blossoms) each spring.

Now delightful cherry blossom festivals are held in communities throughout the United States.

You can commemorate this ancient celebration by hosting your own springtime picnic that showcases an impressive assortment of fabulous East Asia-inspired fare.

Ideas include Veggie Sushi Rolls, Cucumber and Shrimp Sunomono, Spicy Edamame and Cold Sesame Noodles. For a refreshing beverage, try Sparkling Ginger Iced Tea.

A TWIST ON TAKEOUT
(PICTURED AT RIGHT)

Veggie Sushi Rolls (p. 204)
Spicy Edamame (p. 201)
Cold Sesame Noodles (p. 202)
Cucumber and Shrimp Sunomono (p. 202)
Sparkling Ginger Iced Tea (p. 203)

cherry blossoms
CELEBRATION

caramelized onion & pork potstickers

*My boyfriend and I enjoy making these yummy potstickers. You can use
egg roll wrappers if you prefer, just cut off the corners to make them round.*

Sarah Steinhilber | INVER GROVE HEIGHTS, MN

FILLING:

1 large onion, chopped

1-1/2 teaspoons canola oil, divided

3 unpeeled garlic cloves

1 cup finely chopped fresh mushrooms

2 tablespoons water

1 teaspoon cornstarch

1 teaspoon sesame oil

1/4 teaspoon salt

Dash white pepper

1 pound bulk pork sausage

ASSEMBLY:

1 package (14 ounces) potsticker
dumpling wrappers

2 tablespoons canola oil, divided

1 cup water, divided

Reduced-sodium soy sauce

In a small skillet, saute onion in 1 teaspoon canola oil until softened. Reduce heat to medium-low; cook for 30 minutes or until deep golden brown, stirring occasionally.

Meanwhile, place garlic on a double thickness of heavy-duty foil. Drizzle with remaining canola oil. Wrap foil around garlic. Bake at 425° for 15-20 minutes. Cool for 10-15 minutes.

Squeeze softened garlic into a large bowl. Add the mushrooms, water, cornstarch, sesame oil, salt, pepper and caramelized onion; mix well. Crumble sausage over mixture and mix well.

Place 1 tablespoon of filling in the center of each wrapper. (Until ready to use, keep wrappers covered with a damp towel to prevent them from drying out.) Moisten entire edge with water. Fold wrapper over filling to form a semicircle. Press edges firmly to seal, pleating the front side to form three to five folds.

Holding sealed edges, stand each dumpling on an even surface; press to flatten bottom. Curve ends to form a crescent shape. Repeat with remaining wrappers and filling.

In a large skillet, heat 1-1/2 teaspoons oil over medium-high heat. In batches, arrange dumplings flat side down in pan; cook for 1 to 2 minutes or until bottoms are lightly browned. Add 1/4 cup water; cover and steam for 4-6 minutes or until water is almost evaporated and filling is no longer pink.

Uncover; cook about 1 minute longer or until water is evaporated and bottoms are crisp. Transfer to a serving platter; keep warm. Repeat process using remaining dumplings. Serve with soy sauce. **YIELD:** 4 dozen.

tonkatsu

(PICTURED AT RIGHT)

My dear friend Junie shared the recipe for these breaded pork cutlets years ago. Her mom owned a food stand and served this traditional dish.

Yuko Shibata | MONTEREY PARK, CA

4 boneless pork loin chops (6 ounces each)

3 tablespoons all-purpose flour

1 tablespoon garlic salt

2 eggs

2 cups panko (Japanese) bread crumbs

Oil for deep-fat frying

SAUCE:

1/4 cup ketchup

2 tablespoons Worcestershire sauce

1 tablespoon sugar

1 tablespoon reduced-sodium soy sauce

2 teaspoons prepared hot mustard

Flatten pork chops to 1/4-in. thickness. In a shallow bowl, combine flour and garlic salt. In a separate shallow bowl, whisk eggs. Place bread crumbs in a third bowl. Coat pork with flour mixture, then dip in eggs and coat in crumbs.

In an electric skillet, heat 1/4 in. of oil to 375°. Fry pork chops for 2-3 minutes on each side or until crisp and juices run clear. Drain on paper towels.

Meanwhile, in a small bowl, combine the sauce ingredients; serve with pork. **YIELD:** 4 servings.

spicy edamame

(PICTURED ABOVE AND ON PAGE 199)

Edamame (pronounced ay-duh-MAH-may) are young soybeans in their pods. Here, our Test Kitchen staff boiled and seasoned them with salt, ginger, garlic powder and red pepper flakes.

1 package (16 ounces) frozen edamame pods

2 teaspoons kosher salt

3/4 teaspoon ground ginger

1/2 teaspoon garlic powder

1/4 teaspoon crushed red pepper flakes

Place edamame in a large saucepan and cover with water. Bring to a boil. Cover and cook for 4-5 minutes or until tender; drain. Transfer to a large bowl. Add the seasonings; toss to coat. **YIELD:** 6 servings.

cold sesame noodles

(PICTURED ON PAGE 199)

Even my kids can't resist this unique salad with its peanut butter dressing.
To make it a hearty main dish, stir in some cubed cooked chicken.

Elizabeth Perez | FLOWER MOUND, TX

12 ounces uncooked linguine

1/3 cup creamy peanut butter

1/4 cup canola oil

3 tablespoons water

3 tablespoons soy sauce

1 tablespoon red wine vinegar

1 tablespoon sesame oil

1 teaspoon ground ginger

3 to 4 garlic cloves, minced

1/8 to 1/4 teaspoon crushed red pepper flakes

1 cup julienned carrots

8 green onions, thinly sliced

Peanuts or sesame seeds, optional

Cook the linguine according to package directions. Meanwhile, in a blender, combine the peanut butter, canola oil, water, soy sauce, red wine vinegar, sesame oil, ginger, garlic and pepper flakes; cover and process until blended.

Drain linguine; place in a large bowl. Drizzle with three-fourths of the peanut sauce; add carrots and onions. Toss to combine. Refrigerate until serving.

Just before serving, add the remaining peanut sauce; toss to coat. Garnish with peanuts or sesame seeds if desired. **YIELD:** 6 servings.

cucumber and shrimp sunomono

(PICTURED ON PAGE 198)

While studying Japanese culture in the 4th grade, our class celebrated with a big feast,
where I shared this crunchy salad. It adds a special touch to any meal.

Pam Chicou | SAN JOSE, CA

3 medium cucumbers, thinly sliced

2-2/3 cups bean sprouts

1 package (4 ounces) frozen cooked salad shrimp, thawed

1/4 cup rice vinegar

2 tablespoons reduced-sodium soy sauce

2 teaspoons sugar

In a large bowl, combine the cucumbers, bean sprouts and shrimp. In a small bowl, whisk the vinegar, soy sauce and sugar; pour over salad and toss to coat. Refrigerate until serving. Serve with a slotted spoon. **YIELD:** 7 servings.

CUCUMBER CAPERS

Although the cucumber peel is edible, the varieties found in grocery stores usually have a waxy coating that should be removed. If you want to use unpeeled cucumbers in a recipe, pick up organic produce at a local farmers' market.

Look for cucumbers that are free of blemishes and soft spots. Store in the refrigerator for about one week.

miso soup with tofu and enoki

(PICTURED AT RIGHT)

*This traditional Japanese soup has
a mild flavor but is so comforting.
Sliced green onions provide a bit of color.*
Bridget Klusman | OTSEGO, MI

2 packages (3-1/2 ounces each) fresh enoki
mushrooms or 1/2 pound sliced fresh
mushrooms

1 medium onion, chopped

2 garlic cloves, minced

1 teaspoon minced fresh gingerroot

1 tablespoon canola oil

4 cups water

1/4 cup miso paste

1 package (16 ounces) firm tofu, drained and
cut into 3/4-inch cubes

Thinly sliced green onions

In a Dutch oven, saute the mushrooms, onion, garlic and ginger in oil until tender. Add the water and miso paste. Bring to a boil. Reduce heat; simmer, uncovered, for 15 minutes. Add tofu; heat through. Ladle into bowls; garnish with green onions. **YIELD:** 5 servings.

   EDITOR'S NOTE: Miso paste is available in natural food stores or Asian markets.

sparkling ginger iced tea

(PICTURED ON PAGE 199)

Our Test Kitchen staff created a pleasant gingerroot syrup for a refreshing, fizzy beverage.

2 cups sugar

2 cups water

1/2 cup sliced fresh gingerroot

1 cup fresh mint leaves

2 bottles (1 liter each) club soda, chilled

In a large saucepan, bring sugar, water and ginger to a boil. Reduce heat; simmer, uncovered, for 30 minutes. Transfer to a bowl; add mint. Refrigerate until chilled.

   Strain syrup; pour into a large pitcher. Stir in club soda. Serve immediately. **YIELD:** 10 servings.

veggie sushi rolls

(PICTURED ON PAGE 199)

These sushi rolls are great a finger food, side or even main course.
They're versatile and can be made with any veggies you like. Kids have fun assembling them.

Sarah Christenson | SAN DIEGO, CA

2 cups sushi rice, rinsed and drained

2 cups water

1/4 cup rice vinegar

2 tablespoons sugar

1/2 teaspoon salt

7 fresh asparagus spears, trimmed

Bamboo sushi mat

7 nori sheets

1 small cucumber, julienned

1 small carrot, julienned

2 jalapeno peppers, seeded and julienned

1/4 cup julienned daikon radish

1 medium ripe avocado, peeled and thinly sliced

Reduced-sodium soy sauce and prepared wasabi

In a large saucepan, combine rice and water; let stand for 30 minutes. Bring to a boil. Reduce heat to low; cover and simmer for 15-20 minutes or until water is absorbed and rice is tender. Remove from the heat. Let stand, covered, for 10 minutes.

Meanwhile, in small bowl, combine the vinegar, sugar and salt, stirring until sugar is dissolved.

Transfer rice to a large shallow bowl; drizzle with vinegar mixture. With a wooden paddle or spoon, stir rice with a slicing motion to cool slightly. Cover with a damp cloth to keep moist. (Rice mixture may be made up to 6 hours ahead and stored at room temperature, covered with a damp towel. Do not refrigerate.)

Place asparagus in a steamer basket; place in a large saucepan over 1 in. of water. Bring to a boil; cover and steam for 3-5 minutes or until crisp-tender.

Place sushi mat on a work surface so mat rolls away from you; line with plastic wrap. Place 2/3 cup rice on plastic; with moistened fingers, press rice into an 8-in. square. Top with one nori sheet.

Arrange a small amount of vegetables and avocado about 1-1/2 in. from bottom edge of nori sheet. Lifting bottom edge of the bamboo mat, roll up the rice mixture jelly-roll style, being sure to lift plastic from rice. Roll bamboo mat over sushi roll, pressing firmly to make a compact roll. When the roll is complete, tighten the roll to make more compact. Remove mat; cover roll and set aside. Repeat with remaining ingredients to make seven rolls.

Cut each into six pieces. Serve with soy sauce and wasabi.
YIELD: 7 rolls.

EDITOR'S NOTE: We recommend wearing disposable gloves when cutting hot peppers. Avoid touching your face.

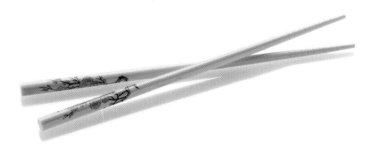

onigiri (rice balls)

(PICTURED AT RIGHT)

Because Japanese rice balls are so easy to eat, they're perfect to use in lunch boxes. Our Test Kitchen's version features tuna and a touch of spicy wasabi.

2 cups sushi rice, rinsed and drained

2 cups water

1 can (5 ounces) light water-packed tuna, drained and flaked

2 tablespoons reduced-sodium soy sauce

1/2 teaspoon prepared wasabi

In a large saucepan, combine rice and water; let stand for 30 minutes. Bring to a boil. Reduce heat to low; cover and simmer for 15-20 minutes or until water is absorbed and rice is tender. Remove from the heat. Let stand, covered, for 10 minutes.

In a small bowl, combine the tuna, soy sauce and wasabi. With wet hands, shape 1/2 cup rice into a patty. Place 1 tablespoon tuna mixture in the center. Shape rice around tuna to enclose filling, forming a triangle. Repeat with remaining ingredients. Serve immediately. **YIELD:** 8 appetizers.

lychee green tea milkshakes

My family can't get enough of milkshakes. Everyone is happy when I prepare this vibrant-colored beverage and pass it alongside a plate of fortune cookies.

Amy Dodson | COLUMBIA, MO

1 can (15 ounces) lychees

1 cup 2% milk

4 cups vanilla ice cream

1 can (8-1/2 ounces) cream of coconut

2 tablespoons matcha (green tea powder)

3/4 cup whipped topping

1 tablespoon finely chopped crystallized ginger

Drain lychees, reserving 1/2 cup syrup. Divide lychees among six chilled glasses.

In a blender, combine half of the milk, ice cream, cream of coconut, matcha and reserved lychee syrup; cover and process until smooth. Pour into three of the prepared glasses; top with whipped topping and ginger. Repeat with remaining ingredients. Serve immediately. **YIELD:** 6 servings.

chicken yakitori with noodles

Yakitori is the word for a Japanese kabob traditionally made with chicken.
I'm vegetarian, so I prepare mine with 14 ounces of extra-firm tofu.

Kim Arrington | COLLEGEDALE, TN

1/2 cup plus 3 tablespoons reduced-sodium soy sauce, divided

1/3 cup vegetable broth

2 tablespoons honey

1 teaspoon garlic powder

1/4 teaspoon ground ginger

1 pound boneless skinless chicken breasts, cut into 1-inch cubes

3 cups fresh broccoli florets

4 quarts water

5 packages (3 ounces each) ramen noodles

3 garlic cloves, minced

1 tablespoon sesame oil

2 tablespoons sake

4 green onions, thinly sliced

In a small bowl, combine 1/2 cup soy sauce, broth, honey, garlic powder and ginger. Pour 1/2 cup marinade into a large resealable plastic bag. Add the chicken and broccoli; seal bag and turn to coat. Refrigerate for at least 3 hours. Cover and refrigerate the remaining marinade.

Drain chicken and broccoli; discard marinade. On eight metal or soaked wooden skewers, alternately thread chicken and broccoli. Moisten a paper towel with cooking oil; using long-handled tongs, lightly coat the grill rack. Grill, covered, over medium heat or broil 4 in. from the heat for 5-7 minutes or until chicken is no longer pink, turning once.

In a Dutch oven, bring water to a boil. Add the noodles (discard seasoning packets or save for another use); cook for 2-3 minutes or just until tender.

Meanwhile, in a large skillet, saute garlic in oil for 1 minute. Add sake; bring to a boil. Cook until liquid is reduced by half; stir in remaining soy sauce. Drain noodles; add noodles and green onions to pan. Toss to coat.

Heat reserved marinade; drizzle over yakitori and noodles. **YIELD:** 4 servings.

salmon teriyaki

Salmon is a hearty fish that easily stands up to the robust teriyaki flavor in this recipe
from our Test Kitchen. The short prep time will appeal to busy cooks.

1/2 cup reduced-sodium soy sauce

1/4 cup sake

3 tablespoons brown sugar

2 tablespoons mirin (sweet rice wine)

4 salmon fillets (6 ounces each)

1 tablespoon olive oil

In a small bowl, combine the soy sauce, sake, brown sugar and mirin. Pour 1/2 cup marinade into a large resealable plastic bag. Add the salmon; seal bag and turn to coat. Refrigerate for at least 30 minutes. Cover and refrigerate remaining marinade.

Drain salmon and discard marinade. In a large skillet, cook salmon in oil over medium heat for 4-5 minutes on each side or until fish flakes easily with a fork. Remove from pan; keep warm.

Add the reserved marinade to the pan. Bring to a boil; cook until the liquid is reduced by half, about 6 minutes. Serve with the salmon. **YIELD:** 4 servings.

EDITOR'S NOTE: Look for mirin in the Asian condiments section.

all about
bento boxes

(PICTURED AT RIGHT)

When you plan your picnic under the beautiful blooms of the flowering cherry trees, consider packing box lunches for your guests. But skip the ugly brown bag!

Instead, use traditional Japanese bento boxes, which are small containers meant for carrying light, individual meals.

In Japan, moms often try to outdo each other in assembling the most attractive bento boxes for the lunches their kids take to school. Most bento meals contain rice, fish or meat and some type of vegetable. For your picnic, be sure to tote the boxes in a cooler if refrigeration is necessary.

BENTO BOX OPTIONS. From basic bamboo to lovely lacquered, bento boxes come in a variety of shapes, styles and sizes that appeal to kids as well as adults. Some places even sell disposable boxes.

BENTO ACCESSORIES. Enhance box lunches with fun additions, such as plastic picks (instead of utensils), containers for soy sauce and such, silicone dividers (which keep wet foods away from dry foods) and molds for shaping rice balls.

TRANSPORTING BENTO BOXES. For an attractive way to carry filled bento boxes to your picnic, wrap them in colorful cloths called furoshiki. Stick a pair of chopsticks into the knot at the top to complete your picnic package.

You can easily find bento boxes and accessories online.

*I*t's true what they say—money can't buy love. So skip the pricey night on the town and express your devotion to one another with a romantic afternoon picnic.

It's the perfect way to celebrate your journey, whether you're at the beginning of your relationship or you've been together for years.

Make a toast with bubbly Sparkling Summer Champagne, and reminisce while enjoying a few bites of Berry Almond Bruschetta and yummy Pistachio Chocolate Macarons. (All recipes shown at right.)

When more of a meal is in order, this chapter offers other enticing options, such as Tangy Feta Herb Dip, Roast Beef Garden Pitas and Nicoise Salad.

AN ALFRESCO AFFAIR
(PICTURED AT RIGHT)

Sparkling Summer Champagne (p. 211)
Berry Almond Bruschetta (p. 210)
Pistachio Chocolate Macarons (p. 212)

romantic
PICNIC FOR TWO

roast beef garden pitas

(PICTURED AT FAR RIGHT)

*Showcasing lots of fresh veggies that are coated with horseradish mayonnaise,
these packed pitas appeal to all. Men will especially like the hearty addition of roast beef.*

Nicole Filizetti | GRAND MARAIS, MI

3 whole wheat pita pocket halves

1/3 pound thinly sliced deli roast beef

1/4 cup chopped fresh broccoli

1/4 cup frozen corn, thawed

1/4 cup chopped seeded peeled cucumber

2 tablespoons shredded carrot

2 tablespoons finely chopped celery

2 tablespoons thinly sliced green onion

DRESSING:

1-1/2 teaspoons prepared horseradish

1-1/2 teaspoons mayonnaise

1-1/2 teaspoons reduced-fat sour cream

1/2 teaspoon Dijon mustard

1/8 teaspoon salt

1/8 teaspoon pepper

Line pita halves with roast beef. In a small bowl, combine the broccoli, corn, cucumber, carrot, celery and onion.

In another bowl, combine the dressing ingredients. Pour over vegetable mixture; toss to coat. Fill pita halves. **YIELD:** 3 servings.

berry almond bruschetta

(PICTURED ON PAGE 209)

*I've made Italian-style bruschetta as an appetizer for years,
but this berry version is unbeatable! It can be served as a snack or a dessert.*

Mary Ann Marino | WEST PITTSBURG, PA

4 ounces cream cheese, softened

1/4 cup sugar

2 tablespoons half-and-half cream

2 tablespoons almond paste

4 teaspoons grated orange peel

1 tablespoon orange liqueur

1 teaspoon vanilla extract

Dash ground nutmeg

12 slices French bread baguette
(1/2 inch thick)

2 tablespoons butter, melted

1-1/2 cups mixed fresh berries

1/2 cup chopped almonds, toasted

Place the first eight ingredients in a food processor; cover and process until smooth. Set aside.

Lightly brush both sides of bread with butter; place on an ungreased baking sheet. Broil 3-4 in. from the heat for 1-2 minutes on each side or until golden brown. Spread cream cheese mixture over toast; top with berries and sprinkle with almonds. **YIELD:** 1 dozen.

HOW TO TOAST NUTS

Toasting nuts before using them in a recipe intensifies their flavor. Spread the nuts on a baking sheet and bake at 350° for 5 to 10 minutes or until lightly toasted. Be sure to watch them carefully so they don't burn.

chilled beet salad

(PICTURED AT RIGHT)

*We enjoy fresh beets all summer long.
This ruby-red dish is an excellent change
from the typical tossed salad and
pairs well with any sandwich or entree.*

Roberta Bozentka | HAMDEN, CT

1/2 pound fresh beets

1/4 small red onion

3 tablespoons balsamic vinegar

1 tablespoon canola oil

1-1/2 teaspoons minced fresh basil

1 small garlic clove, minced

1/4 teaspoon salt

1/8 teaspoon pepper

Scrub beets and trim tops to 1 in. Place in a small saucepan and cover with water. Bring to a boil. Reduce heat; cover and simmer for 30-60 minutes or until tender. Remove from the water; cool.

Peel the beets and thinly slice. Transfer to a small bowl. Add all of the remaining ingredients; toss to coat. Cover and chill overnight. YIELD: 2 servings.

sparkling summer champagne

(PICTURED ON PAGE 209)

*Sipping this drink reminds me of sitting on the back porch in summer and
enjoying a good conversation with friends. I use tonic water for a nonalcoholic version.*

Corey Carbery | MOKENA, IL

1 medium lemon, cut into wedges

1 bottle (750 milliliters) Champagne
or other sparkling wine, chilled

1/2 cup thawed orange juice concentrate

Squeeze the juice from the lemon into a small pitcher; drop lemon into pitcher. Stir in Champagne and orange juice concentrate. YIELD: 4 servings.

pistachio chocolate macarons

(PICTURED ON PAGE 209)

*Traditional macarons are confections made with egg whites, sugar and almonds.
Our version calls for pistachios and features a luscious chocolate filling.*

3 egg whites

1-1/4 cups confectioners' sugar

3/4 cup pistachios

Dash salt

1/4 cup sugar

CHOCOLATE FILLING:

4 ounces bittersweet chocolate, chopped

1/2 cup heavy whipping cream

2 teaspoons corn syrup

1 tablespoon butter

Place egg whites in a small bowl; let stand at room temperature for 30 minutes. Place confectioners' sugar and pistachios in a food processor. Cover and process until pistachios become a fine powder.

Add salt to egg whites; beat on medium speed until soft peaks form. Gradually add sugar, 1 tablespoon at a time, beating on high until stiff peaks form. Fold in pistachio mixture.

Place the mixture in a heavy-duty resealable plastic bag; cut a small hole in a corner of bag. Pipe 1-in.-diameter cookies 1 in. apart onto parchment paper-lined baking sheets. Bake at 350° for 10-12 minutes or until lightly browned and firm to the touch. Cool completely on pans on wire racks.

Place chocolate in a small bowl. In a small saucepan, bring cream and corn syrup just to a boil. Pour over chocolate; whisk until smooth. Whisk in butter. Cool, stirring occasionally, to room temperature or until filling reaches a spreading consistency, about 45 minutes. Spread on the bottoms of half of the cookies; top with remaining cookies. **YIELD:** 16 cookies.

tangy feta herb dip

*I often prepare this make-ahead dip for get-togethers. As a physician and mother,
I love the idea of using yogurt as a healthy, low-fat alternative to sour cream or cream cheese.*

Amy Fountian | COOPERSTOWN, NY

2 cups (16 ounces) plain yogurt

1/2 cup crumbled feta cheese

1-1/2 teaspoons olive oil

1 small garlic clove, minced

1 teaspoon minced fresh parsley

1/2 teaspoon dried oregano

1/4 teaspoon salt

1/8 teaspoon pepper

Baked pita chips and/or assorted
fresh vegetables

Line a strainer with four layers of cheesecloth or one coffee filter and place over a bowl. Place yogurt in prepared strainer; cover yogurt with edges of cheesecloth. Refrigerate for 8 hours or overnight. Remove yogurt from cheesecloth and discard liquid from bowl.

In a large bowl, combine the yogurt, cheese, oil, garlic, parsley, oregano, salt and pepper. Chill until serving. Serve with pita chips and/or vegetables. **YIELD:** 1 cup.

nicoise salad

(PICTURED AT RIGHT)

This garden-fresh salad is a feast for the eyes as well as the palate. Add some crusty bread and you have a mouthwatering meal.

Marla Fogderud | MASON, MI

1/3 cup olive oil

3 tablespoons white wine vinegar

1-1/2 teaspoons Dijon mustard

1/8 teaspoon each salt, onion powder and pepper

SALAD:

2 small red potatoes

1/2 cup cut fresh green beans

3-1/2 cups torn Bibb lettuce

1/2 cup cherry tomatoes, halved

10 Greek olives, pitted and halved

2 hard-cooked eggs, quartered

1 can (5 ounces) white water-packed tuna, drained

In a small bowl, whisk the oil, vinegar, mustard, salt, onion powder and pepper; set aside.

Place potatoes in a small saucepan and cover with water. Bring to a boil. Reduce heat; cover and simmer for 15-20 minutes or until tender. Drain and cool; cut into quarters.

Place beans in another saucepan and cover with water. Bring to a boil. Cover and cook for 3-5 minutes or until crisp-tender; drain and rinse in cold water.

Divide lettuce between two salad plates; top with potatoes, beans, tomatoes, olives, eggs and tuna. Drizzle with the dressing. **YIELD:** 2 servings.

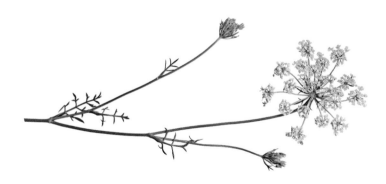

You don't have to attend the school of hard knocks when entertaining a crowd to celebrate your special graduate.

Chart a course for success by hosting a barbecue that's as easy as 1-2-3!

Shredded Pork Barbecue cooks on the grill, allowing you to keep your cool in the kitchen. (You can even assemble the recipe a day in advance and then reheat it in a slow cooker.)

Salsa Criolla (used as a refreshing relish on the sandwiches) and Spicy Antipasto Salad can both be made ahead and chilled until serving.

A crowd-pleasing dessert, Raspberry Pie Squares will receive high marks from all of your honored guests.

MAKE THE GRADE MENU
(PICTURED AT RIGHT)

Shredded Pork Barbecue (p. 216)
with Salsa Criolla (p. 220)
Spicy Antipasto Salad (p. 216)
Raspberry Pie Squares (p. 218)

congrats
TO THE GRADUATE

shredded pork barbecue

(PICTURED ON PAGE 215)

Pork shoulder roast is rubbed with seasonings and grilled, creating a crispy exterior that's lip-smacking good! The meat is moist by itself but can also be topped with your favorite barbecue sauce.

Amanda McLemore | MARYVILLE, TN

1-1/2 teaspoons each white pepper, paprika and black pepper

1 teaspoon each onion powder, garlic powder and cayenne pepper

1 teaspoon dried thyme

1/2 teaspoon salt

1 boneless pork shoulder roast (4 to 5 pounds)

16 hard rolls, split

Barbecue sauce, optional

Combine seasonings; rub over roast. Prepare grill for indirect heat, using a drip pan with 1 in. of water. Grill roast, covered, over medium-low heat for 3-1/2 to 4 hours or until meat is tender.

When cool enough to handle, shred meat with two forks. Spoon 1/2 cup onto each bun; serve with barbecue sauce if desired. **YIELD:** 16 servings.

spicy antipasto salad

(PICTURED ON PAGE 215)

Packed with inviting ingredients and fabulous flavors, this salad is a favorite at all family picnics. Dried herbs can be used in a pinch.

Jennifer Banahan | LEXINGTON, KY

2 large tomatoes, seeded and chopped

1 can (14 ounces) water-packed artichoke hearts, rinsed, drained and quartered

12 pepperoncinis

1-1/2 cups cubed part-skim mozzarella cheese

1 cup cubed salami

1 cup minced fresh parsley leaves

1 cup pitted Greek olives, sliced

1 small red onion, thinly sliced

1/2 cup sliced pepperoni

1/2 cup capers, drained

3/4 cup olive oil

1/4 cup white balsamic vinegar

2 tablespoons minced fresh basil

2 tablespoons minced fresh oregano

2 teaspoons crushed red pepper flakes

1 teaspoon salt

1 teaspoon pepper

In a large bowl, combine the first 10 ingredients. In a small bowl, whisk the oil, vinegar, basil, oregano, pepper flakes, salt and pepper; pour over salad and toss to coat. Cover and refrigerate for at least 1 hour to allow flavors to blend. **YIELD:** 16 servings (1/2 cup each).

watermelon cups

(PICTURED AT RIGHT)

Our Test Kitchen staff created this lovely appetizer that's almost too pretty to eat! Sweet watermelon cubes hold a refreshing topping showcasing cucumber, red onion and fresh herbs.

16 seedless watermelon cubes (1 inch)

1/3 cup finely chopped cucumber

5 teaspoons finely chopped red onion

2 teaspoons minced fresh mint

2 teaspoons minced fresh cilantro

1/2 to 1 teaspoon lime juice

Using a small melon baller or measuring spoon, scoop out the center of each watermelon cube, leaving a 1/4-in. shell (save pulp for another use).

In a small bowl, combine the remaining ingredients; spoon into watermelon cubes.
YIELD: 16 appetizers.

curry snack mix

I coat three kinds of cereal with a blend of zesty seasonings for a savory snack that's hard to stop eating. Microwave cooking keeps the kitchen cool on hot days.

Mona Lynn Hahn | EVANSTON, IL

2 cups Corn Chex

2 cups Rice Chex

2 cups Wheat Chex

1/2 cup butter, melted

1 teaspoon curry powder

1 teaspoon hot pepper sauce

1/2 teaspoon ground cumin

1/2 teaspoon crushed red pepper flakes

2 cups salted cashews

1/4 cup sesame seeds

In a large microwave-safe bowl, combine the cereals. In a small bowl, combine the butter, curry powder, pepper sauce, cumin and pepper flakes; pour over cereal and toss to coat.

Microwave on high for 2 minutes, stirring every minute. Stir in cashews and sesame seeds. Cook 2 minutes longer, stirring once. Spread on waxed paper to cool. Store in an airtight container.
YIELD: 2 quarts.

EDITOR'S NOTE: This recipe tested in a 1,100-watt microwave.

raspberry pie squares

(PICTURED ON PAGE 214)

Making pie for a crowd may seem impossible—but it's not when you turn to this crowd-pleasing recipe from our home economists! The sweet-tart raspberry filling pairs well with a flaky homemade pastry.

3-3/4 cups all-purpose flour

4 teaspoons sugar

1-1/2 teaspoons salt

1-1/2 cups cold butter

1/2 to 1 cup cold water

FILLING:

2 cups sugar

2/3 cup all-purpose flour

1/4 teaspoon salt

8 cups fresh or frozen
unsweetened raspberries

1 tablespoon lemon juice

5 teaspoons heavy whipping cream

1 tablespoon coarse sugar

In a large bowl, combine the flour, sugar and salt; cut in butter until crumbly. Gradually add the water, tossing with a fork until the dough forms a ball.

Divide dough in half so that one portion is slightly larger than the other; wrap each in plastic wrap. Refrigerate for 1-1/4 hours or until easy to handle. Roll out larger portion of dough between two large sheets of waxed paper into a 17-in. x 12-in. rectangle. Transfer to an ungreased 15-in. x 10-in. x 1-in. baking pan. Press pastry onto the bottom and up the sides of pan; trim pastry even with edges.

For filling, in a large bowl, combine the sugar, flour and salt. Add raspberries and lemon juice; toss to coat. Spoon over pastry.

Roll out remaining pastry; place over filling. Trim and seal edges. Cut slits in pastry. Brush top with cream and sprinkle with coarse sugar. Place pan on a baking sheet. Bake at 375° for 40-45 minutes or until golden brown. Cool completely on a wire rack. Cut into squares. **YIELD:** 24 servings.

EDITOR'S NOTE: If using frozen raspberries, use without thawing to avoid discoloring the batter.

grilled shrimp panzanella

(PICTURED AT RIGHT)

I like to add appeal to typical tossed salad with tender grilled shrimp, bread cubes and feta cheese. This colorful dish is an attractive addition to party buffets.

Veronica Callaghan | GLASTONBURY, CT

1-1/2 cups Italian salad dressing, divided

1 pound uncooked jumbo shrimp, peeled and deveined

1 loaf (14 ounces) ciabatta bread, halved lengthwise

8 cups torn mixed salad greens

3 plum tomatoes, quartered

1 cup (4 ounces) crumbled feta cheese

1 medium red onion, chopped

1/2 cup chopped ripe olives

4 garlic cloves, minced

Pour 1 cup salad dressing in a large resealable plastic bag. Add the shrimp; seal bag and turn to coat. Refrigerate for 30 minutes.

Meanwhile, brush bread with 1/4 cup of the salad dressing. Grill, uncovered, over medium heat for 2-3 minutes on each side or until lightly toasted. Cut bread into cubes; set aside.

Drain and discard marinade. Thread shrimp on four metal or soaked wooden skewers. Grill, covered, over medium heat for 5-8 minutes or until shrimp turn pink, turning once.

In a large bowl, combine salad greens and remaining dressing; toss to coat. Add the tomatoes, feta cheese, onion, olives, garlic, shrimp and bread cubes; toss to combine. **YIELD:** 21 servings (3/4 cup each).

inside-out bacon cheeseburgers

(PICTURED AT FAR RIGHT)

During grilling season, these sandwiches often appear on my menus. Cheese and bacon are stuffed inside tender burgers, which are then topped with caramelized onions.

Mary Bilyeu | ANN ARBOR, MI

12 bacon strips, chopped

2 whole garlic bulbs

2 tablespoons Worcestershire sauce

2 teaspoons pepper

1 teaspoon salt

5 pounds ground beef

12 slices Swiss cheese, quartered

2 large onions, halved and thinly sliced

12 kaiser rolls, split

In a large skillet, cook bacon over medium heat until crisp. Remove to paper towels with a slotted spoon and drain, reserving 1/2 cup drippings.

Remove papery outer skin from garlic (do not peel or separate cloves). Cut tops off of garlic bulbs. Brush with 1 tablespoon bacon drippings. Wrap each bulb in heavy-duty foil. Bake at 425° for 30-35 minutes or until softened. Cool for 10-15 minutes.

Squeeze softened garlic into a large bowl; add the Worcestershire sauce, pepper and salt. Crumble beef over mixture and mix well. Shape into 24 patties. Layer 2 pieces of cheese, bacon and remaining cheese onto the center of each of 12 patties. Top with remaining patties and press edges firmly to seal.

In a large skillet, cook onions in remaining reserved drippings over medium heat for 15-20 minutes or until golden brown, stirring occasionally.

Meanwhile, grill the burgers, covered, over medium heat for 5-7 minutes on each side or until a meat thermometer reads 160° and juices run clear. Grill rolls, uncovered, for 1-2 minutes or until toasted. Serve burgers on rolls with onions. **YIELD:** 12 servings.

salsa criolla

(PICTURED ON PAGE 215)

My family piles this versatile relish on sandwiches, chicken and even enchiladas! Prepare it the night before your party to avoid last-minute prep and to let the flavors blend.

Trisha Kruse | EAGLE, ID

1 large sweet onion, peeled and thinly sliced

1 medium red onion, peeled and thinly sliced

4 garlic cloves, minced

1 can (4 ounces) chopped green chilies

2 tablespoons minced fresh cilantro

2 tablespoons lemon juice

1 tablespoon olive oil

1 teaspoon sugar

1/2 teaspoon salt

1/4 teaspoon coarsely ground pepper

In a large bowl, combine the first five ingredients. In a small bowl, whisk the lemon juice, oil, sugar, salt and pepper. Pour over onion mixture; toss to coat. Refrigerate until chilled. Serve with a slotted spoon. **YIELD:** 3 cups.

SWEET ONION SECRETS

Because of their high sugar content, Vidalia and other sweet onions are not suited for long-term storage. You should use them within several weeks of purchase. To store, wrap onions separately in foil or paper towels. Then place in a single layer in the vegetable bin of your refrigerator.

grilled sweet potato & jicama

(PICTURED AT RIGHT)

My dad used to grill sweet potatoes and serve them with a simple vinaigrette. I've tweaked his recipe over the years to give this special side a little Southern twist.

Laureen Pittman | RIVERSIDE, CA

4 medium sweet potatoes

1/2 cup plus 2 tablespoons olive oil, divided

1/2 cup lime juice

1/2 cup minced fresh cilantro

1/4 cup honey

2 tablespoons white wine vinegar

2 garlic cloves, peeled

1 chipotle pepper in adobo sauce, seeded

1 medium jicama, peeled and julienned

Place sweet potatoes in a Dutch oven; cover with water. Bring to a boil. Reduce heat; cover and cook for 20-25 minutes or until almost tender. Drain; cool slightly.

Place 1/2 cup oil, lime juice, cilantro, honey, vinegar, garlic and chipotle pepper in a blender; cover and process until blended. Transfer to a small bowl; add jicama and toss to coat.

Peel and slice sweet potatoes; brush with remaining oil. Grill, covered, over medium heat for 2-3 minutes on each side or until slices have grill marks and are tender.

Arrange potatoes on a serving platter. With a slotted spoon, top with jicama. Drizzle salad with remaining dressing. **YIELD:** 16 servings.

rocky road brownies

Ooey, gooey and good accurately describe these family-favorite brownies!
Nuts and chocolate chips add extra richness and a little crunch.

Wendy Cox | GRANITE FALLS, WA

1 cup butter, cut up

8 ounces unsweetened chocolate, chopped

5 eggs

3 cups sugar

2 teaspoons instant espresso powder

1 tablespoon vanilla extract

1-2/3 cups all-purpose flour

1/2 teaspoon salt

1 cup chopped walnuts

1/2 cup semisweet chocolate chips

TOPPING:

2 cups miniature marshmallows

1 cup chopped walnuts

1 cup (6 ounces) semisweet chocolate chips

In a microwave, melt butter and chocolate; stir until smooth. Cool slightly. In a large bowl, beat the eggs, sugar and espresso powder until thickened, about 5 minutes. Stir in vanilla and chocolate mixture. Combine flour and salt; gradually add to chocolate mixture. Fold in walnuts and chocolate chips.

Transfer to a greased 13-in. x 9-in. baking pan. Bake at 350° for 25-30 minutes or until a toothpick inserted near the center comes out with moist crumbs (do not overbake).

For topping, in a large bowl, combine the marshmallows, walnuts and chocolate chips. Sprinkle over top. Bake 4-6 minutes longer or until marshmallows are lightly browned. Cool on a wire rack. Cut into bars. YIELD: 3 dozen.

southwestern pasta salad

When I first served this jazzed-up pasta salad for my mom's birthday dinner, it was so
well-received that I couldn't wait to make it again. Choose the flavor of salsa to suit your family's taste.

Jackie Berry | PALMYRA, VA

8 ounces uncooked spiral pasta

1 can (15 ounces) black beans, rinsed and drained

3/4 cup chopped sweet red pepper

3/4 cup chopped green pepper

1/2 cup chopped red onion

SALAD DRESSING:

1 cup ranch salad dressing

1 cup salsa

1/8 to 1/4 teaspoon cayenne pepper

Cook pasta according to package directions. Rinse in cold water; drain. In a large salad bowl, combine the pasta, black beans, peppers and onion. Combine the salad dressing, salsa and cayenne. Pour over pasta mixture; toss to coat. Cover and refrigerate for 1 hour or until chilled. YIELD: 9 servings.

school days display

(PICTURED AT RIGHT)

The decor for your backyard graduation barbecue doesn't have to be elaborate and expensive. With these elementary ideas, you can set a stunning table.

CHALK IT UP TO FUN! If your party is for a small number of guests, consider setting the table out back, complete with fun and festive place cards. Mini chalkboards are the perfect size. Put the guest of honor in a seat in the middle so he or she can talk to everyone.

"A" IS FOR APPLE. Polish up colorful red and green apples and scatter them on the table. Encourage guests to indulge in one or to take some home.

HIT THE BOOKS. Stack schoolbooks or yearbooks on the table. Top with a few mementos, such as a school letter, diploma and graduation cap and tassel. For a special touch, tuck in framed pictures of the graduate through the years...maybe photos from the first days of school.

LUNCH BOX BEAUTY. Play into the theme by using metal lunch boxes as vases for displaying flowers. To prevent leaks, first line the boxes with plastic bags. Add floral foam, tuck in a variety of flowers in school colors and then add water.

*B*usy farmers markets are a sure sign of summer. But once you return home with all that farm fresh produce, what do you do with it?

Try whipping up the scrumptious seasonal fare we've gathered here, then inviting friends and family over to enjoy the harvest!

Greet guests with a refreshing glass of White Wine Strawberry Sangria, then let the veggies take center stage. Lemony Green and Wax Beans, Garden Spinach-Potato Salad and Grilled Corn with Bloody Mary Butter are sure to pique the interest—and appetites—of your guests.

Complete your meal by presenting juicy, flavorful Roasted Lime Chicken, which features a lovely medley of fresh herbs.

From appetizers and sides to main dishes and desserts, the recipes on the following pages close the gap between farm and table.

SUMMER HARVEST
(PICTURED AT RIGHT)

Garden Spinach-Potato Salad (p. 226)
Grilled Corn with Bloody Mary Butter (p. 228)
Lemony Green and Wax Beans (p. 226)
Roasted Lime Chicken (p. 228)
White Wine Strawberry Sangria (p. 227)

summer harvest
GET TOGETHER

garden spinach-potato salad

(PICTURED ON PAGE 224)

Not only is this summer dish something to look at, it's a treat for the taste buds, too. The medley of textures and garden-fresh ingredients perfectly complement one another for a delightfully different potato salad.

Marilyn Haynes | SYLACAUGA, AL

2 large cucumbers, chopped

1 small red onion, sliced

1/2 cup white wine vinegar, divided

2 pounds small red potatoes, halved

2 garlic cloves, minced

1-1/2 teaspoons salt

1/2 teaspoon celery seed

1/2 teaspoon coarsely ground pepper

1 package (6 ounces) fresh baby spinach

8 bacon strips, cooked and crumbled

1/2 cup snipped fresh dill

1/4 cup olive oil

In a small bowl, combine the cucumbers, onion and 1/4 cup vinegar. Let stand for 20 minutes.

Meanwhile, place potatoes in a large saucepan and cover with water. Bring to a boil. Reduce heat; cover and simmer for 10-15 minutes or until tender. Drain. Transfer to a large bowl. Drizzle with remaining vinegar; sprinkle with garlic, salt, celery seed and pepper. Cool.

Add the spinach, bacon, dill, oil and cucumber mixture; toss to coat. Serve at room temperature or chilled. **YIELD:** 12 servings (1 cup each).

lemony green and wax beans

(PICTURED ON PAGE 224)

Showcase your garden's bounty in this delectable side. A combination of fresh green beans and wax beans are tossed with a tasty herb- and lemon-infused dressing for perked-up flavor.

Donna Noel | GRAY, ME

1/2 pound fresh wax beans, trimmed

1/2 pound fresh green beans, trimmed

2 tablespoons minced fresh mint

2 tablespoons lemon juice

2 tablespoons olive oil

1 garlic clove, minced

1 teaspoon grated lemon peel

1/4 teaspoon salt

1/8 teaspoon pepper

1/4 cup chopped pistachios

1/4 cup chopped hazelnuts

In a large saucepan, bring 8 cups water to a boil. Add wax and green beans; cover and cook for 4 minutes. Drain and immediately place beans in ice water. Drain and pat dry.

Place beans in a large bowl. In a small bowl, combine the mint, lemon juice, oil, garlic, lemon peel, salt and pepper. Pour over beans; toss to coat. Cover and refrigerate for at least 1 hour.

Just before serving, stir in the pistachios and hazelnuts. **YIELD:** 6 servings.

caprese salad

(PICTURED AT RIGHT)

My husband and I love this salad, but not the high prices we pay for it in restaurants. Here, we created our own version which tastes incredibly good.

Melissa Pearson | SANDY, UT

4 medium tomatoes, sliced

1/2 pound fresh mozzarella cheese, sliced

1/4 cup fresh basil leaves

BALSAMIC VINAIGRETTE:

2 tablespoons olive oil

2 tablespoons balsamic vinegar

1 teaspoon ground mustard

1/8 teaspoon salt

1/8 teaspoon pepper

Arrange the tomatoes, fresh mozzarella cheese and basil on a serving platter. Whisk the vinaigrette ingredients; drizzle over salad. **YIELD:** 4 servings.

white wine strawberry sangria

(PICTURED ABOVE AND ON PAGE 224)

I cannot have people over without someone requesting this perfectly refreshing beverage. Sliced fresh strawberries take the presentation over the top.

Tanya Jones | OKLAHOMA CITY, OK

1 bottle (750 milliliters) white wine

1/2 cup strawberry schnapps liqueur

1/4 cup sugar

2 cups sliced fresh strawberries

Ice cubes

In a 2-qt. pitcher, stir wine, liqueur and sugar until sugar is dissolved; add sliced strawberries. Chill for at least 2 hours. Serve over ice. **YIELD:** 6 servings.

grilled corn with bloody mary butter

(PICTURED ON PAGE 225)

At the peak of the season, sweet corn makes a regular appearance on our dinner table. Basting it with this unique, slightly spicy spread makes it a real treat.

Betty Fulks | ONIA, AR

1/2 cup spicy Bloody Mary mix

1/4 cup butter, cubed

3 tablespoons minced fresh cilantro

1 jalapeno pepper, seeded and finely chopped

2 teaspoons hot pepper sauce

1 garlic clove, minced

1/4 teaspoon salt

8 medium ears sweet corn, husks removed

In a small saucepan, combine the first seven ingredients; cook and stir until butter is melted.

Grill corn, covered, over medium heat for 10-12 minutes or until tender, turning and basting occasionally with the butter mixture. **YIELD:** 8 servings.

EDITOR'S NOTE: We recommend wearing disposable gloves when cutting hot peppers. Avoid touching your face.

roasted lime chicken

(PICTURED ON PAGE 225)

The subtle lime flavor infused throughout this moist and juicy roasted chicken makes it a frequent request for family dinners. It's a tasty way to showcase fresh herbs such as rosemary, sage, thyme and parsley.

Kathy Martinez | SPRING VALLEY, CA

1/2 cup Dijon mustard

1/4 cup lime juice

1/4 cup soy sauce

2 tablespoons minced fresh parsley
or 2 teaspoons dried parsley flakes

2 tablespoons minced fresh rosemary
or 2 teaspoons dried rosemary, crushed

2 tablespoons minced fresh sage
or 2 teaspoons rubbed sage

2 tablespoons minced fresh thyme
or 2 teaspoons dried thyme

1 teaspoon white pepper

1 teaspoon ground nutmeg

1 roasting chicken (6 to 7 pounds)

4 medium limes, cut into wedges

In a small bowl, combine the first nine ingredients. Cover and refrigerate 1/4 cup marinade; pour remaining marinade into a 2-gallon resealable plastic bag. Add the chicken; seal bag and turn to coat. Refrigerate for at least 4 hours.

Drain chicken and discard marinade. Place lime wedges inside the cavity. Tuck wings under chicken; tie drumsticks together. Place chicken breast side up on a rack in a shallow roasting pan. Brush reserved marinade over chicken.

Bake at 350° for 2 to 2-1/2 hours or until a meat thermometer reads 180°, basting occasionally with pan juices. Cover loosely with foil if chicken browns too quickly. Let stand for 15 minutes before carving. **YIELD:** 8 servings.

tomato-squash appetizer pizza

(PICTURED AT RIGHT)

I was looking for quick weeknight meals that would use the fresh herbs from my windowsill garden when I decided to create this seasonal flatbread pizza. To my surprise, I discovered it also makes a fabulous appetizer.

Andrea Tovar | NEW YORK, NY

1 loaf (1 pound) frozen bread dough, thawed

1/4 teaspoon salt

1 tablespoon olive oil

1-1/2 cups (6 ounces each) shredded part-skim mozzarella cheese

1 large yellow summer squash, sliced

1 large tomato, sliced

4 teaspoons shredded Parmesan cheese

1/4 teaspoon pepper

1 teaspoon each minced fresh basil, oregano and chives

Roll dough into a 14-in. x 8-in. rectangle. Transfer to a greased baking sheet. Prick dough thoroughly with a fork. Sprinkle with salt. Bake at 425° for 8-10 minutes or until lightly browned.

Brush crust with oil. Top with mozzarella cheese, squash, tomato, Parmesan cheese, pepper and herbs. Bake 5-10 minutes longer or until cheese is melted. **YIELD:** 24 pieces.

COOKING WITH FRESH BASIL

Homegrown basil is a wonderful addition to recipes, such as Tomato-Squash Appetizer Pizza, and it can be used as a pretty garnish, too. But chopping one leaf at a time can be tedious. To quickly chop a lot of basil, and end up with attractive results, create basil chiffonade, which is just a fancy term for thin, shredded strips. Before cutting basil chiffonade, sprinkle a few drops of vegetable oil on the leaves and gently rub to evenly coat the leaves. This will prevent them from darkening. Stack several basil leaves and roll them into a tight tube. Slice the leaves widthwise into narrow pieces to create long, thin strips. If you'd like smaller pieces, simply chop the strips.

pickled green tomato relish

When I'm left with green tomatoes at the end of summer, I reach for this recipe. Friends and family are so happy to receive the sweet-and-sour relish that they often return the empty jar and ask for a refill!

Mary Gill | FLORENCE, OR

7 pounds green tomatoes (about 20 medium)

4 large onions

2 large red onions

3 large green peppers

2 large sweet red peppers

4 teaspoons canning salt

5 cups cider vinegar

4 cups sugar

2 tablespoons celery seed

4 teaspoons mustard seed

Cut the tomatoes, onions and peppers into wedges. In a food processor, cover and process vegetables in batches until finely chopped. Stir in salt. Divide mixture between two strainers and place each over a bowl. Let stand for 3 hours.

Discard liquid from bowls. Place vegetables in a stockpot; stir in the vinegar, sugar, celery seed and mustard seed. Bring to a boil. Reduce heat; simmer, uncovered, for 30-35 minutes or until thickened.

Carefully ladle hot mixture into hot pint jars, leaving 1/2-in. headspace. Remove air bubbles; wipe rims and adjust lids. Process for 15 minutes in a boiling-water canner. **YIELD:** 8 pints.

EDITOR'S NOTE: The processing time listed is for altitudes of 1,000 feet or less. For altitudes up to 3,000 feet, add 5 minutes; 6,000 feet, add 10 minutes; 8,000 feet, add 15 minutes; 10,000 feet, add 20 minutes.

roasted peppers on goat cheese

Everyone adores this summery appetizer that looks upscale but is really quite simple to prepare. It's a great way to use seasonal produce picked right from the garden.

McKenzie Muscat | POWAY, CA

1 each medium green, sweet red and yellow peppers

1 log (11 ounces) fresh goat cheese

1 large sweet onion, thinly sliced

1/4 cup olive oil

6 garlic cloves, minced

4-1/2 teaspoons chopped seeded jalapeno pepper

1 teaspoon paprika

1 teaspoon pepper

1/2 teaspoon salt

3 tablespoons minced fresh parsley

Sliced French bread baguette

Broil peppers 4 in. from heat until skins blister, about 5 minutes. With tongs, rotate peppers a quarter turn. Broil and rotate until all sides are blistered and blackened. Immediately place peppers in a large bowl; cover and let stand for 20 minutes.

Peel off and discard charred skins. Remove stems and seeds. Thinly slice peppers. Place log of cheese in a greased 2-qt. baking dish. Bake at 350° for 8-10 minutes or just until heated through.

Meanwhile, in a large skillet, saute onion in oil until tender. Add garlic, jalapeno, paprika, pepper and salt; cook 2 minutes longer. Stir in peppers and parsley. Spoon over cheese. Serve with baguette. **YIELD:** 20 servings.

EDITOR'S NOTE: We recommend wearing disposable gloves when cutting hot peppers. Avoid touching your face.

eggplant bruschetta

(PICTURED AT RIGHT)

*One word describes this pretty appetizer...
outstanding! The crispy exterior of
tender eggplant slices and the robust taste
of tomato and basil topping create a
dynamic flavor duo. It's delicious served
chilled or at room temperature.*

Corinne Nicoette | WARWICK, RI

2 eggs, beaten

1/2 cup all-purpose flour

1/4 teaspoon salt

1/4 teaspoon pepper

1 cup seasoned bread crumbs

2 tablespoons grated Parmesan cheese

1 large eggplant, peeled and cut
into 1/2-inch slices

1/3 cup olive oil

4 medium tomatoes, finely chopped

1/4 cup finely chopped red onion

1/2 cup minced fresh basil

8 ounces fresh mozzarella cheese,
cut into 1/4-inch slices

1/2 cup balsamic vinaigrette

Place eggs in a shallow bowl. In a separate shallow bowl, combine
the flour, salt and pepper. In another bowl, combine bread crumbs
and Parmesan cheese. Dip eggplant in the flour mixture, eggs, then
bread crumb mixture.

In a large skillet, cook eggplant in batches in oil for 4-5 minutes
on each side or until tender. Drain on paper towels.

In a small bowl, combine the tomatoes, onion and basil. Top each
eggplant slice with mozzarella cheese and tomato mixture. Drizzle
with vinaigrette. **YIELD:** 1 dozen.

peach blackberry pavlovas

(PICTURED AT FAR RIGHT)

It's hard to decide whether it's the presentation or the taste that makes this dessert tops. Juicy berries rest on a pillow of homemade meringue for a finale that sums up why we love summer in one delicious bite.

Charlene Chambers | ORMOND BEACH, FL

6 egg whites

1 teaspoon vanilla extract

1/2 teaspoon cream of tartar

1/8 teaspoon salt

1-1/2 cups sugar

TOPPING:

4 large peaches, peeled and sliced

2 cups fresh blackberries

1/2 cup sugar

2 tablespoons peach schnapps liqueur

1/2 cup heavy whipping cream

1 teaspoon confectioners' sugar

1/2 teaspoon vanilla extract

Additional fresh blackberries

Place egg whites in a small bowl; let stand at room temperature for 30 minutes. Add the vanilla, cream of tartar and salt; beat on medium speed until soft peaks form. Gradually beat in sugar, 2 tablespoons at a time, on high until stiff peaks form.

Drop meringue into six mounds on parchment paper-lined baking sheets. Shape into 3-1/2-in. cups with the back of a spoon. Bake at 225° for 1 to 1-1/4 hours or until set and dry. Turn oven off; leave meringues in oven for 1-1/2 hours.

In a large saucepan, combine the peaches, blackberries, sugar and liqueur. Bring to a boil. Reduce heat; simmer, uncovered, for 3-4 minutes or until sugar is dissolved. In a large bowl, beat cream until it begins to thicken. Add confectioners' sugar and vanilla; beat until stiff peaks form.

Spoon fruit mixture into meringue shells; top with whipped cream. Garnish with additional blackberries. YIELD: 6 servings.

balsamic-goat cheese grilled plums

(PICTURED AT FAR RIGHT)

For a dessert that is sure to make a statement at the end of your dinner party, look no further. Ripe plums are grilled, then dressed up with a balsamic reduction and sprinkled with tangy goat cheese.

Ariana Abelow | HOLLISTON, MA

1 cup balsamic vinegar

2 teaspoons grated lemon peel

4 medium firm plums, halved and pitted

1/2 cup crumbled goat cheese

In a small saucepan, combine vinegar and lemon peel. Bring to a boil; cook until mixture is thickened and reduced to about 1/3 cup.

Grill plums, covered, over medium heat for 2-3 minutes on each side or until tender. Drizzle with vinegar mixture; sprinkle with goat cheese. YIELD: 8 servings.

watermelon gazpacho

(PICTURED AT RIGHT)

Nothing cools off the dog days of summer like a bowl of this refreshing watermelon chilled soup. Its subtle sweetness, touch of mint and pretty pink color make it especially appealing.

Jill Sparrow | INDIANAPOLIS, IN

1/2 cup sugar

1/2 cup water

12 cups seeded chopped watermelon

2 cups chopped honeydew

1/2 cup fresh mint leaves

1/4 cup lime juice

1 teaspoon salt

TOPPING:

1/2 cup sour cream

2 tablespoons sugar

In a small saucepan, combine sugar and water. Bring to a boil over medium heat. Reduce heat; simmer, uncovered, for 2-3 minutes or until sugar is dissolved, stirring occasionally. Remove from the heat; cool to room temperature.

Working in batches if necessary, place the sugar mixture, watermelon, honeydew, mint, lime juice and salt in a food processor. Cover and process until smooth. Refrigerate for at least 2 hours.

Combine sour cream and sugar. Garnish each serving with topping. YIELD: 9 servings (2-1/4 quarts).

PIPING MERINGUE PILLOWS

Add a bit of flair to your presentation of Peach Blackberry Pavlovas by piping the meringue pillows.

Cut a small hole in the corner of a pastry or resealable plastic bag. Insert a 1/2-in. round decorating tip (#A1) and fill bag about half full with meringue. Smooth the filling down toward the tip to eliminate air bubbles. Twist top of bag shut.

Hold the pastry bag up, and position the tip about 1/8 to 1/4 in. above a baking sheet lined with parchment or waxed paper. Starting at the middle of a circle, pipe meringue in a spiral until the circle is completely filled.

herb garden zucchini

(PICTURED AT FAR RIGHT)

*Full of crunch and flavor, my easy side dish is an appetizing sidekick to
grilled chicken or steak. The flecks of fresh herbs make it visually appealing, too.*

Dana Roberts | PRINCETON, KY

3 large zucchini, thinly sliced

1 teaspoon salt

1/2 cup olive oil

1/4 cup fresh basil leaves

1/4 cup packed fresh parsley sprigs

1/4 cup minced fresh rosemary

1/4 cup fresh thyme

1/4 cup lemon juice

3 tablespoons honey

2 tablespoons Dijon mustard

4 garlic cloves, peeled

Place zucchini in a colander over a plate; sprinkle with salt and toss. Let stand for 30 minutes. Rinse and drain well; pat dry. Place the oil, herbs, lemon juice, honey, mustard and garlic in a food processor; cover and process until smooth.

Transfer zucchini to a large bowl. Drizzle 1/4 cup dressing over zucchini; toss to coat. Cover and refrigerate remaining dressing for up to 2 days. **YIELD:** 6 servings plus 1 cup leftover dressing.

pickled green onions

*Whether you grow your own green onions or get them from the farmers market, pickled green onions
provide a unique and tasty treat. They're a tasty alternative to ordinary pickles on a relish tray.*

Nancy Dentler | GREENSBORO, NC

4 cups cider vinegar

1 cup water

1/2 cup sugar

2 jalapeno peppers, seeded and chopped

3 garlic cloves, peeled and sliced

1 teaspoon ground cinnamon

1 teaspoon ground allspice

5 bunches green onions, trimmed

In a Dutch oven, combine the first seven ingredients. Bring to a boil over medium heat; cook and stir for 5 minutes. Add onions; return to a boil. Reduce heat; simmer, uncovered, for 2 minutes.

Transfer onion mixture to a bowl; cool. Cover and refrigerate for 8 hours or overnight. Store in the refrigerator for up to 2 weeks. **YIELD:** 1-1/2 quarts.

EDITOR'S NOTE: We recommend wearing disposable gloves when cutting hot peppers. Avoid touching your face.

fried green tomato blts

(PICTURED AT RIGHT)

You might call this Southern-inspired sandwich comfort food with a twist. The chipotle mayonnaise adds a little kick, while the peppered bacon really punches up the flavor.

Neilla Roe | KINGSTON, WA

1 package thick-sliced peppered bacon strips (24 ounces)

1 cup all-purpose flour

1 cup cornmeal

4-1/2 teaspoons seafood seasoning

1 teaspoon pepper

1/8 teaspoon salt

1 cup buttermilk

8 medium green tomatoes, cut into 1/4-inch slices

Oil for deep-fat frying

16 slices Texas toast

1/2 cup reduced-fat chipotle mayonnaise

8 Boston lettuce leaves

In a large skillet, cook bacon over medium heat until crisp. Remove to paper towels to drain. In a small shallow bowl, combine the flour, cornmeal, seafood seasoning, pepper and salt. Place buttermilk and flour mixture in shallow bowl. Dip tomatoes in buttermilk, then coat with flour mixture.

In an electric skillet or deep fryer, heat oil to 375°. Fry tomatoes, a few slices at a time, for 1 minute on each side or until golden brown. Drain on paper towels.

Serve tomatoes on Texas toast with mayonnaise, bacon and lettuce. **YIELD:** 8 servings.

There's a lot at "stake" when you host a vampire party on Halloween. Not only does your nest need to be decked out in the best night-of-the-living-undead decor, but the bites and beverages need to be dazzling as well.

There's no need to put your neck on the line. Become kindred spirits with your coven of friends with a spirited drink like a Candy Apple Martini.

Paired with flavorful Garlic and Shallot Mashed Potatoes, Steak-through-the-Heart Bites will keep enemy vampires at bay during your immortal masquerade.

And test tubes filled with Roasted Tomato Soup will quench the appetite of any type of blood-thirsty ghoul.

CREEPY CUISINE
(PICTURED AT RIGHT)

Candy Apple Martini (p. 241)
Roasted Tomato Soup (p. 240)
Steak-through-the-Heart Bites (p. 238)
Garlic and Shallot Mashed Potatoes (p. 240)

vampire themed
HALLOWEEN

steak-through-the-heart bites

(PICTURED ON PAGE 237)

Our Test Kitchen staff enhances the already fabulous flavor of beef kabobs by topping them with a colorful roasted red pepper sauce. Guests will fall in love with these appetizers!

4 large sweet red peppers

1/4 cup olive oil

1 tablespoon white wine vinegar

2 anchovy fillets

2 teaspoons minced fresh thyme or 1/2 teaspoon dried thyme

KABOBS:

2 tablespoons olive oil

2 teaspoons paprika

1 teaspoon minced fresh thyme or 1/4 teaspoon dried thyme

3/4 teaspoon salt

1/2 teaspoon coarsely ground pepper

2 pounds beef tenderloin, cut into eight pieces

Broil peppers 4 in. from the heat until skins blister, about 5 minutes. With tongs, rotate peppers a quarter turn. Broil and rotate until all sides are blistered and blackened. Immediately place peppers in a large bowl; cover and let stand for 20 minutes.

Peel off and discard charred skins; remove stems and seeds. Place peppers in a food processor. Add the oil, vinegar, anchovies and thyme. Cover and process until blended.

For kabobs, combine the oil, paprika, thyme, salt and pepper; rub over beef. Grill, covered, over medium heat or broil 4 in. from the heat for 6-8 minutes or until the meat reaches desired doneness, turning once. Thread beef onto skewers. Serve with red pepper sauce. **YIELD:** 8 kabobs (2 cups sauce).

bloody-mary seafood cocktail

When planning impromptu parties, I rely on this recipe. After a quick stop at the supermarket, I can create an hors d'oeuvre that both impresses and satisfies.

Shari Foster | LOCKHART, TX

2 pounds peeled and deveined cooked medium shrimp

1 jar (12 ounces) chili sauce

1 cup spicy Bloody Mary mix

1 large red onion, finely chopped

1 large sweet red pepper, finely chopped

2/3 cup minced fresh cilantro

1/4 cup lemon juice

1/4 cup olive oil

3 jalapeno peppers, seeded and minced

5 garlic cloves, minced

2 medium ripe avocados, peeled and cubed

In a large bowl, combine the first 10 ingredients. Chill until serving. Just before serving, stir in avocado. **YIELD:** 14 servings (1/2 cup each).

EDITOR'S NOTE: We recommend wearing disposable gloves when cutting hot peppers. Avoid touching your face.

THE SKINNY ON DEVEINING SHRIMP

Start on the underside by the head area. Pull legs and first section of shell to one side. Continue pulling shell up around the top and to the other side. (You can pull off shell by tail if desired, too.) Remove the black vein running down the shrimp's back by making a shallow slit with a paring knife along the back from head to tail. Rinse under cold water to remove the vein.

black-hearted candy apples

(PICTURED AT RIGHT)

The glossy coating of these old-fashioned candy apples is hard, not soft like the more common caramel variety. It's best to lick them like a lollipop. You can also cut into wedges with a sharp knife, but the candy coating may crack.

Agnes Ward | STRATFORD, ON

4 medium red apples

4 Popsicle or decorative lollipop sticks

2 cups sugar

1 cup water

2/3 cup light corn syrup

1/2 teaspoon ground cinnamon, divided

Red food coloring

Black food coloring

Wash and dry apples; remove stems. Insert Popsicle sticks into apples. Place on a waxed paper-lined baking sheet; set aside.

In a large heavy saucepan, combine the sugar, water and corn syrup. Cook and stir over medium heat until sugar is dissolved. Bring to a boil. Cook, without stirring, until a candy thermometer reads 290° (soft-crack stage).

Remove from the heat and pour into two small bowls; stir 1/4 teaspoon cinnamon and red food coloring into one bowl. Stir black food coloring and the remaining cinnamon into other bowl.

Working quickly, dip the apples into the hot sugar mixtures to completely coat. Place on prepared baking sheet; let stand until set. YIELD: 4 servings.

roasted tomato soup

(PICTURED ON PAGE 236)

Using canned whole tomatoes means this recipe can easily be served throughout the year, not just Halloween. The secret to the soup's great taste is fresh basil...the more the better as far as I'm concerned!

Sala Houtzer | GOLDSBORO, NC

2 cans (28 ounces each) whole tomatoes, undrained

1 carton (32 ounces) chicken broth

1 can (28 ounces) crushed tomatoes

1 can (10-1/2 ounces) condensed chicken broth, undiluted

1 can (6 ounces) tomato paste

1/3 cup balsamic vinegar

1/4 cup thinly sliced fresh basil leaves

3 fresh thyme sprigs

1 large onion, finely chopped

1/4 cup plus 2 tablespoons packed brown sugar, divided

Drain whole tomatoes, pouring juice into a Dutch oven; set tomatoes aside. Add the chicken broth, crushed tomatoes, condensed chicken broth, tomato paste, vinegar, basil and thyme to the pan. Bring to a boil. Reduce heat; simmer, uncovered, for 50-60 minutes or until slightly thickened.

Pierce reserved tomatoes; place in a greased 15-in. x 10-in. x 1-in. baking pan. Sprinkle with onion and 1/4 cup brown sugar. Bake at 450° for 20-30 minutes or until onion is tender. Cool slightly and chop.

Discard thyme sprigs from soup. Stir in roasted tomato mixture and remaining brown sugar; heat through. Serve warm or cold. **YIELD:** 11 servings.

garlic and shallot mashed potatoes

(PICTURED ON PAGE 237)

Roasting garlic gives it a mellow taste, so it's not overpowering in these marvelous mashed potatoes. A touch of cream cheese provides just the right amount of devilish richness.

Dana Nelson | OTTAWA, OH

1 whole garlic bulb

1 shallot

1 tablespoon olive oil

2-1/2 pounds Yukon Gold potatoes (about 8 medium), peeled and cut into wedges

1/2 cup 2% milk

3 tablespoons butter, softened

2 ounces cream cheese, softened

1 teaspoon salt

1/4 teaspoon coarsely ground pepper

Cayenne pepper or paprika, optional

Remove papery outer skin from garlic (do not peel or separate cloves) and the shallot. Cut tops off of garlic bulb and shallot; brush with oil. Wrap each in heavy-duty foil. Bake at 425° for 30-35 minutes or until softened. Cool for 10-15 minutes.

Meanwhile, place potatoes in a large saucepan and cover with water. Bring to a boil. Reduce heat; cover and simmer for 15-20 minutes or until tender. Drain; place in a large bowl.

Squeeze softened garlic into bowl. Finely chop shallot; add to potatoes. Add the milk, butter, cream cheese, salt and pepper; mash potatoes. Sprinkle with cayenne if desired. **YIELD:** 6 servings.

kiss from a vampire cookies

(PICTURED AT RIGHT)

Raspberry jam eerily oozes from our home economists' soft butter cookies. One bite and you'll have a hard time stopping.

3/4 cup butter, softened

1/2 cup sugar

1 egg

1/2 teaspoon vanilla extract

1/8 teaspoon almond extract

1-1/2 cups all-purpose flour

1/4 teaspoon salt

1/2 cup seedless raspberry jam

In a large bowl, cream butter and sugar until light and fluffy. Beat in egg and extracts. Combine flour and salt; gradually add to creamed mixture and mix well. Flatten into a disk. Wrap in plastic wrap and refrigerate for 30 minutes.

On a lightly floured surface, roll dough to 1/8-in. thickness. Cut with a floured 2-in. round cookie cutter.

Place half of the circles on greased baking sheets. Place 1 teaspoon of jam in center of each circle; top with remaining circles and press edges lightly to seal. Use a toothpick to poke two small holes (resembling a vampire bite) in the top of each cookie.

Bake at 325° for 10-12 minutes or until cookies are set. (Jam will escape from tops of cookies as they bake.) Cool for 5 minutes before removing from pans to wire racks. YIELD: 2 dozen.

candy apple martini

(PICTURED ON PAGE 236)

Surprise the ghouls and goblins at your Halloween party with these thirst-quenching martinis. Cranberry juice and sour apple liqueur make them tart yet terrific.

Crystal Bruns | ILIFF, CO

1-1/2 to 2 cups ice cubes

2 ounces vodka

2 ounces sour apple liqueur

2 ounces cranberry juice

1/2 ounce butterscotch schnapps liqueur

Fill a shaker three-fourths full with ice. Add the vodka, apple liqueur, cranberry juice and butterscotch schnapps.

Cover and shake for 10-15 seconds or until condensation forms on the outside of shaker. Strain into a chilled cocktail glass. YIELD: 1 serving.

strawberry fondue

A friend shared this recipe with me more than 35 years ago. It tastes as great today as it did then. The luscious dip clings wonderfully to pieces of angel food cake.

Janice Goble Caloia | ROCHESTER HILLS, MI

2 packages (10 ounces each) frozen sweetened sliced strawberries, thawed

2 teaspoons cornstarch

1 tablespoon cold water

1-1/2 teaspoons maraschino cherry juice

1/2 cup heavy whipping cream

4-1/2 teaspoons confectioners' sugar

1/8 teaspoon almond extract

Cubed angel food cake

Place strawberries in a food processor; cover and process until pureed. Transfer to a small saucepan. Combine cornstarch and water; stir into the pan. Bring to a boil; cook and stir for 1-2 minutes or until thickened. Stir in cherry juice. Transfer to a fondue pot; keep warm.

In a small bowl, beat cream until it begins to thicken. Add confectioners' sugar and extract; beat until stiff peaks form. Serve fondue with cake and whipped cream. YIELD: 1-1/2 cups fondue (1 cup cream).

layered mediterranean dip

Family and friends will dive into this delightful dip with an Italian flair. Black olives bring a bit of saltiness to the creamy, layered mixture.

Mary Frucelli | JACKSONVILLE, FL

2 cans (15 ounces each) pinto beans, rinsed and drained

1/3 cup prepared pesto

2 cups (16 ounces) reduced-fat sour cream

1 package (8 ounces) reduced-fat cream cheese

1-1/2 teaspoons Italian seasoning

1/2 teaspoon pepper

4 plum tomatoes, seeded and finely chopped

1 medium green pepper, finely chopped

3 green onions, finely chopped

2 cups (8 ounces) shredded Italian cheese blend

1 cup crumbled feta cheese

2 cans (2-1/4 ounces each) sliced ripe olives, drained

Baked pita chips

Place beans in a large bowl; stir in pesto until blended. Spread into a 13-in. x 9-in. dish.

In another bowl, beat the sour cream, cream cheese, Italian seasoning and pepper until smooth; layer over bean mixture. Sprinkle with vegetables, cheeses and olives. Refrigerate for at least 30 minutes. Serve with chips. YIELD: 10 cups.

FETA FACTS

Feta is a white, salty, semi-firm cheese. Traditionally, it was made from sheep's or goat's milk, but it is now also made with cow's milk. After feta is formed in a special mold, it's sliced into large pieces, salted and soaked in brine. Although feta cheese is mostly associated with Greek cooking, "feta" comes from the Italian word "fette", meaning slice of food.

pickled eggs

(PICTURED AT RIGHT)

Because my grandmother didn't measure anything when she cooked, I had to guess when I decided to duplicate her recipe for pickled eggs. The fun color becomes more intense the longer they marinate.

Judie Thurstenson | COLCORD, OK

1 can (15 ounces) whole beets, undrained

4 cups cider vinegar

12 hard-cooked eggs

8 pickled hot cherry peppers

6 pearl onions

2 garlic cloves, sliced

1/2 teaspoon salt

Drain beets, reserving 1/2 cup juice. Place in a large glass bowl; add the remaining ingredients. Cover; chill overnight. **YIELD:** 12 servings.

radicchio salad cups

Radicchio leaves serve as edible cups for a fresh-tasting salad. A tangy mustard and vinegar dressing partners well with apples and Gorgonzola cheese.

Deb Williams | PEORIA, AZ

1-1/3 cups crumbled Gorgonzola cheese

2/3 cup chopped walnuts

1 medium apple, chopped

1/4 cup olive oil

2 teaspoons white wine vinegar

1 teaspoon Dijon mustard

1/8 teaspoon pepper

8 radicchio leaves

In a large bowl, combine the cheese, walnuts and apple. In a small bowl, whisk the oil, vinegar, mustard and pepper. Drizzle over salad; gently toss to coat. Spoon 1/3 cup onto each radicchio leaf. Serve immediately. **YIELD:** 8 servings.

sweet and spicy chili

This recipe for Sweet and Spicy Chili is the result of much experimentation.
I knew I had perfected it when my husband took a pot to work, where one guy ate five bowls himself!

Kristin McPherson | WEST PLAINS, MO

3/4 pound beef sirloin tip steak, cubed

2 tablespoons canola oil

1 pound ground beef

2 medium onions, chopped

3 garlic cloves, minced

4 cans (16 ounces each) kidney beans, rinsed and drained

3 cans (14-1/2 ounces each) diced tomatoes with mild green chilies, undrained

2 cans (6 ounces each) tomato paste

1 can (12 ounces) root beer

1 cup strong brewed coffee

1 cup beef broth

2 jalapeno peppers, seeded and chopped

1/4 cup packed brown sugar

3 tablespoons chili powder

1 tablespoon ground cumin

1 tablespoon baking cocoa

1 teaspoon garlic salt

1 teaspoon cayenne pepper

1 teaspoon Creole seasoning

1 teaspoon dried oregano

In a Dutch oven, brown steak in oil. Remove and set aside. Add the ground beef, onions and garlic to the pan; cook and stir over medium heat until meat is no longer pink. Drain.

Return steak to the pan; stir in the remaining ingredients. Bring to a boil. Reduce heat to low. Simmer, uncovered, for 2 hours or until beef is tender. **YIELD:** 13 servings (1 cup each).

EDITOR'S NOTE: When cutting hot peppers, disposable gloves are recommended. Avoid touching your face. The following spices may be substituted for 1 teaspoon Creole seasoning: 1/4 teaspoon each salt, garlic powder and paprika; and a pinch each of dried thyme, ground cumin and cayenne pepper.

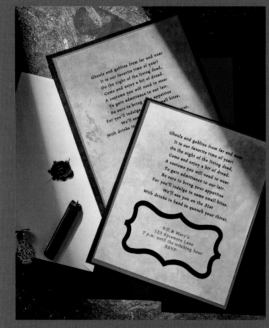

EERIE INVITATION

Personalize the invitations for your vampire gala by making your own on the computer. We suggest using the following wording:

Ghouls and goblins from far and near
It is our favorite time of year!
On the night of the living dead,
Come and enjoy a bit of dread.
A costume you will need to wear
To gain admittance to our lair.
Be sure to bring your appetites
For you'll indulge in some small bites.
We'll see you on the 31st
With drinks in hand to quench your thirst.

For an extra formal touch, use blood-red sealing wax and a spooky seal to close the envelopes. You can find wax and seals wherever stationery is sold.

creepy candleholders

(PICTURED AT RIGHT)

Because vampires are sensitive to light, illuminate your soiree with the soft glow of candles resting in wax-dripped candleholders, which are fashioned to resemble dripping blood.

Clear empty bottles in various shapes and sizes

Gloss enamel paint in various dark colors

Acrylic paint with glitter in various dark colors

Red and black taper candles

Squeeze the paints into each bottle, using a straw to spread the paint around. (You can also cover the bottle openings with paper towel and shake them.) Use multiple colors to get a fun effect. Repeat several times so that the entire insides of all the bottles are covered. Let dry completely.

Place the bottles on a protected surface. Insert a candle into each bottle. Light the candles, letting the wax drip down the outsides of the bottles. (You may need to hold a lit candle in your hand over the top of each bottle and have the wax drip down.) Let dry completely.

Insert the same used candles into each bottle. Light just before guests arrive.

EDITOR'S NOTE: We used a combination of Americana Gloss Enamels and Folk Art Extreme Glitter to achieve this look. Make sure the candles sit securely in the bottle openings before lighting. Never leave a lit candle unattended.

reference index

Use this index as a guide to the many helpful hints, food facts, decorating ideas and step-by-step instructions throughout the book.

CANDIES

Storing homemade candy, 73
Using a candy thermometer, 69

CENTERPIECES & TABLE TOPPERS

Bells of Ireland beauty, 197
Fast & festive decor, 23
Heavenly illuminated centerpieces, 85
School days display, 223
Stunning squash vase, 117

DECORATING IDEAS

All about bento boxes, 207
Cheering station setup, 179
Clover cutlery, 196
Creepy candleholders, 245
Glass jar chandelier, 147
Wine pairing cards, 45

DESSERTS

Fast cupcake fixes, 185
Fluted edges are as easy as pie, 116
Piping meringue pillows, 233

FRUIT

Sectioning a citrus fruit, 21
Using fresh citrus peel, 154

HERBS & SPICES

Cooking with fresh basil, 229
Freezing fresh rosemary, 42
Fresh gingerroot facts, 92
Trimming cilantro, 164

INVITATIONS & PARTY FAVORS

Eerie invitation, 244
Penalty flag favors, 179

MEAL & PARTY PLANNING

Countdown to Christmas dinner, 8
Easter dinner agenda, 140
Easy outline for a no-fuss Christmas meal, 18
Holiday dinner planner, 78
How much wine to buy?, 39
Thanksgiving timeline, 110

MISCELLANEOUS FOOD & COOKING TIPS

Crushing peppermint candy, 60
Feta facts, 242
Freezer pleasers, 150
How much pork to purchase, 103
How to toast nuts, 210
Make-ahead shepherd's pie, 190

Making a water bath, 99
Safely storing leftovers, 120
Simple spaghetti, 80
So what is sazon?, 104
Softening brown sugar, 177
Stir-fry secret, 124
The skinny on deveining shrimp, 238
What are capers?, 54

NAPKIN FOLDS & PLACE CARDS

Christmas cracker napkin fold, 15
Under-glass place card, 15

VEGETABLES

About butternut squash, 128
Asparagus tips, 160
Choosing the best, 12
Cucumber capers, 202
Make time for jicama, 32
Preparing asparagus, 144
Slicing shallots, 49
Squeezing spinach dry, 89
Sweet onion secrets, 220
The dish on radishes, 163
Trim green beans in no time, 112

general recipe index

This handy index lists every recipe by food category, major ingredient and/or cooking method.

APPETIZERS & SNACKS

Cold Appetizers
Berry Almond Bruschetta, 210
Bloody-Mary Seafood Cocktail, 238
Pickled Eggs, 243
Shrimp & Artichoke Spring Rolls with Lemon Aioli, 146
Veggie Sushi Rolls, 204
Watermelon Cups, 217

Dips
Artichoke, Spinach & Sun-Dried Tomato Dip, 89
Beer Fondue, 195
Cheese Crisps with Ricotta Dip, 36
Layered Mediterranean Dip, 242
Oil & Vinegar Dipping Sauce, 19
Shrimp Salsa, 101
Spicy Apple Dip, 19
Tangy Feta Herb Dip, 212

Hot Appetizers
Bacon-Jalapeno Mushrooms with Ranch Sauce, 176
Baked Figs, 40
Beef Tenderloin Lollipops, 39
Brie Toasts with Cranberry Compote, 79
Caprese Scallop Stacks, 37
Caramelized Onion & Pork Potstickers, 200
Eggplant Bruschetta, 231
Focaccia Party Sandwich, 172
Goat Cheese and Spinach Stuffed Mushrooms, 84
Meatballs with Cranberry Sauce, 120
Onion Tarts with Balsamic Onion Jam, 41
Peppery Herb Flatbread, 94
Polenta Mushroom Appetizers, 44
Puttanesca Meatball Sliders, 173
Roasted Garlic & Sun-Dried Tomato Toast, 38
Roasted Peppers on Goat Cheese, 230
Salmon & Cream Cheese Potatoes, 40
Smoky Chicken Nachos, 172
Spring Brunch Bruschetta, 144
Steak-through-the Heart Bites, 238
Tomato-Squash Appetizer Pizza, 229
Tostones, 100
Warm Olive Bruschetta, 38

Snack Mixes, Crackers and Chips
Buffalo Wing Munch Mix, 178
Curry Snack Mix, 217
Garlic-Herb Mini Flatbreads, 43
Rainbow Potato Chips with Creamy Onion Dip, 178
Roasted Curry Chickpeas, 44
Sweet & Spicy Kettle Corn, 93

Spreads
Maple Sausage Cheesecake, 94
Onion-Date Baked Brie, 14
Parmesan Truffles, 42
Tomato Rosemary Hummus, 42

APPLES
Apple-Cinnamon Shortcakes, 133
Apple-Glazed Holiday Ham, 10
Black-Hearted Candy Apples, 239
Gorgonzola Baked Apples with Balsamic Syrup, 113
Hot Apple Pie Sipper, 92
Pecan Sausage Stuffing, 114
Radicchio Salad Cups, 243
Spicy Apple Dip, 19
Stuffed Apples with Honey Creme Fraiche, 132

ARTICHOKES
Artichoke, Spinach & Sun-Dried Tomato Dip, 89
Shrimp & Artichoke Spring Rolls with Lemon Aioli, 146
Spicy Antipasto Salad, 216
Spinach and Artichoke Bread Pudding, 141

ASPARAGUS
Dijon Roasted Asparagus, 160
Spring Brunch Bruschetta, 144
Springtime Asparagus Pizza, 146

BACON & PANCETTA
Bacon-Jalapeno Mushrooms with Ranch Sauce, 176
BLT Wedge Salad, 22
Dark Chocolate Bacon Cupcakes, 185
Fried Green Tomato BLTs, 235
Inside-Out Bacon Cheeseburgers, 220
Peppered Bacon and Cheese Scones, 154
Poached Egg Salads with Pancetta Vinaigrette, 81

BANANAS & PLANTAINS
Bananas Foster Baked French Toast, 29
Bananas Foster Surprise Cupcakes, 183
Tostones, 100

BARS & BROWNIES
Blondie Sundaes, 177
Layered Gingerbread Bars, 95
Nanaimo Bars, 75
Rocky Road Brownies, 222

BEANS *(also see Green Beans & Soybeans)*
Fish in Rosemary Broth, 52
Habichuelas (Red Beans), 104
Layered Mediterranean Dip, 242
Pasta and White Bean Soup with Sun-Dried Tomatoes, 57
Roasted Curry Chickpeas, 44
Southwestern Pasta Salad, 222
Tomato Rosemary Hummus, 42

BEEF & GROUND BEEF

Main Dishes
Braised Short Ribs, 53
Cranberry-Stuffed Beef Tenderloin, 50
Eat-Twice Chili Pizza, 176
Four-Pepper Ribeye Roast, 54
Mozzarella-Stuffed Meatballs, 52
Steak au Poivre, 20

Sandwiches
Loaded Philly Cheese Steaks, 174
Puttanesca Meatball Sliders, 173
Roast Beef Garden Pitas, 210

Snacks
Beef Tenderloin Lollipops, 39
Steak-through-the Heart Bites, 238

Soup and Chili
Beef & Barley Soup, 88
Sweet and Spicy Chili, 244

BEVERAGES
Candy Apple Martini, 241
Coconut-Caramel Hot Cocoa, 93
Coquito, 99
Creamy Mocha Cocktail, 195

BEVERAGES *(continued)*
Family-Favorite Pina Coladas, 98
Gingerbread Fizz, 92
Hot Apple Pie Sipper, 92
Irish Whiskey Float, 190
Lychee Green Tea Milkshakes, 205
Sparkling Ginger Iced Tea, 203
Sparkling Summer Champagne, 211
Strawberry Citrus Slushies, 28
Vanilla Bean Fizz, 82
White Wine Sangria, 9
White Wine Strawberry Sangria, 227

BISCUITS & SCONES
Butterscotch Maple Scones, 27
Flaky Biscuits with Herb Butter, 156
Peppered Bacon and Cheese Scones, 154

BLUEBERRIES
Overnight Baked Oatmeal, 30
Overnight Yeast Pancakes with
  Blueberry Syrup, 26

BREADS *(see Biscuits & Scones; Muffins;
Quick Breads; Waffles, Pancakes & French Toast;
Yeast Breads & Rolls)*

BROCCOLI & BROCCOLINI
Beer Fondue, 195
Chicken Yakitori with Noodles, 206
Lemon-Scented Broccolini, 14

CABBAGE & SAUERKRAUT
Colcannon with Onions and Leek, 193
Corned Beef & Cabbage for the Wine
  Lover, 192

CAKES *(also see Cheesecakes; Cupcakes)*
Coconut Chiffon Cake, 145
Flourless Chocolate Cake with Peanut
  Butter Ice Cream, 13
Grand Marnier Cranberry Pound
  Cake, 131
Layered Peppermint Icebox Cake, 60
Malted Chocolate & Stout Layer
  Cake, 194
Mint Angel Cake, 65

CANDIES
Black-Hearted Candy Apples, 239
Candy Cane Fudge, 62
Candy Cane Truffle Lollipops, 74
Chocolate Caramels, 73
Choco-Tato Truffles, 125
Macadamia Peanut Butter Cups, 70
Orange-Almond Chocolate Logs, 68
Pistachio Brittle, 69

CARAMEL
Bananas Foster Surprise Cupcakes, 183
Chocolate Caramels, 73
Coconut-Caramel Hot Cocoa, 93
Salted Caramel Cupcakes, 182

CASSEROLES
Main Dishes
Ham & Cheese Strata with Sun-Dried
  Tomatoes, 31
Overnight Baked Eggs Bruschetta, 33
West Virginia Shepherd's Pie, 190
Side Dishes
Oven-Roasted Spring Vegetable
  Medley, 167
Pecan Sausage Stuffing, 114
Rich Onion Gratin, 166
Roasted Cauliflower, 12
Spectacular Fingerling Potatoes, 22
Spinach and Artichoke Bread
  Pudding, 141
Squash au Gratin, 9
Three-Cheese Stuffed Onions, 80

CHEESE
Breads and Spreads
Asiago Bagels, 152
Mini Cheddar Bread Bowls, 88
Parmesan Butter, 79
Peppered Bacon and Cheese Scones, 154
Rosemary-Parmesan Biscotti, 90
Desserts
Balsamic-Goat Cheese Grilled
  Plums, 232
Butternut Cheesecake, 128
Cappuccino Cheesecake, 83
Gin & Tonic Cupcakes, 184 (frosting)
White Chocolate Peppermint
  Cheesecake, 64
Main Dishes
Ham & Cheese Strata with Sun-Dried
  Tomatoes, 31
Mozzarella-Stuffed Meatballs, 52
Pork Scallopini with Caper Sauce, 54
Salads
Caprese Salad, 227
Radicchio Salad Cups, 243

Sandwiches
Inside-Out Bacon Cheeseburgers, 220
Loaded Philly Cheese Steaks, 174
Sides Dishes
Cheese-Stuffed Twice-Baked
  Potatoes, 10
Gorgonzola Baked Apples with
  Balsamic Syrup, 113
Gruyere-Turnip Mashed Potatoes, 113
Pumpkin with Walnuts & Blue
  Cheese, 111
Shiitake & Goat Cheese Rustic
  Tart, 160
Squash au Gratin, 9
Three-Cheese Stuffed Onions, 80
Snacks
Artichoke, Spinach & Sun-Dried
  Tomato Dip, 89
Beer Fondue, 195
Berry Almond Bruschetta, 210
Brie Toasts with Cranberry Compote, 79
Cheese Crisps with Ricotta Dip, 36
Eggplant Bruschetta, 231
Goat Cheese and Spinach Stuffed
  Mushrooms, 84
Layered Mediterranean Dip, 242
Maple Sausage Cheesecake, 94
Onion-Date Baked Brie, 14
Parmesan Truffles, 42
Roasted Peppers on Goat Cheese, 230
Salmon & Cream Cheese Potatoes, 40
Spicy Apple Dip, 19
Tangy Feta Herb Dip, 212
Warm Olive Bruschetta, 38
Soups
Brie and Wild Mushroom Soup, 36
Potato Cheese Soup, 175

CHEESECAKES
Butternut Cheesecake, 128
Cappuccino Cheesecake, 83
White Chocolate Peppermint
  Cheesecake, 64

CHICKEN
Chicken Yakitori with Noodles, 206
Creamy Chicken Gnocchi Soup, 91
Phyllo-Wrapped Pesto Chicken, 50
Pistachio-Crusted Chicken Breasts, 55
Pollo Guisado (Chicken Stew), 100
Roasted Lime Chicken, 228
Smoky Chicken Nachos, 172

CHOCOLATE
Bars and Brownies
Nanaimo Bars, 75
Rocky Road Brownies, 222

Beverages
Coconut-Caramel Hot Cocoa, 93
Creamy Mocha Cocktail, 195
Bread
Chocolate Panini, 157
Cakes and Cupcakes
Chocolate and Red Wine
  Cupcakes, 186
Dark Chocolate Bacon Cupcakes, 185
Flourless Chocolate Cake with Peanut
  Butter Ice Cream, 13
Layered Peppermint Icebox Cake, 60
Malted Chocolate & Stout Layer
  Cake, 194
Peppermint Red Velvet Cupcakes, 60
Candies
Candy Cane Fudge, 62
Candy Cane Truffle Lollipops, 74
Choco-Tato Truffles, 125
Chocolate Caramels, 73
Macadamia Peanut Butter Cups, 70
Orange-Almond Chocolate Logs, 68
Cookies
Double Chocolate Chipotle Cookies, 174
Lace Cookies with Chocolate
  Middles, 70
Linzer Tarts, 71
Mayan Chocolate Biscotti, 72
Pistachio Chocolate Macarons, 212

Desserts and Pie
Bourbon Chocolate Pecan Pie, 135
Chocolate Mint Truffle Tart, 64
Meringue Torte with Peppermint
  Cream, 61
White Chocolate Panna Cotta with
  Espresso Syrup, 134
White Chocolate Peppermint
  Cheesecake, 64

COCONUT
Coconut Bread, 156
Coconut-Caramel Hot Cocoa, 93
Coconut Chiffon Cake, 145
Coconut Cranberry Yummies, 68
Coconut Tres Leches Cupcakes, 182

Coconut Waffles, 28
Coquito, 99
Family-Favorite Pina Coladas, 98
Lime Muffins with Coconut Streusel, 151
Nanaimo Bars, 75
Puerto Rican Coconut Pudding, 105

CONDIMENTS & RELISHES
Chive Horseradish Sauce, 193
Herb Garden Zucchini, 234
Parmesan Butter, 79
Pearl Onion, Cherry & Pear Chutney, 114
Pickled Green Onions, 234
Pickled Green Tomato Relish, 230
Salsa Criolla, 220
Sofrito, 104

COOKIES *(also see Bars & Brownies)*
Coconut Cranberry Yummies, 68
Double Chocolate Chipotle Cookies, 174
Ginger Shortbread Cookies, 72
Kiss from a Vampire Cookies, 241
Lace Cookies with Chocolate
  Middles, 70
Lemon Pistachio Wreaths, 74
Linzer Tarts, 71
Mayan Chocolate Biscotti, 72
Pistachio Chocolate Macarons, 212

CORN
Grilled Corn with Bloody Mary Butter, 228
Jalapeno Popper Corn Cupcakes, 187

CRANBERRIES
Brie Toasts with Cranberry Compote, 79
Coconut Cranberry Yummies, 68
Corned Beef & Cranberry Hash, 30
Cranberry Focaccia, 111
Cranberry Ice Cream Pie, 124
Cranberry Meringue Pie, 132
Cranberry Sherbet, 130
Cranberry-Stuffed Beef Tenderloin, 50
Grand Marnier Cranberry Pound
  Cake, 131
Meatballs with Cranberry Sauce, 120

CUCUMBERS
Cucumber and Shrimp Sunomono, 202
Shrimp Salsa, 101
Watermelon Cups, 217

CUPCAKES
Bananas Foster Surprise Cupcakes, 183
Chocolate and Red Wine
  Cupcakes, 186
Coconut Tres Leches Cupcakes, 182
Dark Chocolate Bacon Cupcakes, 185
Gin & Tonic Cupcakes, 184

Jalapeno Popper Corn Cupcakes, 187
Orange Creamsicle Cupcakes, 186
Pad Thai Cupcakes, 184
Peppermint Red Velvet Cupcakes, 60
Salted Caramel Cupcakes, 182

DESSERTS *(also see specific kinds)*
Apple-Cinnamon Shortcakes, 133
Balsamic-Goat Cheese Grilled Plums, 232
Candy Cane Souffle, 63
Chocolate Mint Truffle Tart, 64
Holiday Baked Alaska, 62
Meringue Torte with Peppermint
  Cream, 61
Peach Blackberry Pavlovas, 232
Strawberry Fondue, 242
Stuffed Apples with Honey Creme
  Fraiche, 132
Triple Nut Tart, 130

DRESSING *(see Stuffing)*

EGGS
Ham & Cheese Strata with Sun-Dried
  Tomatoes, 31
Nicoise Salad, 213
Overnight Baked Eggs Bruschetta, 33
Pickled Eggs, 243
Poached Egg Salads with Pancetta
  Vinaigrette, 81
Spinach and Artichoke Bread
  Pudding, 141
Spring Brunch Bruschetta, 144

FISH & SEAFOOD
Main Dishes
Fish in Rosemary Broth, 52
Halibut with Citrus-Olive Sauce, 49
Pan-Fried Scallops with White Wine
  Reduction, 82
Salmon Teriyaki, 206
Seared Salmon with Pomegranate-
  Thyme Butter, 56
Salads, Soup and Side Dish
Cucumber and Shrimp
  Sunomono, 202
Grilled Shrimp Panzanella, 219
Nicoise Salad, 213
Onigiri (Rice Balls), 205
Seafood Bisque, 90
Snacks
Bloody-Mary Seafood Cocktail, 238
Caprese Scallop Stacks, 37
Chive Horseradish Sauce, 193
Salmon & Cream Cheese Potatoes, 40
Shrimp & Artichoke Spring Rolls with
  Lemon Aioli, 146
Shrimp Salsa, 101

FRUIT (also see specific kinds)
Balsamic-Goat Cheese Grilled
    Plums, 232
Berries in Yogurt Cream, 26
Berry Almond Bruschetta, 210
Grapefruit in Honey-Thyme
    Sauce, 21
Peach Blackberry Pavlovas, 232
South of the Border Citrus Salad, 32
Tahitian Fruit Salad, 161

GREEN BEANS & SOYBEANS
Lemony Green and Wax Beans, 226
Sizzling Green Beans, 112
Spicy Edamame, 201

GRILLED RECIPES
Balsamic-Goat Cheese Grilled
    Plums, 232
Chicken Yakitori with Noodles, 206
Four-Pepper Ribeye Roast, 54
Grilled Corn with Bloody Mary
    Butter, 228
Grilled Shrimp Panzanella, 219
Grilled Sweet Potato & Jicama, 221
Inside-Out Bacon
    Cheeseburgers, 220
Shredded Pork Barbecue, 216
Steak-through-the Heart Bites, 238

HAM & PROSCIUTTO
Apple-Glazed Holiday Ham, 10
Focaccia Party Sandwich, 172
Ham & Cheese Strata with Sun-Dried
    Tomatoes, 31
Pork Scallopini with Caper Sauce, 54

HERBS
Flaky Biscuits with Herb Butter, 156
Garlic-Herb Mini Flatbreads, 43
Herb-Crusted Rack of Lamb with
    Mushroom Sauce, 51
Herb-Crusted Tomatoes & Sweet
    Peas, 143
Herb Garden Zucchini, 234
Lemon Herb Quinoa, 164
Peppery Herb Flatbread, 94
Tangy Feta Herb Dip, 212

ICE CREAM & SHERBET
Blondie Sundaes, 177
Cranberry Ice Cream Pie, 124
Cranberry Sherbet, 130
Flourless Chocolate Cake with Peanut
    Butter Ice Cream, 13
Holiday Baked Alaska, 62
Hot Apple Pie Sipper, 92
Irish Whiskey Float, 190
Lychee Green Tea Milkshakes, 205

LAMB
Herb-Crusted Rack of Lamb with
    Mushroom Sauce, 51
Rosemary Roasted Lamb, 142
West Virginia Shepherd's Pie, 190

LEMON & LIME
Gin & Tonic Cupcakes, 184
Hazelnut & Lemon-Crusted Turkey
    Breast, 56
Lemon and Honey Mustard
    Vinaigrette, 144
Lemon-Butter Brussels Sprouts, 20
Lemon Herb Quinoa, 164
Lemon Pistachio Wreaths, 74
Lemon-Scented Broccolini, 14
Lemon Spaghetti, 80
Lemon Thyme Bread, 152
Lemony Green and Wax Beans, 226
Lime Muffins with Coconut Streusel, 151
Mixed Greens with Lemon Champagne
    Vinaigrette, 11
Roasted Lime Chicken, 228
Shrimp & Artichoke Spring Rolls with
    Lemon Aioli, 146
Strawberry Citrus Slushies, 28
Tarragon Peas with Lemon-Thyme
    Butter, 165

MARSHMALLOWS & MARSHMALLOW CREME
Orange Creamsicle Cupcakes, 186
Rocky Road Brownies, 222

MELON
Watermelon Cups, 217
Watermelon Gazpacho, 233

MEATBALLS
Meatballs with Cranberry Sauce, 120
Mozzarella-Stuffed Meatballs, 52
Puttanesca Meatball Sliders, 173

MICROWAVE RECIPES
Buffalo Wing Munch Mix, 178
Candy Cane Fudge, 62
Curry Snack Mix, 217
Turkey & Rice Tostadas, 122

MINT & PEPPERMINT
Candy Cane Fudge, 62
Candy Cane Souffle, 63
Candy Cane Truffle Lollipops, 74
Chocolate Mint Truffle Tart, 64
Holiday Baked Alaska, 62
Layered Peppermint Icebox Cake, 60
Meringue Torte with Peppermint
    Cream, 61
Mint Angel Cake, 65

Peppermint Red Velvet Cupcakes, 60
White Chocolate Peppermint
    Cheesecake, 64

MUFFINS
Breakfast Sausage & Sweet Potato
    Muffins, 123
Lime Muffins with Coconut Streusel, 151

MUSHROOMS
Bacon-Jalapeno Mushrooms with Ranch
    Sauce, 176
Brie and Wild Mushroom Soup, 36
Goat Cheese and Spinach Stuffed
    Mushrooms, 84
Herb-Crusted Rack of Lamb with
    Mushroom Sauce, 51
Miso Soup with Tofu and Enoki, 203
Poached Egg Salads with Pancetta
    Vinaigrette, 81
Polenta Mushroom Appetizers, 44
Portobello-Stuffed Pork Roast, 48
Shiitake & Goat Cheese Rustic Tart, 160
Steak au Poivre, 20

NUTS & PEANUT BUTTER
Bourbon Chocolate Pecan Pie, 135
Brown Sugar & Almond Pumpkin
    Custard, 116
Creamy Penne Pasta with Walnuts, 166
Curry Snack Mix, 217
Flourless Chocolate Cake with Peanut
    Butter Ice Cream, 13
Hazelnut & Lemon-Crusted Turkey
    Breast, 56
Lemon Pistachio Wreaths, 74
Linzer Tarts, 71
Macadamia Peanut Butter Cups, 70
Mayan Chocolate Biscotti, 72
Mom's Almond-Filled Coffee Rings, 150
Orange-Almond Chocolate Logs, 68
Pad Thai Cupcakes, 184
Pecan Sausage Stuffing, 114
Pistachio Brittle, 69
Pistachio Chocolate Macarons, 212
Pistachio-Crusted Chicken Breasts, 55
Pumpkin with Walnuts & Blue Cheese, 111
Rocky Road Brownies, 222
Triple Nut Tart, 130

OLIVES

Greek Olive Bread, 12
Halibut with Citrus-Olive Sauce, 49
Layered Mediterranean Dip, 242
Warm Olive Bruschetta, 38

ONIONS, LEEKS & SHALLOTS

Caramelized Onion & Pork
   Potstickers, 200
Chive Horseradish Sauce, 193
Colcannon with Onions and Leek, 193
Garlic and Shallot Mashed
   Potatoes, 240
Irish Onion Soup, 196
Onion-Date Baked Brie, 14
Onion Tarts with Balsamic Onion
   Jam, 41
Pearl Onion, Cherry & Pear
   Chutney, 114
Pickled Green Onions, 234
Rainbow Potato Chips with Creamy
   Onion Dip, 178
Rich Onion Gratin, 166
Salsa Criolla, 220
Sofrito, 104
Three-Cheese Stuffed Onions, 80

ORANGE

Carrot Soup with Orange and
   Tarragon, 142
Halibut with Citrus-Olive Sauce, 49
Nanaimo Bars, 75
Orange-Almond Chocolate Logs, 68
Orange Creamsicle Cupcakes, 186
Sparkling Summer Champagne, 211
Strawberry Citrus Slushies, 28
Sunshine State Orange Bread, 154

OVEN ENTREES

Beef
Cranberry-Stuffed Beef Tenderloin, 50
Four-Pepper Ribeye Roast, 54
Mozzarella-Stuffed Meatballs, 52

Chicken
Phyllo-Wrapped Pesto Chicken, 50
Roasted Lime Chicken, 228

Fish
Fish in Rosemary Broth, 52

Lamb
Herb-Crusted Rack of Lamb with
   Mushroom Sauce, 51
Rosemary Roasted Lamb, 142

Pork and Ham
Apple-Glazed Holiday Ham, 10
Pork Scallopini with Caper Sauce, 54
Portobello-Stuffed Pork Roast, 48
Roasted Pork Shoulder, 103

Turkey

Bistro Turkey Calzone, 121
Hazelnut & Lemon-Crusted Turkey
   Breast, 56
Rosemary Roasted Turkey, 115

OVERNIGHT RECIPES

Bananas Foster Baked French
   Toast, 29
Big Sweet Potato Flan, 134
Butternut Cheesecake, 128
Candy Cane Souffle, 63
Cappuccino Cheesecake, 83
Chilled Beet Salad, 211
Corned Beef & Cranberry Hash, 30
Four-Pepper Ribeye Roast, 54
Ham & Cheese Strata with Sun-Dried
   Tomatoes, 31
Holiday Baked Alaska, 62
Layered Peppermint Icebox
   Cake, 60
Make-Ahead Monkey Bread, 32
Maple Sausage Cheesecake, 94
Overnight Baked Oatmeal, 30
Overnight Yeast Pancakes with
   Blueberry Syrup, 26
Pickled Eggs, 243
Pollo Guisado (Chicken Stew), 100
Roasted Pork Shoulder, 103
Spinach and Artichoke Bread
   Pudding, 141
Vanilla Flan, 98
White Chocolate Peppermint
   Cheesecake, 64

PASTA & NOODLES

Chicken Yakitori with Noodles, 206
Cold Sesame Noodles, 202
Creamy Penne Pasta with
   Walnuts, 166
Fish in Rosemary Broth, 52
Lemon Spaghetti, 80
Pasta and White Bean Soup with Sun-
   Dried Tomatoes, 57
Southwestern Pasta Salad, 222

PEAS

Arroz con Gandules (Rice with Pigeon
   Peas), 102
Herb-Crusted Tomatoes & Sweet
   Peas, 143
Szechuan Sugar Snap Peas, 164
Tarragon Peas with Lemon-Thyme
   Butter, 165
Three-Pea Salad with Creamy Tarragon
   Dressing, 162

PEPPERS & CHILIES

Bacon-Jalapeno Mushrooms with Ranch
   Sauce, 176
Double Chocolate Chipotle
   Cookies, 174
Jalapeno Popper Corn Cupcakes, 187
Roasted Peppers on Goat
   Cheese, 230
Salsa Criolla, 220
Sofrito, 104
Southwestern Pasta Salad, 222
Sweet and Spicy Chili, 244

PIES

Bourbon Chocolate Pecan Pie, 135
Brown Sugar & Almond Pumpkin
   Custard, 116
Cranberry Ice Cream Pie, 124
Cranberry Meringue Pie, 132
Pear Pie with Cardamom Cream, 129
Raspberry Pie Squares, 218

PIZZAS

Eat-Twice Chili Pizza, 176
Springtime Asparagus Pizza, 146
Tomato-Squash Appetizer Pizza, 229

POMEGRANATE

Mixed Greens with Lemon Champagne
   Vinaigrette, 11
Seared Salmon with Pomegranate-
   Thyme Butter, 56

PORK (also see Bacon & Pancetta; Ham & Prosciutto; Sausage)

Pork Scallopini with Caper Sauce, 54
Portobello-Stuffed Pork Roast, 48
Puttanesca Meatball Sliders, 173
Roasted Pork Shoulder, 103
Shredded Pork Barbecue, 216
Tonkatsu, 201

POTATOES (also see Sweet Potatoes)

Main Dishes
Corned Beef & Cranberry Hash, 30
Fish in Rosemary Broth, 52
West Virginia Shepherd's Pie, 190

POTATOES *(continued)*

Salad
Garden Spinach-Potato Salad, 226

Side Dishes
Cheese-Stuffed Twice-Baked Potatoes, 10
Colcannon with Onions and Leek, 193
Garlic and Shallot Mashed Potatoes, 240
Gruyere-Turnip Mashed Potatoes, 113
Spanish Smashed Potatoes with Cilantro Sauce, 102
Spectacular Fingerling Potatoes, 22

Snacks
Choco-Tato Truffles, 125
Rainbow Potato Chips with Creamy Onion Dip, 178
Salmon & Cream Cheese Potatoes, 40

Soups
Creamy Chicken Gnocchi Soup, 91
Irish Onion Soup, 196
Potato Cheese Soup, 175
Potato Chive Soup, 122

PUDDING & CUSTARD
Big Sweet Potato Flan, 134
Puerto Rican Coconut Pudding, 105
Vanilla Flan, 98
White Chocolate Panna Cotta with Espresso Syrup, 134

PUMPKIN
Brown Sugar & Almond Pumpkin Custard, 116
Pumpkin Gnocchi in Sage Butter, 121
Pumpkin with Walnuts & Blue Cheese, 111

QUICK BREADS
Boston Brown Bread, 192
Coconut Bread, 156
Lemon Thyme Bread, 152
Peppery Herb Flatbread, 94
Rosemary-Parmesan Biscotti, 90
Sunshine State Orange Bread, 154

RASPBERRIES
Kiss from a Vampire Cookies, 241
Raspberry Pie Squares, 218

RICE, BARLEY & QUINOA
Arroz con Gandules (Rice with Pigeon Peas), 102
Beef & Barley Soup, 88
Curried Turkey Soup, 120
Lemon Herb Quinoa, 164
Onigiri (Rice Balls), 205
Turkey & Rice Tostadas, 122
Veggie Sushi Rolls, 204

SALADS & SALAD DRESSINGS

Dressing
Lemon and Honey Mustard Vinaigrette, 144

Fruit Salads
Radicchio Salad Cups, 243
South of the Border Citrus Salad, 32
Tahitian Fruit Salad, 161

Green Salads
Arugula Salad with Berry Dressing, 165
BLT Wedge Salad, 22
Mixed Greens with Lemon Champagne Vinaigrette, 11
My Underground Vegetable Salad, 191
Poached Egg Salads with Pancetta Vinaigrette, 81
Three-Pea Salad with Creamy Tarragon Dressing, 162

Main-Dish Salads
Cucumber and Shrimp Sunomono, 202
Grilled Shrimp Panzanella, 219
Nicoise Salad, 213

Pasta and Potato Salads
Garden Spinach-Potato Salad, 226
Southwestern Pasta Salad, 222

Vegetable Salads
Caprese Salad, 227
Chilled Beet Salad, 211
Italian Fennel Salad, 141
Lemony Green and Wax Beans, 226
Ravishing Radish Salad, 163
Spicy Antipasto Salad, 216

SANDWICHES
Focaccia Party Sandwich, 172
Fried Green Tomato BLTs, 235
Inside-Out Bacon Cheeseburgers, 220
Loaded Philly Cheese Steaks, 174
Puttanesca Meatball Sliders, 173
Roast Beef Garden Pitas, 210
Shredded Pork Barbecue, 216

SAUSAGE
Arroz con Gandules (Rice with Pigeon Peas), 102
Breakfast Sausage & Sweet Potato Muffins, 123
Caramelized Onion & Pork Potstickers, 200
Focaccia Party Sandwich, 172
Maple Sausage Cheesecake, 94
Meatballs with Cranberry Sauce, 120
Pecan Sausage Stuffing, 114
Spicy Antipasto Salad, 216

SIDE DISHES *(also see Casseroles)*

Fruit
Berries in Yogurt Cream, 26
Gorgonzola Baked Apples with Balsamic Syrup, 113
Grapefruit in Honey-Thyme Sauce, 21

Miscellaneous
Habichuelas (Red Beans), 104
Pumpkin Gnocchi in Sage Butter, 121
Shiitake & Goat Cheese Rustic Tart, 160

Pasta and Quinoa
Cold Sesame Noodles, 202
Creamy Penne Pasta with Walnuts, 166
Lemon Herb Quinoa, 164
Lemon Spaghetti, 80

Potatoes
Cheese-Stuffed Twice-Baked Potatoes, 10
Colcannon with Onions and Leek, 193
Garlic and Shallot Mashed Potatoes, 240
Spanish Smashed Potatoes with Cilantro Sauce, 102

Rice
Arroz con Gandules (Rice with Pigeon Peas), 102
Onigiri (Rice Balls), 205

Vegetables
Dijon Roasted Asparagus, 160
Grilled Corn with Bloody Mary Butter, 228
Grilled Sweet Potato & Jicama, 221
Herb-Crusted Tomatoes & Sweet Peas, 143
Lemon-Butter Brussels Sprouts, 20

Lemon-Scented Broccolini, 14
Maple-Ginger Glazed Carrots, 162
Pumpkin with Walnuts & Blue
    Cheese, 111
Sizzling Green Beans, 112
Spicy Edamame, 201
Szechuan Sugar Snap Peas, 164
Tarragon Peas with Lemon-Thyme
    Butter, 165

SKILLET & STOVETOP SUPPERS

Corned Beef & Cranberry Hash, 30
Day-After-Thanksgiving Turkey
    Stir-Fry, 124
Halibut with Citrus-Olive Sauce, 49
Pan-Fried Scallops with White Wine
    Reduction, 82
Pistachio-Crusted Chicken Breasts, 55
Salmon Teriyaki, 206
Seared Salmon with Pomegranate-
    Thyme Butter, 56
Steak au Poivre, 20

SLOW COOKER RECIPES

Braised Short Ribs, 53
Corned Beef & Cabbage for the Wine
    Lover, 192
Curried Turkey Soup, 120

SOUPS, STEWS & CHILI

Beef & Barley Soup, 88
Brie and Wild Mushroom Soup, 36
Carrot Soup with Orange and
    Tarragon, 142
Creamy Chicken Gnocchi Soup, 91
Curried Turkey Soup, 120
Irish Onion Soup, 196
Miso Soup with Tofu and
    Enoki, 203
Pasta and White Bean Soup with
    Sun-Dried Tomatoes, 57
Pollo Guisado (Chicken Stew), 100
Potato Cheese Soup, 175
Potato Chive Soup, 122
Roasted Sweet Potato Soup, 112
Roasted Tomato Soup, 240
Seafood Bisque, 90
Sweet and Spicy Chili, 244
Watermelon Gazpacho, 233

SPINACH & GREENS

Artichoke, Spinach & Sun-Dried
    Tomato Dip, 89
Arugula Salad with Berry Dressing, 165
Creamy Chicken Gnocchi Soup, 91
Garden Spinach-Potato Salad, 226
Goat Cheese and Spinach Stuffed
    Mushrooms, 84

Radicchio Salad Cups, 243
Shrimp & Artichoke Spring Rolls with
    Lemon Aioli, 146
Spinach and Artichoke Bread
    Pudding, 141

SQUASH & ZUCCHINI

Butternut Cheesecake, 128
Caprese Scallop Stacks, 37
Herb Garden Zucchini, 234
Squash au Gratin, 9
Tomato-Squash Appetizer Pizza, 229

STRAWBERRIES

Arugula Salad with Berry
    Dressing, 165
Strawberry Citrus Slushies, 28
Strawberry Fondue, 242
White Wine Strawberry Sangria, 227

STUFFING

Meatballs with Cranberry
    Sauce, 120
Pecan Sausage Stuffing, 114

SWEET POTATOES

Big Sweet Potato Flan, 134
Breakfast Sausage & Sweet Potato
    Muffins, 123
Grilled Sweet Potato & Jicama, 221
Roasted Sweet Potato Soup, 112

TOMATOES & SUN-DRIED TOMATOES

Artichoke, Spinach & Sun-Dried
    Tomato Dip, 89
BLT Wedge Salad, 22
Caprese Salad, 227
Eggplant Bruschetta, 231
Fried Green Tomato BLTs, 235
Ham & Cheese Strata with Sun-Dried
    Tomatoes, 31
Herb-Crusted Tomatoes & Sweet
    Peas, 143

Pasta and White Bean Soup with Sun-
    Dried Tomatoes, 57
Pickled Green Tomato Relish, 230
Roasted Garlic & Sun-Dried Tomato
    Toast, 38
Roasted Tomato Soup, 240
Shrimp Salsa, 101
Sofrito, 104
Tomato Rosemary Hummus, 42
Tomato-Squash Appetizer Pizza, 229

TURKEY

Bistro Turkey Calzone, 121
Curried Turkey Soup, 120
Day-After-Thanksgiving Turkey
    Stir-Fry, 124
Hazelnut & Lemon-Crusted Turkey
    Breast, 56
Meatballs with Cranberry Sauce, 120
Rosemary Roasted Turkey, 115
Turkey & Rice Tostadas, 122

VEGETABLES (also see specific kinds)

Day-After-Thanksgiving Turkey
    Stir-Fry, 124
Eggplant Bruschetta, 231
Fish in Rosemary Broth, 52
Grilled Sweet Potato & Jicama, 221
Gruyere-Turnip Mashed Potatoes, 113
Italian Fennel Salad, 141
Lemon-Butter Brussels Sprouts, 20
My Underground Vegetable
    Salad, 191
Nicoise Salad, 213
Oven-Roasted Spring Vegetable
    Medley, 167
Ravishing Radish Salad, 163
Roast Beef Garden Pitas, 210
Spicy Antipasto Salad, 216
Veggie Sushi Rolls, 204

WAFFLES, PANCAKES & FRENCH TOAST

Bananas Foster Baked French Toast, 29
Coconut Waffles, 28
Overnight Yeast Pancakes with
    Blueberry Syrup, 26

YEAST BREADS & ROLLS

Asiago Bagels, 152
Cardamom Twist, 155
Chocolate Panini, 157
Cranberry Focaccia, 111
Greek Olive Bread, 12
Italian Easter Bread, 153
Make-Ahead Monkey Bread, 32
Mini Cheddar Bread Bowls, 88
Mom's Almond-Filled Coffee Rings, 150
Rosemary-Garlic Dinner Rolls, 84

alphabetical index

Refer to this index for a complete alphabetical listing of all recipes in this book.

A

Apple-Cinnamon Shortcakes, 133
Apple-Glazed Holiday Ham, 10
Arroz con Gandules (Rice with Pigeon Peas), 102
Artichoke, Spinach & Sun-Dried Tomato Dip, 89
Arugula Salad with Berry Dressing, 165
Asiago Bagels, 152

B

Bacon-Jalapeno Mushrooms with Ranch Sauce, 176
Baked Figs, 40
Balsamic-Goat Cheese Grilled Plums, 232
Bananas Foster Baked French Toast, 29
Bananas Foster Surprise Cupcakes, 183
Beef & Barley Soup, 88
Beef Tenderloin Lollipops, 39
Beer Fondue, 195
Berries in Yogurt Cream, 26
Berry Almond Bruschetta, 210
Big Sweet Potato Flan, 134
Bistro Turkey Calzone, 121
Black-Hearted Candy Apples, 239
Blondie Sundaes, 177
Bloody-Mary Seafood Cocktail, 238
BLT Wedge Salad, 22
Boston Brown Bread, 192
Bourbon Chocolate Pecan Pie, 135
Braised Short Ribs, 53
Breakfast Sausage & Sweet Potato Muffins, 123
Brie and Wild Mushroom Soup, 36
Brie Toasts with Cranberry Compote, 79
Brown Sugar & Almond Pumpkin Custard, 116
Buffalo Wing Munch Mix, 178
Butternut Cheesecake, 128
Butterscotch Maple Scones, 27

C

Candy Apple Martini, 241
Candy Cane Fudge, 62
Candy Cane Souffle, 63
Candy Cane Truffle Lollipops, 74
Cappuccino Cheesecake, 83
Caprese Salad, 227
Caprese Scallop Stacks, 37

Caramelized Onion & Pork Potstickers, 200
Cardamom Twist, 155
Carrot Soup with Orange and Tarragon, 142
Cheese Crisps with Ricotta Dip, 36
Cheese-Stuffed Twice-Baked Potatoes, 10
Chicken Yakitori with Noodles, 206
Chilled Beet Salad, 211
Chive Horseradish Sauce, 193
Choco-Tato Truffles, 125
Chocolate and Red Wine Cupcakes, 186
Chocolate Caramels, 73
Chocolate Mint Truffle Tart, 64
Chocolate Panini, 157
Coconut Bread, 156
Coconut-Caramel Hot Cocoa, 93
Coconut Chiffon Cake, 145
Coconut Cranberry Yummies, 68
Coconut Tres Leches Cupcakes, 182
Coconut Waffles, 28
Colcannon with Onions and Leek, 193
Cold Sesame Noodles, 202
Coquito, 99
Corned Beef & Cabbage for the Wine Lover, 192
Corned Beef & Cranberry Hash, 30
Cranberry Focaccia, 111
Cranberry Ice Cream Pie, 124
Cranberry Meringue Pie, 132
Cranberry Sherbet, 130
Cranberry-Stuffed Beef Tenderloin, 50
Creamy Chicken Gnocchi Soup, 91
Creamy Mocha Cocktail, 195
Creamy Penne Pasta with Walnuts, 166
Cucumber and Shrimp Sunomono, 202
Curried Turkey Soup, 120
Curry Snack Mix, 217

D

Dark Chocolate Bacon Cupcakes, 185
Day-After-Thanksgiving Turkey Stir-Fry, 124
Dijon Roasted Asparagus, 160
Double Chocolate Chipotle Cookies, 174

E

Eat-Twice Chili Pizza, 176
Eggplant Bruschetta, 231

F

Family-Favorite Pina Coladas, 98
Fish in Rosemary Broth, 52
Flaky Biscuits with Herb Butter, 156
Flourless Chocolate Cake with Peanut Butter Ice Cream, 13
Focaccia Party Sandwich, 172
Four-Pepper Ribeye Roast, 54
Fried Green Tomato BLTs, 235

G

Garden Spinach-Potato Salad, 226
Garlic and Shallot Mashed Potatoes, 240
Garlic-Herb Mini Flatbreads, 43
Gin & Tonic Cupcakes, 184
Ginger Shortbread Cookies, 72
Gingerbread Fizz, 92
Goat Cheese and Spinach Stuffed Mushrooms, 84
Gorgonzola Baked Apples with Balsamic Syrup, 113
Grand Marnier Cranberry Pound Cake, 131
Grapefruit in Honey-Thyme Sauce, 21
Greek Olive Bread, 12
Grilled Corn with Bloody Mary Butter, 228
Grilled Shrimp Panzanella, 219
Grilled Sweet Potato & Jicama, 221
Gruyere-Turnip Mashed Potatoes, 113

H

Habichuelas (Red Beans), 104
Halibut with Citrus-Olive Sauce, 49
Ham & Cheese Strata with Sun-Dried Tomatoes, 31
Hazelnut & Lemon-Crusted Turkey Breast, 56
Herb-Crusted Rack of Lamb with Mushroom Sauce, 51
Herb-Crusted Tomatoes & Sweet Peas, 143
Herb Garden Zucchini, 234
Holiday Baked Alaska, 62
Hot Apple Pie Sipper, 92

I

Inside-Out Bacon Cheeseburgers, 220
Irish Onion Soup, 196

Irish Whiskey Float, 190
Italian Easter Bread, 153
Italian Fennel Salad, 141

J

Jalapeno Popper Corn Cupcakes, 187

K

Kiss from a Vampire Cookies, 241

L

Lace Cookies with Chocolate
   Middles, 70
Layered Gingerbread Bars, 95
Layered Mediterranean Dip, 242
Layered Peppermint Icebox Cake, 60
Lemon and Honey Mustard
   Vinaigrette, 144
Lemon-Butter Brussels Sprouts, 20
Lemon Herb Quinoa, 164
Lemon Pistachio Wreaths, 74
Lemon-Scented Broccolini, 14
Lemon Spaghetti, 80
Lemon Thyme Bread, 152
Lemony Green and Wax Beans, 226
Lime Muffins with Coconut
   Streusel, 151
Linzer Tarts, 71
Loaded Philly Cheese Steaks, 174
Lychee Green Tea Milkshakes, 205

M

Macadamia Peanut Butter Cups, 70
Make-Ahead Monkey Bread, 32
Malted Chocolate & Stout Layer
   Cake, 194
Maple-Ginger Glazed Carrots, 162
Maple Sausage Cheesecake, 94
Mayan Chocolate Biscotti, 72
Meatballs with Cranberry Sauce, 120
Meringue Torte with Peppermint
   Cream, 61
Mini Cheddar Bread Bowls, 88
Mint Angel Cake, 65
Miso Soup with Tofu and Enoki, 203
Mixed Greens with Lemon Champagne
   Vinaigrette, 11
Mom's Almond-Filled Coffee Rings, 150
Mozzarella-Stuffed Meatballs, 52
My Underground Vegetable Salad, 191

N

Nanaimo Bars, 75
Nicoise Salad, 213

O

Oil & Vinegar Dipping Sauce, 19
Onigiri (Rice Balls), 205
Onion-Date Baked Brie, 14
Onion Tarts with Balsamic Onion Jam, 41
Orange-Almond Chocolate Logs, 68
Orange Creamsicle Cupcakes, 186
Oven-Roasted Spring Vegetable
   Medley, 167
Overnight Baked Eggs Bruschetta, 33
Overnight Baked Oatmeal, 30
Overnight Yeast Pancakes with
   Blueberry Syrup, 26

P

Pad Thai Cupcakes, 184
Pan-Fried Scallops with White Wine
   Reduction, 82
Parmesan Butter, 79
Parmesan Truffles, 42
Pasta and White Bean Soup with Sun-
   Dried Tomatoes, 57
Peach Blackberry Pavlovas, 232
Pear Pie with Cardamom Cream, 129
Pearl Onion, Cherry & Pear Chutney, 114
Pecan Sausage Stuffing, 114
Peppered Bacon and Cheese Scones, 154
Peppermint Red Velvet Cupcakes, 60
Peppery Herb Flatbread, 94
Phyllo-Wrapped Pesto Chicken, 50
Pickled Eggs, 243
Pickled Green Onions, 234
Pickled Green Tomato Relish, 230
Pistachio Brittle, 69
Pistachio Chocolate Macarons, 212
Pistachio-Crusted Chicken Breasts, 55
Poached Egg Salads with Pancetta
   Vinaigrette, 81
Polenta Mushroom Appetizers, 44
Pollo Guisado (Chicken Stew), 100
Pork Scallopini with Caper Sauce, 54
Portobello-Stuffed Pork Roast, 48
Potato Cheese Soup, 175
Potato Chive Soup, 122
Puerto Rican Coconut Pudding, 105
Pumpkin Gnocchi in Sage Butter, 121
Pumpkin with Walnuts & Blue
   Cheese, 111
Puttanesca Meatball Sliders, 173

R

Radicchio Salad Cups, 243
Rainbow Potato Chips with Creamy
   Onion Dip, 178
Raspberry Pie Squares, 218
Ravishing Radish Salad, 163

Rich Onion Gratin, 166
Roast Beef Garden Pitas, 210
Roasted Cauliflower, 12
Roasted Curry Chickpeas, 44
Roasted Garlic & Sun-Dried Tomato
   Toast, 38
Roasted Lime Chicken, 228
Roasted Peppers on Goat Cheese, 230
Roasted Pork Shoulder, 103
Roasted Sweet Potato Soup, 112
Roasted Tomato Soup, 240
Rocky Road Brownies, 222
Rosemary-Garlic Dinner Rolls, 84
Rosemary-Parmesan Biscotti, 90
Rosemary Roasted Lamb, 142
Rosemary Roasted Turkey, 115

S

Salmon & Cream Cheese Potatoes, 40
Salmon Teriyaki, 206
Salsa Criolla, 220
Salted Caramel Cupcakes, 182
Seafood Bisque, 90
Seared Salmon with Pomegranate-
   Thyme Butter, 56
Shiitake & Goat Cheese Rustic Tart, 160
Shredded Pork Barbecue, 216
Shrimp & Artichoke Spring Rolls with
   Lemon Aioli, 146
Shrimp Salsa, 101
Sizzling Green Beans, 112
Smoky Chicken Nachos, 172
Sofrito, 104
South of the Border Citrus Salad, 32
Southwestern Pasta Salad, 222
Spanish Smashed Potatoes with Cilantro
   Sauce, 102
Sparkling Ginger Iced Tea, 203
Sparkling Summer Champagne, 211
Spectacular Fingerling Potatoes, 22
Spicy Antipasto Salad, 216
Spicy Apple Dip, 19
Spicy Edamame, 201
Spinach and Artichoke Bread
   Pudding, 141
Spring Brunch Bruschetta, 144
Springtime Asparagus Pizza, 146
Squash au Gratin, 9
Steak au Poivre, 20
Steak-through-the Heart Bites, 238
Strawberry Citrus Slushies, 28
Strawberry Fondue, 242
Stuffed Apples with Honey Creme
   Fraiche, 132
Sunshine State Orange Bread, 154
Sweet and Spicy Chili, 244
Sweet & Spicy Kettle Corn, 93
Szechuan Sugar Snap Peas, 164

T

Tahitian Fruit Salad, 161
Tangy Feta Herb Dip, 212
Tarragon Peas with Lemon-Thyme
 Butter, 165
Three-Cheese Stuffed Onions, 80
Three-Pea Salad with Creamy
 Tarragon Dressing, 162
Tomato Rosemary Hummus, 42
Tomato-Squash Appetizer Pizza, 229

Tonkatsu, 201
Tostones, 100
Triple Nut Tart, 130
Turkey & Rice Tostadas, 122

V

Vanilla Bean Fizz, 82
Vanilla Flan, 98
Veggie Sushi Rolls, 204

W

Warm Olive Bruschetta, 38
Watermelon Cups, 217
Watermelon Gazpacho, 233
West Virginia Shepherd's Pie, 190
White Chocolate Panna Cotta with
 Espresso Syrup, 134
White Chocolate Peppermint
 Cheesecake, 64
White Wine Sangria, 9
White Wine Strawberry Sangria, 227

Here's Your Chance to Be Published!

Send us your special-occasion recipes, and you could have them featured in a future edition of this classic cookbook.

Year after year, the recipe for success at every holiday party or special-occasion celebration is an attractive assortment of flavorful food. So we're always on the lookout for mouthwatering appetizers, entrees, side dishes, breads, desserts and more...all geared toward the gatherings you attend or host throughout the year.

Here's how you can enter your family-favorite holiday fare for possible publication in a future *Holiday & Celebrations Cookbook*:

- Print or type each recipe on one sheet of 8-1/2-in. x 11-in. paper. Please include your name, address and daytime phone number on each page. Be specific with directions, measurements and sizes of cans, packages and pans.
- Please include a few words about yourself, when you serve your dish, reactions it has received from family and friends and the origin of the recipe.
- Send to "Celebrations Cookbook," 5400 S. 60th Street, Greendale WI 53129 or email to recipes@reimanpub.com. Write "Celebrations Cookbook" on the subject line of all email entries and include your full name, postal address and phone number on each entry.

Contributors whose recipes are printed will receive a complimentary copy of the book—so the more recipes you send, the better your chances of being published!